OPERATING AND EVALUATING SCHOOL LIBRARY MEDIA PROGRAMS

A HANDBOOK FOR ADMINISTRATORS AND LIBRARIANS

Bernice L. Yesner and **Hilda L. Jay**

Neal-Schuman Publishers, Inc.
New York   London

Published by Neal-Schuman Publishers, Inc.
100 Varick Street
New York, NY 10013
Copyright ©1998 by Bernice L. Yesner and Hilda L. Jay

Printed and bound in the United States of America

Library of Congress Cataloging-in-Publication Data

Yesner, Bernice L.
    Operating and evaluating school library media programs : a
handbook for administrators and librarians / by Bernice L.
Yesner and Hilda L. Jay.
        p.   cm.
    ISBN 1–55570–250–3
    1. School libraries—United States—Administration. 2. School
libraries—United States—Evaluation. 3. Instructional materials
centers—United States—Administration. 4. Instructional materials
centers—United States—Evaluation. I. Jay, Hilda L. 1921–
II. Title.
Z675.S3.Y465   1998
025.1'978—dc21   98–11469
                                                            CIP

Dedication

To Ray and John who have provided between them more than a hundred years of support to the authors.

Table of Contents

Preface

Administrators responsible for the supervision of school library media teachers and for the evaluation of school library media center programs have an important and influential assignment. The school library media center—including its print and nonprint materials, attendant hardware, microforms collection, security system, and computerized functions within the center and throughout the building—represents one of the largest cost centers in the entire school system. Effective selection, budgeting, purchasing, processing, circulating, and other use of these materials, as well as the development of their integrated instructional use by the entire school population, call for certified personnel whose salaries also must be included. Qualified library media teachers have engaged in extensive curricular and specialized education in teaching as well as in library and media work; most often this training requires a master's degree in library and information science.

Many administrators have received little, if any, course work during their professional preparation programs to help with their school library media center responsibilities. Neither basic classes designed for the classroom teacher nor advanced classes dealing with curriculum, supervision, and administration have provided them with the necessary background. When administrators have sought assistance in carrying out school library media center-related oversight by looking to the literature of education, they have found little to help them. Their educational administration journals have infrequently, and minimally, addressed this aspect of their responsibilities. When they have talked with the school library media teacher and requested tools to assist with the task, most such tools have centered on job descriptions of the school library media center personnel and not on evaluation of the program, its operation within the school, and its integration into the total school program.

We would like to encourage the restructuring of standard initial training experiences and subsequent staff development programs made available to classroom teachers and administrators concerning the administration and use of the school library media center program. We hope that in the future there will be far wider recognition of the value of including school library media teachers on curriculum revision and design committees. Too many curriculum modifications are put into effect without consideration of a suitable match between the demands the new courses would create and the availability of school library media center materials to support those needs.

Meanwhile, here is a tool that can be used by both the school library media teacher and the supervising administrator to identify problems and potentials, recognize clues to positive and negative aspects, and to set goals and objectives. It can also be used to structure evaluation plans and to initiate improvements in school library media center programs. University-level instructors who wish to include a unit on the school library media center program in education courses designed for the preparation of classroom teachers and administrators will also find the book useful.

Currently, there is increasing awareness that the successful school library media center program provides an excellent opportunity to create significant learning experiences, especially those that require mental applications of the higher orders in the thinking taxonomies. This is an additional reason for administrators to accept the triple responsibility of being (1) informed about the scope and purpose of the school library media center program, (2) supportive of its personnel and program, and (3) determined to realize its full educational benefits through effective supervision and evaluation of all school personnel. Whenever administrators are supportive of and visibly involved in the functioning of the school library media center program, the chances are bettered that the program will be a constantly evolving one geared to the educational needs of the school. If it truly follows that the quality of the school library media center program is an accurate measure of the quality of the entire school, then it should just as logically follow that the quality of that program is a trustworthy indicator of the educational leadership of the school administrator. The authors address this book to all administrators who embrace these concepts and whose classroom and school library media center faculties team with them to create programs that contribute significantly to children's learning.

Introduction

This book is designed to assist the principal, curriculum coordinator, or any administrator whose responsibilities include supervising and evaluating school library media programs in understanding the scope of the task. In addition to the quality of the materials and the effectiveness of facilities, of classroom teachers, and of school library media teachers, there is an even more important factor to be evaluated: the educational use made of the total school library media program by students. Guides for evaluating school library media center *materials* and *equipment* are readily available. Assistance with the evaluation of school library media *personnel*, while less easily located, can be found in the literature. Much less has been written about the need for accurate methods of evaluating school library media *programs*, their attendant activities, and their degree of integration into the school's curriculum. All of these have a distinct bearing upon the students' grasp of information usage, an essential key to job and life success in an information age.

DEFINITION AND SCOPE

The probable reason for the lack of material relating to programs is the range of perceptions of what school library media programs are and should be. Philosophical development, changing educational needs, advancing technology, proliferation of information, upgrading of certification requirements to enhance school library media teachers' capabilities—all have contributed to confusing definitions, terminology, and varied interpretations.

When educational technology introduced films, filmstrips, transparencies, recordings of various sorts, and these came to have frequent use in classrooms, economic decisions had to be made. Just as creating a central collection of books within the school and sharing them for the benefit of all made sense, it was logical to do the same with nonprint materials. In the beginning, dual service was often provided by separate units known as the "library" and the "AV department." Gradually, in schools that made the best educational use of these materials, it became evident that teachers and students would be served more efficiently if the two services were operated from a single department. A "unified philosophy" was embraced. The preservice training of library media professionals came to include attention to existing nonprint media long before TV studios, videocassettes, and computers were factors.

Vocabulary pertaining to these audiovisual media came into being along with their use. The school library became known as a "media center," a "resource center," or a "learning resources center" in an effort to indicate that audiovisual materials were now housed, cataloged, and dispensed from the same place as books. To make certain that books were included when the word *media* was used and not overlooked in the midst of all the "glamor" technology, the awkward term *books and other media* was often used. Educators were encouraged to use the terms *print* and *nonprint* media when they wanted to talk about one or the other type of materials. Similarly, "school librarians" became "media specialists" whether or not the program offered in the school truly reflected the unified philosophy. There has been continuing controversy over use of the terms *specialist, generalist,* and *teacher* to describe the professionals in these positions.

The changes in terminology were meant to reflect more than just the inclusion of nonprint media with printed materials in the school library media center's arsenal of learning tools and resources. It was aimed also at doing away with the stodgy, traditional images attached to the words *library*—a storehouse for dusty books—and *librarian*—the protective keeper of those books, more anxious to enforce rules than to help students to learn. These out-moded images included a vision of the school library as static, trapped within its walls, and of the librarian as ready to "supple-ment" or "enrich" curriculum when called upon, but never taking the lead in innovation, in discovery, or as a member of the teaching team within the instructional program. The library bespoke the place where classes were taken in lockstep, periodically, whether they needed it or not, to receive some add-on experiences that had little to do with their classroom instruction. The changes in terminology were central to the strategy of school library leaders for raising expectations of the school library professional, vastly enlarging the scope of the job, and remaking the image of the librarian from reactive to proactive. They were aimed at project-ing the school library program itself as integrated with the cur-riculum and essential to independent learning, ready for small groups and individuals throughout the school day, a place where the classroom teacher could expect to work hand-in-glove with the library professional rather than "dumping" students there and taking a preparation or rest period.

The strategy worked well. Administrators who seldom had given a thought to the library (if they had one in the school), were proud of their modern media centers. And yet *media center* had little meaning for the average parent, community member, or public official; it seemed that the term could never gain the recognition value or the respect that the concept of *library* commanded. There came, in the seventies, the growing sense that the baby had been thrown out with the bathwater, and *library* was reincorporated in the rather redundant but more widely understood term *library media center*. As the role of the school library media center has emerged as part of the network of information sources and a part-ner with all other types of libraries, and the latter have expanded their mission and meaning, we have become proud to use the word again.

We prefer to use the term *school library media teacher* to iden-tify the professionals who are based in the center where print and nonprint media are collected and organized for use, together with the hardware needed for listening, viewing, and networking. They are truly teachers as they design instructional units, teach individuals and groups of students, and become increasingly important to the implementation of educational goals throughout the school building. Their interaction with all the knowledge and communications resources—now often including television studios, the production of audio and video tapes or cassettes, and the management of computers networked around the world—as well as with students, faculty, and the instructional program in all subject fields at all levels, is identified as "the school library media program."

NEED FOR EVALUATION

Increased attention to evaluation of all aspects of the school's programs has been a natural outgrowth of the insistent demand for accountability. It has become abundantly apparent that every school must have a constructive system for evaluating all levels of personnel.

> Effective management requires the use of evaluation systems that reflect the actual activities of workers. When the focus is on specific activities, evaluation can provide constructive feedback that has the potential to improve job performance. In education, however, teachers' jobs are inadequately designed, and expected outcomes are often ambiguous and conflicting. Therefore, evaluators spend disproportionate amounts of time appraising the individual rather than identifying obstacles that prevent a person from meeting job expectations.[1]

Samuel B. Bacharach and Sharon C. Conley comment that "organizations in the private sector spend large sums on the development of performance appraisal and job evaluation systems, and they devote considerable time to the training of evaluators. Education does neither of these things. More often than not, the systems of appraisal and evaluation in education are governed by the personal idiosyncrasies of the evaluators."[2]

There are many reasons for carrying out a careful evaluation of school library media programs. Concern for excellence in education requires knowledge of all functions of the school's program. In addition, administrators want to be convinced (so that they are on firm ground in assuring citizens, for one thing) that the most educational return is received for the funds invested.

There are other reasons for careful evaluation. Educators are continually looking for programs that lead to better preparation of their students for tomorrow's world. There is growing consensus that one of the most logical approaches to educating children for a future world we know little of is to teach them to find and process information and to develop a sense of responsibility for their own continuing self-education. The school library media program is a natural element in implementing this educational goal.

There is no conflict between teaching students to accept responsibility for continuing self-education and being able to cope with the fast pace of changing information. However, there are proponents of establishing a common core of knowledge to provide commonality in learning and not leave to chance what students will learn. They are fearful that in an attempt to prepare students to cope with and live in a world of rapid change, while valid in itself, at least one fundamental will be lost. Their concern is that "a wide range of stable fundamental knowledge is the key to rapid adaptation and the learning of new skills. It is precisely *because* the needs of a modern economy are so changeable that one needs broad general knowledge in order to flourish. Only high literacy (which implies broad general knowledge) provides the flexibility to learn new things fast. The only known route to broad general knowledge for all is for a nation's schools to provide all students with a substantial solid core of knowledge."[3] They go on to agree with Stevenson and Stigler that "the most significant diversity faced by our schools is not cultural diversity but, rather, diversity of academic preparation."[4] The school library media program will play an integral part in supplying information of any sort.When attention is given to finding the more efficient ways (time, people, and money saving) of handling both technical and educational aspects of the total school program, technology and its use plays a significant role. The school library media center is the technological center of the school, and this aspect of its role is enlarging rapidly. Through technology, access to information takes on a worldwide scope.

When there are library media programs mandated by local, county, or state agencies, evaluations of these programs are normally required also. There may be overall evaluations to be filed with various government agencies as part of state accreditation or other programs. Additionally, various regional and state accrediting associations are called in to assess the school's program. These associations take a careful look at the school library media center and its program during their deliberations, and self-evaluations before the evaluation team's visit are an important part of the procedure. There has been a noticeable increase in the attention given by these accrediting teams to the use made of the school library media center facilities. These teams want to know about the educational uses made by students and staff of the center as a learning/teaching tool, and the degree of integration of the program into the total learning/teaching experience. Changes in political climate may affect mandates and accompanying standards. However, the independent decision maker supporting the highest principles and standards will not be swayed away from them.

The school library media center, like the classroom, is a learning station, but unlike any other classroom in the school, its program simultaneously covers all grade and curriculum levels and all students. Evaluation of school library media teachers has to be based on much broader criteria than that of classroom teachers. The specific elements to be examined are unique to this professional position. The building level school library media teacher is a true generalist (New Hampshire certification uses this term) concerned with the individual differences of all the students in the school. The guidance counselor and the principal also have this broad responsibility, but their time is often spent on students with educational and other problems rather than on the full range of students. While school library media teachers are responsible for the technical administration of the school library media center, the schoolwide scope and diversity of their teaching duties are better compared to the responsibilities of the guidance counselors and principals than to those of classroom teachers. The standard teacher evaluation form is not adequate or even applicable. A form, customized for addressing the uniqueness of the school library media teacher's responsibilities, is required (see sample in Appendix A).

This book is designed to assist directly those who have been assigned the responsibility for evaluating the school library media program—both administrators and library media teachers—by describing the various aspects of the program from the basic philosophy of service to minute clerical functions. There is no intention of turning the administrators who use this book into school library media teachers, but rather to make known to them what effective school library media center personnel do in a day, month, semester, and year; what the ineffective school library media teacher ought or ought not to be doing and why; possible reasons why expectations are not being met and possible solutions to the identified problems. Practicing school library media teachers should find the book a useful tool when engaging in program or self-evaluation, and those in training may find it of preparatory value.

Attention is called to the responsibilities of the supervising administrators. Before turning to specifics, there are a number of basic philosophic points and educational assumptions to consider. In addition, literature and research addressing the use of school library media center programs contain useful information that should be noted. It is hoped that administrators wishing to promote library media programs within their schools will find materials to support their efforts.

PART ONE
Shared Responsibilities

1.   The Management Chain of Command

BOARDS OF EDUCATION

It is important to recognize and understand the chain of command in the school district. It starts at the top with the local board of education (elected or appointed) which is empowered by law to set policy for the school system. The board of education has the responsibility for presenting the yearly budget to the citizenry, and for hiring and firing the superintendent, who is the agent of the board. It approves other personnel to be hired throughout the school system, and it directs the building and remodeling of school facilities.

Activities within the school such as planning for curricular change, scheduling, purchasing of textbooks and school library media materials, and staff development are initiated on the building level and approved by both the system administration and the board of education. The entire matter of who approves and who initiates is a critical one because, while nothing can be done without its approval, the board of education does not directly initiate in-house matters. Its legal mandate is to establish and carry out policies.

Indirectly, however, members of boards of education can be agents of termination, change, or initiation of activities or programs in the schools. It is their responsibility as representatives of the community to question aspects of the school program and to relay parent and citizen concerns to the administration. As policy makers they must make sure that school programs and activities reflect those policies. The degree to which they are successful "watchdogs" varies widely, but when boards of education become initiators of specific school programs, something is more than amiss: It is unhealthy. The perceptions, regardless of their accuracy, held by members of the board of education about any facet of a school program will influence their decisions and their voting. Members of the board who are parents of children in the school system tend to perceive the instructional program, including that of the school library media center, only as it is interpreted by their children. Accuracy of children's reporting is naturally influenced by their biases, schedules, grade levels, previous experiences, personalities, and academic capabilities and achievements. The child who is an academic disappointment and whose achievement falls short of potential can result in a disgruntled parent on the board. The parent of an average student who believes the school pays too little attention to the middle-range student while giving more attention to upper and lower achievers may also be discontented. Federal and state laws concerning what must be done for the disabled, the gifted, or specific ethnic groups can create bad feelings and divisions on the board.

Disturbed board of education members, whatever the cause of their irritation, may or may not be knowledgeable about the educational problems involved. When the focus is on the school library media center program, there is often little understanding of that program or its scope and purposes. When supervising administrators have no better information to work with than that of the partially informed community, there can be only setbacks for the school library media program.

All too often in the school system, the board of education deals with "the schools" as a group of facilities without having the knowledge or time to recognize the accomplishments of each of the schools or to make comparisons. Careful, periodic, evaluative reports to the board on strengths and areas of needed improvement in particular aspects of each school's program could highlight the individual personalities and atmospheres of the schools and their staffs. An evaluative report on each of the school district's library media centers could be particularly enlightening because the library media program reflects and correlates with the energy, innovation, and success that mark the instructional program as a whole.

SUPERINTENDENTS

Many superintendents were practicing principals for some period of time before being elevated to posts as chief administrators of school systems and agents of boards of education. Their ability to interpret and gain support for school library media programs may depend upon how informed they were as principals about the program's functions, ideals, services, responsibilities, and curricular relationships. The principal has the most direct power to ensure a quality school library media program in a given school. The continued growth, development, and achievement of excellence in the individual school library media program can be enhanced by an understanding, informed, and committed superintendent, or inhibited by one without these characteristics.

The common progression of the budget proposal is from the school library media teacher to the principal, to the superintendent (or delegated district staff), and then to the board of education. Frequently this means that an attempt is made at each level to cut an honest and earnest proposal prepared by the professional who is most directly involved with the needs of the library media center program. Should the budget have to proceed upward from the board of education to the board of finance, the board of selectmen (city council or whatever political leadership body), and then to the public for their vote, what the citizenry actually vote on may be a five times discounted proposal bearing little resemblance to the amounts of money needed to sustain or support the type of program the students need and are entitled to. If budgets listed all the amounts that were presented and cut prior to final presentation to the voters, the citizenry—seeing the whole picture and the progression of cuts—might well want to support the initial request.

"Realistic" often means what administrators think they can get, not what is required educationally. Rates of inflation often appear as rates of real increase in annual budgets. Less often taken into full consideration are increases in student body numbers, innovations in curriculum, new courses, new approaches, and variables such as the growing range of student abilities and interests or shifting faculty concerns. It has been said that 3 percent of students will, like Lincoln, learn in spite of poor teaching, barren facilities, and meager materials. But this is minimal learning. The nation's future may depend upon higher-level learning by this 3 percent, but there must also be concern with optimal learning for all students—including the 97 percent who are not self-directed determined learners. Not all students will take full advantage of the opportunities made available to them, but what might the 3 percent become in a proper learning environment?

The channels through which decision making moves have value. Boards of education, being made up of people with varying community views, represent a continuous interfacing of educational wishes, needs, and goals of the community as a whole. They also reflect to their communities this range of views and desires for action. Each of the positions along the chain of command and those who hold them must relate to the previous one as well as to the one that comes after, and communicate in both directions. The superintendent as the agent of the board of education needs to keep the principals aware of the community's reactions and interpretations of school matters just as the principals' varying programs and views need to be conveyed to the board of education. In this way, the differences as well as similarities of the schools within the system will be brought to the attention of the board of education.

SYSTEM-LEVEL PERSONNEL

In larger school systems there may be a position for a systemwide curriculum director and a systemwide library media supervisor, as well as other subject area supervisors or consultants. When these persons are available on the educational team, some of the responsibility for maintaining the quality of programs falls on them. They also have a role to play in ensuring equality of educational opportunity to students and among schools within the system. District personnel advise, facilitate, and ensure compliance with local, state, and federal mandates relating to their area of responsibility, but the primary responsibility for the success of the individual school still rests with the principal of that school.

Effective systemwide curriculum directors can be instrumental in developing curriculum guides that incorporate school library media center usage into ongoing classroom activity. An overall curricular plan, once developed, must be implemented. There are two ways of addressing the need. One is to place appropriate goals, standards, and references in the curriculum guide for each and every discipline, not just language arts and perhaps social studies. The other option is to create a separate media skills document that applies to all disciplines across the curriculum. Either plan will work, but neither is any better than the supervisory authority that ensures its implementation.

The systemwide library media supervisors may take a direct hand in interpreting the curriculum guides and improving their results through work with individual school library media teachers. They also accept some of the budgetary planning responsibilities that otherwise would fall to the building level library media teacher. They may help tremendously by instituting centralized training, processing, and mass purchasing benefits. Above all, they project as a goal the attainment of a truly modern program. Modern, in this case, means a program devoted to the training and education of all students to be prepared for the world in which they will participate as adults. This program calls for a wide variety of thought processes, search and technical skills, use of proliferating information, fluent communicating abilities, and a sense of responsibility for lifelong learning. District-level personnel should make independent, highly professional efforts to keep up with the changes in materials, technology, and modes of instruction. Without knowledge and understanding of current needs and a constantly updated vision of potential, these people may not demand and support the level of school library media programs the principal needs and wants in the school. Principals should not accept system-level personnel's actions or proposals without question, nor be hesitant to insist on raising program standards in their schools.

PRINCIPALS

The principal is chiefly responsible for what the school is and what it may become. This role is increasingly complex and its responsibilities more diversified due to the changes in society and the effect of these changes on the educational needs of the students. The principal has traditionally been viewed as the key person in the improvement of education. This is most certainly true where school library media center programs are concerned. It is the principal who determines their visibility and importance as perceived in the school. It is also the principal who largely determines the degree to which the library media program is integrated into the instructional program. Small schools and understaffed larger schools create work situations in which, at least during the school day, the library media teacher who works alone has no one to consult with or with whom to share problems or successes. If principals and school library media teachers fail to be a mutually supportive team promoting the program together, the singleton school library media teacher's morale can easily sink.

The importance of the principals' role to the success of school library media programs is in line with their overall leadership and influence. Studies reported in general education and library literature repeatedly underscore this point. Examples of such statements include:

> If we accept the premise that the prime purpose of the school is the establishment of a creative environment wherein the learning process can most effectively be achieved, then we must conclude that the principal's chief role lies in being able to effect such an environment through dynamic leadership. . . . Although the increasing demands upon the principal's time tend to erode his role as an instructional leader, research has indicated this area as the one of greatest concern to principals. It is the one to which principals state they most would like to devote themselves. . . . The supervising principal as an instructional leader must clear avenues for growth and improvement, identify talents and abilities in others, and release the potential within all persons concerned.[5]

In order to become a strongly supportive advocate of the school library media program, able to share expectations of it with the entire faculty and student body, the parents, the community, and the administration, the principal must become committed to the program and be convinced of its importance. How do administrators know what a good library media program is? Well, they might possibly as children have attended schools with good school library media programs at the elementary and high school levels. There is a slight chance (pretty slim, in fact) that some university courses they took included units on what constitutes quality in a school library media program, and what it can do to improve teaching and educational achievement. Perhaps as education majors their practice teaching was done in schools with excellent school library media programs, and master teachers who made good use of them as learning/teaching tools. Maybe the schools in which they were employed as teachers were equipped with high-quality library media centers, and they had the opportunity to use diversified resources to individualize and motivate learning.

What is more likely than any of these, however, is that they have had the chance—perhaps as teachers, perhaps not until they became principals—to visit schools where they could observe the difference that proper library media programs make in achieving overall goals of instruction. Perhaps professional reading, a workshop, conference program, or casual conversation with a colleague led to initial interest, exploration of, and final commitment to the importance of having a good school library media program in every school at every level. Whatever the exposure, however the commitment came about, it is an essential first step.

It is still necessary to learn about the components of the program if, as an administrator, one plans to evaluate what exists and build toward something better. To learn about these elements requires some reading in the literature of the school library media field and the taking of some specialized courses. To date, standard textbooks used in administration classes do little more than mention the school library media center, if that. Few professors of administration place any emphasis on this facet of the school's instructional program, and fewer still have any first-hand knowledge of school library media functions. Professors' personal experience often dates from before the development and reshaping that created the modern school library media center and its program.

The literature of school library media programs deals with the resources needed to create the programs (materials, facilities, staff, and funding), but it deals also with process and product—the objectives and the results to be expected. The literature is full of references to learning taxonomies, critical thinking, and analysis, synthesis, and evaluation of information. The point of the higher-order thinking skills approach is to help equip students to become independent learners.

In the adult world, it is in libraries that much continuing self-education can take place. Granted, technology makes it possible to envision home and office information terminals, but the scope and cost of these services will continue to lead many users to public information sources. Students who have learned in their school library media centers to use the tools of inquiry and to apply the information they acquire through their use, can exercise these skills confidently in all types of libraries throughout their lives. If the students do not become successful users of the school library media centers and able processors of information, the chances are strong that not only will they not be users of libraries or information services beyond their school years, but that they will cripple their abilities to contribute and to compete. So all persons in the school district's chain of management command bear responsibility for providing the best school library media opportunities within their power.

2. Operating the Program: Staff and Other Resources

RESPONSIBILITIES

> Visionaries see a future of telecommuting workers, interactive libraries and multimedia classrooms. They speak of electronic town meetings and virtual communities. Commerce and business will shift from offices and malls to networks and modems. And the freedom of digital networks will make government more democratic. Baloney. Do our computer pundits lack all common sense? The truth is no online database will replace your daily newspaper, no CD-ROM can take the place of a competent teacher and no computer network will change the way government works.[6]

The bottom line is that no amount of technology can supplant the use of the human brain. Educators have the responsibility to students to equip them to live successfully in an unknown world. Comprehension of the effects of technology on society, of its contributions, limitations, and dangers is every bit as important as comprehension of how technology works and what it is capable of doing.

To acquire this comprehension does call for access to technology and the opportunity to learn to use it. It calls for teachers who effectively employ technology as a teaching tool, who refuse to let what they have available go to waste with improper application. "Having enough terminals to go around is one problem. But another important question is what the equipment is used for."[7]

The young have taken to computers quite readily while numbers of the older generation have chosen not to. "These aging choose-nots become a more serious issue when they are teachers in schools. Even if schools manage to acquire state-of-the-art equipment, there is no guarantee that trained adults will be available to understand them."[8]

Herein lies the awesome responsibility for school principals—not only to acquire the equipment but to develop the right kind of curriculum and faculty to implement it so that students get the most educational value from the community's investment. The way that the principal employs evaluation has a great deal to do with the success of not only the school library media program, but the overall school educational program.

The principal who is responsible for supervising and evaluating the school library media center program and its personnel soon realizes that there are no simple answers to the problems and few shortcuts to the goal of securing effective services. There are, of course, many options as to where to start the upgrading process, but the most important thing is that the plan for growth and development be ongoing with short-term objectives and long-range goals. These objectives and goals are an essential part of the evaluation process.

Because of the rapid rate of technological as well as societal changes, the planned program for developing the school library media program must be continuously upgraded. The administrator must keep abreast of changing outlooks in many directions to keep the school library media program dynamic and contemporary. The program must not just reflect or react to developments that affect education as a whole, but anticipate them in order to prepare students for the world into which they will graduate.

Planning for a school library media program begins with the expertise of the school library media teacher as department head. If the school library media teacher fails to function in this capacity, then the immediate supervisor (either the vice-principal who has day-to-day responsibility for the school library media program or the principal) must set this planning into action. The principal will attempt to involve the school library media teacher, but if after reasonable effort to accomplish this has been made and has failed, more direct action must be taken.

The inadequacy of the school library media teacher as a professional is no excuse for a lack of a plan for a developing school library media program. Long- and short-term goals must be related to what is needed for the students and their education, not set on the basis of present provisions. The types and amounts of staff needed to put this plan into operation must be dealt with. Not having a plan has no validity. The school library media program does not exist in a vacuum and therefore is never static. Every change in curriculum, personnel, teaching staff, student population, societal pressures and needs, community interests, the economy, the job market, the percentage of students going on to higher education, and technological advances impacts on the school library media program, both immediately and in the near future. Educational and societal trends must be acknowledged and responded to. The search skills students need today will become even more important in the uncertain future. Once we could prepare students for positions we knew would be available when they had completed their education. Now we have only an incomplete idea of what kinds of jobs will be available to our students when they leave school. Use of databases, online searching, scanning microforms, and seeking out the latest information on a topic is, and will continue to be, required. More important still is the use made of this information. Higher-order intellectual skills, including analytical skills, creative thinking, problem solving, and innovative application of ideas are vital parts of one's everyday world. Equally imperative is the ability to communicate these ideas both in writing and orally. These are the survival skills of today and tomorrow. They are the curricular basics. These skills are learned and polished in the school library media center every bit as much as in the classroom. This is why the integration of the two learning areas—classroom and school library media center—through cooperative planning, instructional design, and teamed instruction becomes imperative.

STAFFING

As the operation of the school library media center program is examined and evaluated, it becomes clear that one person alone is not going to be able to produce all that is wanted. The most supportive, demanding principal working to establish an effective school library media program cannot do it alone. The successful program is a result of teamwork—schoolwide cooperation and integration. But every team has a captain, and the school's captain is the principal. To provide knowledgeable leadership, the principal must understand not only what the results of the program must be, but how to obtain those results. This calls for continuous communication with classroom teachers regarding the use of the school library media center as a learning/teaching tool. It calls for being personally knowledgeable regarding the administrative management, technical processing, and instructional functions of the school library media teachers' roles.

Staff who are inadequate to the tasks required for this progressive program must be brought up to par. Missing or weak skills must be worked on with a measurable outcome required to attest to accomplishments. Staff development or college class enrollment, without corollary evaluation and performance requirements, do not guarantee results. Required outcomes clearly stated and understood by both the staff and the administration are essential. Failure to measure up should lead to a limited period of probation followed by reassignment or dismissal. When agreed-upon improvements take place, close supervisory follow-up should ensure continuing growth and development.

Not every school is blessed with gifted school library media teachers. When this professional is substandard, the principal is the one who must press aggressively for improvement and not settle for mediocrity. This requires full knowledge of what a quality person is and does. When a new school library media teacher is to be hired, the principal needs to know what abilities and attributes to look for, along with what questions to ask in the interview and what promises to make and keep. (See job description and job function documents in Appendix B.) Competency should be examined carefully so that the performance demands made on the school library media teacher will be met and surpassed.

Given the principal's hiring and firing power, it is vital that this administrator thoroughly understand the training, education, capabilities, aptitudes, and temperament required for both the professional and the support staff positions in a school library media center. School library media teachers are by definition and practice fully educated as teachers and librarians. The professional in charge of the school library media program is also a department head, and, as such, a middle-level administrator who, to be effective, should have had previous experience as a building-level school library media staff member.

The hiring of support staff in the school library media center will be done by the principal and/or principal plus the superintendent or someone on the district staff to whom authority is delegated. School library media teachers may make recommendations and suggestions, but it is the principal who often has the final say on who is hired to work in the building. It is imperative that the principal understand that clerical-level personnel for school library media centers cannot be evaluated on the same basis as those who do clerical work in the school office. Typing skills for a school library media center are more concerned with accuracy than speed, and tests for office typists are often based on the criterion of word-per-minute. The parameters and idiosyncrasies of keyboard skills pertaining to catalog card or computer entry, the notations needed for barcodes or transaction cards and pockets and labels for library materials call for special training and aptitudes quite different from those required of most office clerks. While contracts may treat all clerical personnel alike, the aware principal will recognize that the specially trained school library media center support staff should be used where their training is of benefit.

The tasks required for the effective operation of the media center are of both a professional and nonprofessional nature. Professional tasks include instruction, collaborative planning with teachers, interaction with students, selection of materials, excellent reference skills, and other responsibilities that require professional training and judgment. Nonprofessional tasks include, among others, filing, circulating, shelving, mending, delivering, accepting, and processing materials as well as preparing overdues, making copies, and keeping equipment functioning. National professional standards call for two support staff members for every professional, and in fact the nonprofessional tasks divide into technical and user-oriented services. When the recommended staffing pattern is followed, it becomes useful to designate responsibilities and to keep these responsibilities and talents in mind when interviewing and hiring. When there is only one nonprofessional support staff person, the technical side gets the attention first. The school library media teacher accepts responsibility for the users' services normally performed by a nonprofessional in addition to those of a professional nature. Where there are no nonprofessional support staff members, the school library media teacher provides clerical and other support staff services as well as professional services. In this instance, professional time is drawn off from professionally oriented activities and service, and is wastefully misspent on clerical tasks.

When volunteers are recruited to take the place of paid support staff, their presence will further impact on the one and only professional. The volunteer concept is often misleading. Recruitment, selection, training, observation (supervision), and scheduling are all time-consuming responsibilities of the school library media teacher when there is no nonprofessional staff to supervise volunteer work. Even with a volunteer coordinator of volunteers, the on-the-scene responsibilities do consume time. Volunteers, like paid clerical workers, should be assigned tasks in accordance with their proclivities and abilities. Instructional aides and technical aides do different jobs and require specific skills and training. While the school library media teachers may fully understand the desirability of having volunteers, they may be unable to give up the necessary time to make the program viable. The cost in professional time can be exorbitant.

Administrators often fear the presence of volunteers in the school. Even when the school library media teacher is eager and willing to devote personal time to recruitment and training, seeing the long-range value, the administrator may be unwilling to have these "strangers" in the building on a regular basis. The truth is that the vast majority of regular volunteers become boosters for the school program and they are among the best supporters at budget time. On the other hand, there must be a certain degree of valid self-assurance on the part of the administration to make the venture successful. Poorly run programs do invite criticism. Wise principals will keep in touch with the volunteer program so that they may render the necessary praise and thanks as it is due and be aware of trouble spots and criticisms before they get out of hand or "go public."

There is wisdom in calling school library media support staff something other than the generic term *aide* which also applies to classroom helpers and hall monitors. When budget cuts are made across the board and aides are abolished, the effect of the loss on the school library media center can be significantly more severe than elsewhere. Their specialized skills and training have been acquired at considerable cost and are not readily replaced.

EVALUATING THE SCHOOL
LIBRARY MEDIA PROFESSIONAL

To evaluate school library media teachers adequately requires evaluating the end product—the school library media program—as well. Everything that school library media teachers do as a part of the job should result in bettering the overall learning opportunity for all students. The school library media teachers have been characterized as wearing many hats at the same time and always being "busy" with something. While this may be apt, it makes evaluation difficult. Just how many hats should be worn at any given time? Or one after the other in a day, week, semester, school year, or a couple of years? While school library media teachers want to engage in these multiple roles, wish their attendant responsibilities to be recognized, and want to be evaluated for more than their technical processing and organizing roles, they may become uneasy if the evaluator does not keep all this in perspective. There needs to be clear-cut understanding about what is expected by the evaluator, and how often certain items on the checklist should be carried out. Inability to "do it all" is not necessarily a reflection of a lack of industry, knowledge, skill, or creativity on the part of the school library media teacher. When there is no support staff, or too few professionals for the size of the student body, some activities may seldom occur. It is simply impossible to obtain the full potential from the school library media center program unless four essential facets are in place: space, materials, personnel, and access.

When the evaluating administrator feels he or she is an active part of the school library media center team, this administrator is involved in establishing and implementing goals and objectives, fights the battle of the budget, and understands the impact of administrative decisions. Such an administrator also recognizes the school library media teachers' contributions, understands the demands of the multifaceted library media teacher's role, and is both a frequent visitor to and remains in communication with the center. The result is productive, effective, satisfied school library media teachers. Like all other teachers, library media professionals respond well to principals who demonstrate consistent policies, supportive actions, availability, communication, approachability, impartiality, and who give praise and show appreciation.

Many evaluation forms are designed so that the administrator may consider one "hat" at a time. When the school library media teachers' activities are related to the program, and results are also measured, it becomes possible to evaluate the educational return being received from the school library media center investment. The point of the evaluation is to identify ways to increase return, or to determine that the best possible value is already being received from the interaction of personnel and materials. Long- and short-range plans are clearly dependent upon accurate and honest evaluation.

THE SCHOOL LIBRARY MEDIA PROFESSIONAL
AS AN INFORMATION SPECIALIST

The term *information specialist* is an outgrowth of the proliferation of information carriers. The school library media professional is the school staff member whose speciality is information and as such must be knowledgeable about all types of sources of information, how they may be tapped, and the learning purpose that each will serve best. These types range from the printed page, spoken word recordings, and film to the emerging digital technologies which include microcomputers, laptops, main frames, facsimile transmission, distance learning, satellite, cable television, microwave, modem, videodisc, CD-ROM, electronic databases, and worldwide information networks.

It is to the school library media professional that administrators, faculty, and students should be able to turn for information. Therefore, the library media professional should be conversant with retrieval systems for accurate and efficient access to information resources, knowledgeable about technological developments, and able to assess the potential impact of emerging information and instructional technologies on the school program. If the school is engaging in remodeling or adding to its technology facilities, the library media professional is informed or knows where to go to find the needed information and/or consultants who have the necessary competence.

In short, the staff member who is the "technology coordinator must be a facilitator who assists the administration and teachers with overall design and implementation of programs including finding the appropriate hardware, software, methods, and training needed to integrate technology into the curriculum."[9]

THE SCHOOL LIBRARY MEDIA PROFESSIONAL AS A TEACHER

Informal Student Instruction

There are many clues that students are having difficulty in finding solutions or information. Not all chitchat taking place in the library is idle socializing. There is often reluctance to "interrupt" the librarian, a misunderstanding sometimes shared by the teachers as well. Each student query leads to an individualized teaching opportunity with that student. For each student who asks a question there are nine others who do not formally ask. The well-prepared school library media teacher, sensitive to the students' questions and needs, will be able to guide any student to find pertinent material. Small groups of students, as well as individual students, regardless of how well directed they may be before entering the school library media center, will still need guidance and suggestions if their efforts are to be fruitful. For those who come without any direction from the classroom, there is a still greater teaching obligation on the part of the media professional to help the students recognize their mission, clarify their goals, and identify productive procedures.

Formal Student Instruction

Formal classroom teaching takes place in either the school library media center or in the classrooms of teachers who enlist the assistance of the school library media teacher. Types of formal instruction could include introduction of a new topic—for example, the westward expansion in United States history, elementary or secondary; the use of specific types of materials such as biographies; the use of reference tools that serve special needs such as indexes to poetry or short stories or a specialized handbook of chemistry or physics; bibliography construction; and any number of computer approaches using word processing and networking. Sometimes this instruction is done in the library media center, but it is sometimes more effective when the school library media teacher goes to the classroom or computer lab to teach the lesson. Team teaching with a classroom or subject teacher creates student interest. It allows for the special talents of each teacher to be used to the best advantage, and even better, the setting causes students to recognize the importance placed by the classroom teacher on the information presented by the school library media teacher. Seeing the classroom teacher take notes, and realizing that the classroom teacher knows what material has been covered, further emphasizes the relevance of the library media teacher's lesson to the classroom curriculum assignments.

Multiclass Instruction

In the crowded school schedule it makes no sense to teach the same unit to four different classes in the same week. Two or more classes could be scheduled together. Tape the instruction in the first class and let it be used on tape in the following classes, or by those who were either absent when the instruction was given or who may want to review the material. The live presentations can be staggered throughout the classrooms so that the same class is not always the one taped. Some means by which student questions can be answered must be developed. One way is for the teacher to use the tape in the classroom with the students, noting the questions that are raised. When the areas that are unclear are identified, the school library media teacher can be asked to come to the classroom and discuss the problems with the students. This may take only a few minutes, especially when the classroom teacher has become thoroughly familiar with the material. Most classrooms have direct communication with other rooms in the school, making the school library media teacher only a phone call, intercom, or e-mail communication away.

Orientation for classes new to the building certainly can be accomplished by the use of videocassette programs. These tapes are retained so that transfer students entering the school throughout the year may view them as a part of their orientation as well. Additionally, individualized instruction packets can be made available to students who are late bloomers, ahead of their classes in their needs, or for some other reason simply out of sync and in need of some specialized instruction.

Self-Evaluation

School library media teachers should engage in continuous self-evaluation. The units that are designed to support classroom assignments have clear-cut purposes. However, it is important to determine whether the students got out of the lesson what was intended. Should the unit have been taught by the school library media teacher, or should the classroom teacher have provided the instruction? Should there be some in-service instruction to equip the classroom teacher to handle that unit? Is the same example always used: In the case of *Reader's Guide*, is it always taught in the social studies curriculum? Or should it be treated as a developmental skill taught throughout the grades using varying or different parts of the curriculum for practice? Is it perhaps a unit in the English grammar textbook in which all students are asked to answer identical questions that in time become completely outdated? One example is a question calling for the answer "*Science News Letter*," a magazine that had been renamed *Science News* many years before. The old textbooks, using the old question and providing the answer for the classroom teacher accordingly, cause students confusion and possibly to be marked incorrectly. Unless there is contact with someone who is aware of the changes, a teaching/learning opportunity regarding publishers' practice of changing periodical titles is lost. So, too, is the students' opportunity to learn the impact of title changes on their search approaches and processes.

When the teaching of search skills is associated only with the English curriculum, do students learn to footnote and credit sources only for English papers, ignoring the practice for other subjects? Is there any carryover? Wouldn't there be if such practice were called for also in social studies, art, science, or vocational arts classes?

Is interlibrary loan service brought into use? Are human resources in the area known and brought into the schools? And, if so, are they listed under subject headings in the school library media center catalog so that they will be thought about another time?

To what extent is computerized networking used? Is the school library linked to other libraries in the local area? Within the state or region? Are specialized information networks subscribed to and made available to students? Are CD-ROM materials a part of the students' collection? Do students turn to computerized knowledge banks as easily and as confidently as they turn to print sources?

The increasingly in-depth teaching and practice of search skills in the elementary and secondary grades is of the utmost importance. If students do not learn how to do reference searches for the information they need *before* they get to college, and perhaps to graduate education afterward, the chances are good that they will have missed out on this training for life. When course syllabi were examined (162 of them, representative of all colleges and course levels at Pennsylvania State University in 1982), it was learned that only 8 percent of the courses required much library usage, and 63 percent required none at all. When the advanced courses were examined, only 11.5 percent required much library use, and 56 percent still required absolutely none. This study correlated well with other similar studies.[10] The explanation given is that there is a difference between "search" and "research." Scholars tend to feel that they need to use "primary materials" exclusively, and recommend to their graduate students the use of footnotes in preference to bibliographies for locating information on which to base their own research. Librarians, on the other hand, rely upon bibliographies to identify useful sources.

There may be a sizable amount of information that can be identified on a given subject through the use of bibliographies and indexes. One of the important facets of "search" is the probability of chance discoveries that occur while browsing through library shelves. With the advent of computerized databases there has come the mistaken notion that the machines will produce 100 percent coverage of a field. It should be evident to the trained searcher for references that as with any other type of index, what is to be found depends upon the skill and diligence of the catalogers or indexers and the scope and limitations of their interests and knowledge. Database users must understand from their earliest learning years that database indexes are not all-inclusive and are only as good as the human intelligence that created them. On the other hand, students need to learn early the effect of currency on information that networked databases can provide. Many students complain bitterly about having been "cheated" and ill-prepared by earlier schooling to do the information seeking that is expected of them. Some see, finally, that if they had had the requisite search skills they could have done better work even though they were not required by their professors to use the library. But when people do not know what it is that they do not know there can be little progress. This may explain why comparatively few undergraduate students take advantage of the reference skills instruction that many university libraries offer to first-year students. Coming from schools where an often inadequate effort has been made to give them "library skills," they assume that they know all that they need to know. In fact, they may have absorbed next to nothing about the range of references they have never learned to consult, nor how to use the vast reservoir of materials available to them.

Teaching with Displays

Placing displays both in the school library media center and elsewhere throughout the school is effective teaching that assists teachers and students alike. Choice of the topic, its timeliness, and its integration with curriculum all have impact. Pilgrims at Thanksgiving may be timely so far as the calendar is concerned, but that topic in the curriculum may come at some other time in the year. Why not feature Pilgrims when the curriculum does and when the contribution would be greatest? What if it is October? Come November the emphasis could be on the giving of thanks in various ways around the world and in different eras. The Ides of March theme would work as well with Shakespeare as with the study of Rome. And why not make the display an interactive or involvement type so that students can learn from it in the same way they do from learning centers?

THE SCHOOL LIBRARY MEDIA PROFESSIONAL AS AN INSTRUCTIONAL CONSULTANT

In the role of instructional consultant the library media teacher will need the opportunity to work with teachers in developing the instructional units used in the classrooms. Planning time must be provided if the fullest use is to be made of the instructional teaming that is possible between library media and classroom teachers. Although a valuable exchange can be made during a passing encounter in the corridor, over a lunchtime sandwich, or through a desk-to-desk e-mail scribble, these are no substitute for being able to sit down together to work and think uninterruptedly.

Decisions must be made about the intent and content of the assignment, the needs and abilities of the students, the purpose and design of activities, the materials to be used, the shared methods of presentation and evaluation. Obviously, when the library media teacher operates from a flexible schedule, not only is planning time more available, but the planned activities reflect that same flexibility. The bell does not control the learning opportunity; the educational need does. The teaming teachers can construct learning opportunities that challenge students to do their best work.

Library media and classroom teachers work together to "foster a process of discovery through which students learn how to use information resources effectively while pursuing questions they find meaningful. . . . A learner cannot identify resources—whether print, online, or human—without first having a question to ask, a problem to solve, or a project to complete. . . . If it's the educator's job to 'cover' content, then surrounding the content with resource-based learning activities makes the experience that much more interactive, collaborative, and vivid for learners."[11]

When resource-based learning is to become the way of

instruction in a school, adaptation will be required to meet "the challenges of different grade levels. At the elementary level, efforts may be hampered by inflexible schedules or the tendency of students to stay with one teacher too much. In middle schools, the team-teaching structures that lend themselves to resource-based learning are often in place already. But in high schools, students are often constrained by short class periods and rigid content demands that make it hard for teachers to develop the flexibility needed for resource-based learning."[12]

It follows that the library media teacher must be well informed about educational practice, learning theory, and what is going on in the classroom. The classroom teacher provides clues to the library media teacher regarding the goals of the assignment and how it fits into the curriculum. When they work together, the most effective materials can be identified and incorporated into the lesson plans.

It also follows that the library media teacher must be able to help with and design student assessment right along with the classroom teacher. One of the great changes taking place in the schools has to do with assessment. Throughout the literature one reads that the one thing educators seem certain about is what "good assessment" is not; namely, multiple-choice questions. To the extent that educational reform rejects traditional testing and quizzing in favor of innovative forms of performance-based assessment, all educators are involved. Jorgensen observes: "As education reform begins to take hold across the country, the role of assessment in effecting change is becoming more and more clear. Classroom instruction will not focus on higher-order thinking skills as long as traditional multiple-choice tests measure primarily low-level recall and recognition skills. Thus, an important aspect of reform is developing innovative methods of assessment."[13] The library media teachers must be able to hold their own in creating sound methods of assessment that call for students to exhibit their abilities to use the information they acquire in meaningful ways through performance-based approaches.

Informal Teaching of Teachers

Ideally, the school library media teacher is a master teacher, knowledgeable not only in the curriculum and educational goals of a particular school, but also those of American education in general. The school library media teacher, through working with other teachers and seeing the results of their assignments translated into student search for materials, has a comprehensive idea of the differences in teaching styles used by classroom teachers. By anticipating teachers' needs, the library media teacher, throughout the school year, makes recommendations for the use of specific materials—those already owned, possible to purchase, or soon to be published. Because of having experienced the strain put on the collection when several classes get identical assignments simultaneously, the library media teacher will work with teachers to stagger assignments. These conflicts can be minimized. Placing materials on reserve and/or on curtailed or shortened circulation is a help, but other methods may prove more beneficial in the long run.

When the school library media teacher is an active member of the various department meetings or curriculum committees these problems can be aired, discussed, and dealt with in ways that will benefit both teaching and learning. As the resources expert of the school, the library media teacher should be involved in planning for curriculum revision. When departments fail to utilize this in-house expertise, the bibliographies listed in the newly revised curriculum manual often contain a majority of titles that are out of print or outdated and omit important newer entries. Subject teachers tend to rely on bibliographies found at chapter ends and on book reviews in their professional periodicals. These titles are almost always several years past their publication date when used in a text or when they are reviewed. Frequently, they are difficult to acquire even if still useful. If they are not already owned by the school library media center, or quickly and inexpensively available electronically, students will have difficulty with the assignments they are given.

School library media teachers make suggestions to other teachers about approaches as well as materials to be used in a content area. They initiate this activity and anticipate needs; they do not depend upon classroom teachers coming to them. They look for ways to facilitate and encourage use of the media center's materials collection. As they come to know teachers' strengths, interests, talents, and hobbies, they can feed material to those strengths and interests that can enrich classroom activities.

Additionally, classroom teachers should be made aware and reminded often that many less familiar materials such as charts, maps, posters, the picture in the principal's office, or the letters from soldiers in the Civil War that are in the local historical museum library are cataloged in the library media center as they indeed should be. These can be used to add interest and variety to learning.

Staff Development

There needs to be both formal staff development planning and execution and the daily informal one-on-one upgrading of staff skills, techniques, awareness, and knowledge of materials. The school library media teachers who would maintain a high level of interest in faculty colleagues must share new ideas and methodologies in order to keep alive an enthusiastic attitude toward service. Simply alerting or reminding teachers that you are there for any help that they need will not ensure their coming for that help. Many people view making such a request with some uncertainty about their own adequacy and become defensive. Administrators can help by promoting the desirability of asking for help, but even so, many teachers will not welcome being urged to make public contact with the school library media teacher. While the elementary school child is conditioned to asking adults for help or direction, once students reach junior high school, and perhaps from there on, they are reticent about seeking help from the professional staff. This places greater responsibility on the school library media center staff to offer assistance without being asked and to be on the lookout for students and teachers who would like help but probably will not ask for it. The staff in the library media center must appear ready and eager to assist, but all too often we hear, "I didn't want to interrupt you," or "I know you are busy." The library media teacher who hears this often must make a conscious effort to avoid looking so intently busy with "more important" duties that questions and unspoken needs of patrons are turned off.

In order to carry out the all-important teaching/facilitating role, good time management is a must. There are many paperwork and routine tasks that must be done in order to keep the school library media center running efficiently. A good manager must be extremely well organized, and yet flexible enough to drop what is being worked on to attend to an important immediate need. This takes good planning, so that one is not always running behind and up against deadlines.

THE SCHOOL LIBRARY MEDIA
PROFESSIONAL AS A MANAGER

The Library Media Center

The school library media professional has the responsibility for the library media center, a teaching area representing both a sizable investment and a significant educational return to the taxpayer. It requires business acumen and organizational skills at a level that in the business world would be rated at least as middle management. The head school library media teacher supervises the other media professionals, the nonprofessional support staff, student assistants, and volunteers. While some of these responsibilities can be delegated, the ultimate responsibility resides with the head professional.

Although the ultimate authority for hiring and firing staff members may not be given to the head school library media teachers, they should be involved in these processes. Those who keep up with library media professional activities in the state and region will be aware of other professionals who might be interested in a position that becomes available. Not only are they aware of specific persons, they also understand the kinds of talents, special skills, and character traits required of the applicant. In addition, they know the job description to be given to the administrators as they institute a search for candidates. Even well-trained, experienced persons who are hired will need to be indoctrinated into the specifics of a particular school and its library media center, and the responsibility for this training rests with the head library media professional. (See job description and job function documents in Appendix B.)

From the fiscal point of view, there is much responsibility for the library media teacher, or the head if there are several. The collection in the average high school now costs at least $45 per volume on average. A collection of a mere 22,000 items approaches a million dollars—for books alone. Add to this all the computer lab and other equipment used in computerized programs, the nonprint materials and hardware needed for their use, the furniture, shelving, and other specialized equipment, and it is easy to see that the fiscal responsibility must be in the hands of a knowledgeable, capable, and efficient person.

From the public information point of view, the head of the library media center is the spokesperson for the school library media program. This person must, therefore, demonstrate communication skills of the highest order. They are needed for working with the community, the administration of the school, the classroom teachers, staff, and students. Because this person represents the school library media program, it is vital that this image be a dynamic, active, knowledgeable one. The school library media program is a service operation as well as a force for educational leadership. It is expected that the school library media teachers will be well grounded in the latest developments of the field's specialties, have an eye open toward change and improvement within the school library media center organization and its program, and be a catalyst for disseminating professional literature.

The Technology Responsibility

The library media teacher has varying degrees of responsibility depending on the staffing in the building and at the system level. In some cases total responsibility falls on the library media teachers. In others it is shared among technology teachers, system level coordinators, and technology support personnel.

However the responsibilities are shared, decisions need to be made relative to hardware, furniture, and software purchases, wiring and retrofitting, networking components, future plans, scheduling, curricular application, training, budgeting, and security. Whenever there are multiple personnel working with technology, teamwork is essential. While specific responsibilities may be assigned to individuals, the underlying philosophy of utilization of technology is mutually supported.

FACILITIES DESIGN AND CONFLICTS OF INTEREST

Working together to get the school library media center facility the school truly needs should be a joyous experience, but it often becomes a frustrating one instead. Even when many of the initial steps in planning are properly done, subsequent compromises can severely cripple the potential of the intended program. Mostly, the problem arises from the wide range and disparity of both experience and views held by persons responsible for the planning. Building committee members are not always close to the intended users of the facility, and tend to hold out for features that have special meaning for them. For example, a man who hated the portholed library doors of his youth insisted on glassed corridor walls so that "students could see into the library and be attracted in." Because of the configuration of the area this removed much-needed wall space and also created a disturbance problem when students inside and outside of the glass walls wished to communicate with their friends. Architects have not by definition worked in a school library media center and do not aptly differentiate among maturity levels of students. Constructing an inflexible layout will choke a vibrant and growing school library media program that must change, rearrange, and adapt to educational needs to remain successful. Sometimes school administrators, who should know better, allow themselves to be carried away by the lure of a physical appearance of the room and its furnishings that does not fit the functions. Of course, the atmosphere of the school library media center is of prime importance, influencing its use markedly, but appearance is only one facet of environment. Ultimately, it is the school library media teachers who must make sense out of the center, live in it and make it useful, no matter how it is designed, and who sadly put aside all of the "if onlys" that would have made implementing a first-rate program much easier.

On the other hand, the building committee accepts the architects' final plans and the estimated total cost of the structure. Theirs is the final authority—the signature on the contract. Usually there is a budget ceiling and the cost of the desired features will exceed it. Immediately, cuts begin to be imposed. Priorities differ, causing conflict, frustration, and anger to take over unless a sensible resolution can be achieved. It is a miracle that many school library media centers come off physically as well as they do, but they are rarely as program-oriented as they could be. What is it that gets in the way of success? Often it is the hidden agendas of the decision makers, or the politics of compromise. More often it is the fact that the only member of the team who will work in the facility, the one who knows the students and the program best, usually has the least decision-making authority.

In one instance the building committee instructed the architects to meet with the school library media teacher and secure a list of "musts" to incorporate in the design of the new center. Thirty-six basic essentials were identified. Only three and a half appeared in the finished facility. Building committee members' priorities are concerned with the total school program, the number of students that must be housed, and the budget. The building principal expects the school library media center to be the "showplace of the school," which can result in placing a higher priority on interior decoration than on the learning activities that should take place there.

Architects receive a part of their fees from percentages based on the cost of equipment installed, so they may not be enthusiastic about some of the school library media teachers' preferences that are based on experience and educational utility. There are ample causes for conflict. Even when there is concurrence regarding the end goals, there are multiple ways of setting out to achieve them.

For example, everyone may agree that the ideal is to place the school library media center where it is "centrally located." Does this mean in the physical center of the building? If there are three levels, should the center be on the second? Should it be halfway between ends (including receiving, auditorium, gymnasium, and music wings) rather than in the academic wing? Those who think about program will realize that placing a school library media center any place except on the ground floor will call for increases in steel reinforcements to carry its excessive weight and permit rearrangement of stack areas in response to changes in use and growth. A living school library media program is never static. It is recommended that the facility be located so that it can be closed off from the rest of the school to permit after-school and nighttime use. Thinking ahead to the time when program demands may call for enlarging the facility, planners will want to make sure there is adjacent land to expand onto, and that alterations can be made without spoiling the building's facade.

Architects often turn to manufacturers of library furniture for help with layout. The manufacturers, logically from their point of view, suggest using every specialized piece of furniture in their catalogs. Architects, thinking of commissions, are perfectly happy with that idea as well. Administrators have come to expect oversized charge desks, atlas and dictionary stands, and lounge furniture as part of traditional libraries, and building committees suggest that expensive furnishings be obtained as part of the bond issue, as a capital expense. Perhaps the school library media teacher is requesting a smaller, sectional charge desk that can be relocated as needed. The library media professional's request may be for freestanding metal shelving with bar shelf supports rather than built-in wooden shelving that rests on easily removed pegs. The school library media teacher is placing priority on flexibility and the fact that metal shelving is less expensive than wooden shelving so there can be more of it. There is also the thought that office suppliers may offer a preferred chair, table, stack, desk for the office area, and something other than school or library furniture may be the answer to such needs. One thinks of the elementary school library media center that was equipped with 30 small Boston rockers. Not only did these serve individual students for leisure reading, clustered together they worked very well for group instruction. In another elementary school there are 30 tablet-armed chairs (properly sized) that are usually thought of for use by secondary students. They fit space requirements better than tables and chairs and prove to be more flexible for small- and large-group instruction.

Rarely is sufficient attention given to the storage of periodicals for reference. Space is provided for the current issues and a handful of back copies, but the real reason for periodicals is their reference value. Technology offers some optional answers. Periodicals are available in summarized or full text CD-ROM or database formats. Instead of space for back files, space for computers is required. If retrospective files are to be maintained on microform, then there must be sufficient space to use microform readers and printers. This points up an additional essential need. Few school library media centers are designed with enough electrical power or outlets, and the ones supplied are often inflexible. Outlets are needed for viewing and listening equipment, as well as computers, and they must be placed where they are usable in proximity to the software and hardware required by the activity.

The primary lack in any school library media center is shortage of floor space. When cuts for building or remodeling are imposed, it would be far wiser to retain the space and temporarily bypass some of the equipment. Additional shelving units, display cases, draperies, lounge furniture, and specialized furniture units can be added later through a variety of community efforts. To add floor space is a major undertaking that usually does not happen—certainly not soon.

ROLE OF THE SCHOOL LIBRARY MEDIA PROFESSIONAL IN EDUCATIONAL LEADERSHIP

Whether the collection of professional materials for teachers and other staff members is housed at the central offices or in individual school buildings, the school library media teacher has responsibilities related to it. Included will be titles useful for the classroom teachers, the administrators, the subject department heads, as well as those needed for keeping up with school library media services. The collection must be kept up-to-date, and new materials should be constantly brought to the attention of potential users. This may be done through individualized messages, short reviews in the faculty newsletter, time set aside in faculty meetings, or in department meetings. One device that may be used is to duplicate the contents pages of the new issues and send the copies to departments or individual teachers. The interested recipient need only check the title of the article of interest, return the sheet to the center, and expect to receive a duplicated copy of the article very soon thereafter. In this way, the article, rather than the entire journal issue, may be carried about in pocket or purse and read whenever there are snatches of time that permit reading of materials that are conveniently at hand.

Some school systems authorize the purchase for the professional collection of a single copy of any textbook used by their teachers who are enrolled in university education courses. Articles on staff development do not often discuss the value of the professional collection or how it is to be managed.

Decisions have to be made as to whether the collection will be a single one for systemwide use, kept at the district offices, or whether there will be smaller collections housed in individual schools. Perhaps there can be some of both with the location decision based on potential use. The more esoteric titles would be at the central location. Sometimes a plan is used whereby an ever-changing small collection is placed in teachers' lounges, dining rooms, or workrooms. If the professional collection is to be the valuable tool that it can and should be, users must accept personal responsibility for the return or replacement of these materials. In some larger school districts professional collections are maintained in a teacher resource center under the management of a professional librarian or the district supervisor of school library media programs.

Decisions must also be made regarding access and control. What is the likelihood that faculty members will try to borrow from the collection in a district supervisor's office as contrasted with the ease of access of the school library media center? Unless the collection is cataloged and inventoried, how can users know the subject content or what titles are included? Uncataloged, go-fish types of arrangements often make it difficult to justify an investment in professional materials. It is possible to make a secretary in the curriculum director's area responsible for charging out materials to teachers, but without proper cataloging there is no way to conduct an inventory or maintain an up-to-date collection.

Linkages to educational databases are turning up now in principals' and superintendents' offices. Sometimes these are placed in the high school library media center. Either way, provision must be made for appropriate distribution of the materials. If housed in central offices, it is the nonadministrative information that must be examined and distributed to teachers. If housed in the school library media center, there must be a way to relay the administrative materials to the administrators.

As more and more classroom teachers are being linked by desktop computers to the main office records, private information regarding students' abilities and personal lives must be protected and made available only to the teacher. The necessary software programs must be identified and put into place so that access to files will be limited to the approved users only.

Students may also need to use the professional collection. Many topics used in debates and in search papers deal with educational subjects. Students need to use *Education Index*, the journals, and the new monographs for these purposes. Even when students know that certain materials are at the school district offices, it is unlikely that they will be well served without the intervention of the school library media teacher. Student need should not be overlooked when decisions are made regarding the management of the professional collection.

CONCLUSION

It is imperative that all persons in the management chain of command understand the totality as well as their own segments of the chain. They should also recognize the corresponding responsibilities, capabilities, and talents needed by the individuals at each level.

Supervision of the school library media program should be an ongoing effort, not a series of spasmodic walk-throughs. Administrators who state there is no need for them to visit the library media center because they know the staff is "doing a good job," are in fact undermining the program while sounding complimentary. This attitude clearly indicates that the library media program is a low-priority item.

Both teachers and students respond positively to seeing the principal in the center. When the principal is observed as a patron, using the materials, browsing at the shelves, or reading a periodical, the message is loud and clear that this is a valued part of the school and its educational program.

While supervising administrators are not expected to be trained library media specialists in order to competently evaluate the center and its programs, there are many aspects and factors they must be able to recognize, interpret, and diagnose in order to maximize the potential. The topics addressed in the next section of this book represent ingredients of the school library media program that must be understood by the principal who wants the most effective library media learning program possible for students and teachers and for the benefit of the community.

WHAT OTHERS SAY

Beginning in the mid-1980s, and increasingly as comprehension has grown outside the school library media field, there has been more space in the literature devoted to the roles of the library media program, the teaming of library media and classroom teachers, and the responsibilities of the principal. To the extent that the school's goal is to equip students to act on their own behalf as lifelong learners, the principal, as leader and manager, has a unique opportunity to influence students. Some of the thoughts of prominent educators concerning the library media program, the professional teacher specialist who runs it, and the principal's role in supervising it appear in the following quotations:

> Educating administrators about strong library media centers and their roles has to be a high priority of every library media specialist. Neither the administrator nor the media specialist can work at top effectiveness in isolation from each other (p. 8).
>
> Pauline H. Anderson, *Library Media Leadership in Academic Secondary Schools.* Hamden, Conn.: Shoe String Press, 1985.

> Another way in which the principal can foster a fusing of the media program with the school program is by constantly interpreting, suggesting and illustrating interrelationships to teachers, students, parents and in some instances to those media specialists who have not kept informed about changing educational practices. Rowell believes that "negative or indifferent teacher attitude is due to a lack of understanding of what the media program is, what it can do to support the instructional program, how its resources can be directed to students' use, and what those services and resources are" (p. 41).
>
> Mainstreaming the basics of listening, viewing, and critical reading into a school's teaching program is a crucial purpose of the media program (p. 167).
>
> The unique capability of the library media program to serve as locator-beyond-the-building, an information clearing house and a connection point, is of special consequence. . . . Many of the resources (materials and persons) useful within . . . programs may have to be found at a distance from the school, and the specialist should take the lead in locating and incorporating these into the program (p. 163).
>
> Well-managed media programs do not just endure what-

ever comes their way; they prevail over circumstances because they are led by managers who understand the nature of shifting priorities and changing program focus (p. 61).

The media specialist needs the strong support of the principal in carrying out the media program. In addition, the principal's guidance and counsel and visible support stimulate confidence and provide direction (p. 46).

One way to highlight development of school media programs is through the annual report developed by the superintendent and presented to the school district governing body. In such a document the official leader is able to present data which reflect achievements during the given year and, at the same time, outline needs and goals. In this report there is an opportunity to note the impact of technological changes on school media collections and programs, and the resulting need for more appropriately trained personnel (p. 91).

D. Philip Baker, *The Library Media Program and the School.* Littleton, Colo.: Libraries Unlimited, 1984.

Every elementary school should have a library (p. 24). . . . The librarian should be an integral part of the instructional staff. By leading children to good books, by sponsoring incentive programs and author visits, the librarian can play an essential role in enriching curricula (p. 38). . . . In league with classroom teachers, the librarian can foster in children a taste for good literature and a love of serious study. Good librarians can be great teachers (p. 39). . . . Study Group member Lois Coit tells of one elementary school in which reading scores were lagging; rather than starting a library, which the school lacked, administrators bought the students a workbook series on how to take tests. . . . Obviously, this was a case of assessment gone awry (p. 53). If the school is to function as a "working community," if all the parts are to mesh in an engine of achievement, the principal must act as catalyst. More than any other figure, the principal is able to create conditions for excellence—or what Study Group member Michael Joyce calls "an ethos of shared expectations" (p. 43). . . . Says Professor James Guthrie of the University of California-Berkeley: "[If] you could only change one component of a school in order to make it more effective, finding a dynamic principal is the most important thing you can do" (p. 43).

The most serious problems facing our elementary schools do not derive from a lack of money; they derive from a surfeit of confusion, bureaucratic thinking, and community apathy. . . . The improvement of elementary schools requires fresh approaches, better incentives, and inventive leadership (p. 3).

William J. Bennett [U.S. Secretary of Education], *First Lessons: A Report on Elementary Education in America.* Washington, D.C.: U.S. Department of Education, 1986.

For years now, studies have been pointing to the pivotal role of the principal in bringing about more effective schools. Our own field studies bear out these findings. In schools where achievement was high and where there was a clear sense of community, we found, invariably, that the principal made the difference (p. 219).

Ernest L. Boyer, *High Schools: A Report on Secondary Education in America.* New York: Harper & Row, 1983.

The primary shortcoming of most process-based models is that they tend to isolate the process of information seeking from other information-processing activities. Interactive communication techniques, such as multimedia and networked communication, provide excellent opportunities to break out of this isolation. . . . Models limited to a single aspect of the information process—as search process—made sense in the collection-bound environment of the library media centers of the past, but these models will not provide an adequate basis for understanding the information-processing learning that will take place in the integrated and connected library media center of the near future (p. 93). . . . The physical layout of the environment, the technology that supports it, and day-to-day adult supervision are areas that the library media specialist of the near future will be called upon for expertise. In addition, he or she will need to work in close partnership with the classroom teacher to create assignments, assess students' work, and establish initial collaborative relationships (p. 94). . . . The fostering of collaboration in the library media center, whether face-to-face or computer-mediated, will require fundamental changes in the current models of information gathering and processing, and in the physical environment of the library media center (p. 95). . . . The successful adoption of the new interaction models and incorporation of the emerging technologies will require careful long-range planning and curricula design. Too often in the past, schools have become discouraged by the false promises of the wonders new technologies would bring to learning. Educators, however, must accept the lion's share of the burden of those failures. The emerging technologies, like their predecessors, are tools. To the extent that curricula are designed to use them well, transformation will be seen. Allowing these techniques to sit in classrooms and library media centers collecting dust is the only failure (p. 96).

Kathleen Burnett and Mary Jane McNally, "School Library Media Specialist as Knowledge Navigator: Preparing for the Electronic Environment." *School Library Media Annual*, Littleton, Colo.: Libraries Unlimited, 1994.

The library is at the heart of the educational process; if students are to have the free access they need to resources, the schools cannot have classes rigidly scheduled into the library.

Saul Cooperman [New Jersey Commissioner of Education, 1987], *Check This Out: Flexible Scheduling.* School, Children & Young People's Section of Nebraska Library Association, & Nebraska Educational Media Association, [s.l.], 1990.

Various "low-tech" and "low-cost" forms of virtual reality, include telephone, normal mail, e-mail, and a new kind of emerging instant, interactive mail which is now taking shape in online conversations, forums, and chat sessions. . . . [V]irtual reality is not just the stuff of power gloves, VR helmets with stereoscopic 3–D goggles, and multimedia computers. What makes an experience "virtual" arises out of our most important cyberorgan of all: our imagination (p. 58).

Fred D'Ignazio, "Distance Is a State of Mind," *Computing Teacher* (February 1995).

As society has shifted from an economy based on capital goods (industrial) to an economy based on services (information) there has been a corresponding shift in what is expected from education. Knowing how to ask the right questions may be the single most important step in learning. The process that is conducted in order to find answers to the right question leads to the point at which information becomes knowledge. Information Literacy—the ability to access, evaluate, and use information from a variey of sources—is central to all successful learning and by extension, to all successful living (p. 32).

Christina S. Doyle, "Eric Digest." *Emergency Librarian* (March–April 1995).

Communication systems that connect educator to educator and connect teacher to scientist and researcher change the traditional paradigms of hierarchies in schools. These networks will irrevocably alter the way schools do business (p. 38).

It is well known that once school connectivity and equipment is provided that staff development and technical assistance is needed for effective use of telecommunications (p. 38).

"Education, Access to Telecommunications, Technology, and Equity," *Computing Teacher* (March 1995).

As we move down the multiformat road, however, perhaps it's not enough to be covering [reviewing] a particular format. We need to pay more attention to what format delivers the message best (p. 56).

Francine Fialkoff, "The Medium and the Message," *Library Journal* (15 March 1995).

More recently the works of Edmonds, Brookover, Lezotte, and others have singled out the principal as the most significant individual in the creation of an effective school (p. 3).

Kevin Gallmeier, "The Effectiveness of Principal Leadership Style on Teacher Motivation." Eric Document: ED354591, 1992.

Technology education is quite likely the least understood area of the school curriculum. Many people view technology as the tools used by technicians; some equate technology with computers; and still others think of it as a method of instruction. . . . Unfortunately, none of these perceptions reflects the teaching and learning that occur in a technology education classroom (p. 10).

Anthony F. Gilberti, "Technology Education and Societal Change," *NAASP Bulletin* (September 1994).

[T]he Library of Congress is the seminal knowledge dissemination system on the planet. We should strive for every child in America, in every school in America, no matter how rural, no matter how poor, to have electronic access to the world of knowledge. That is a national asset. We should strive to make it easy for every scholar to interact electronically. That's a national asset. And the work done here and the work done

at other libraries across the country are the most cost effective investment in learning that we make. And they have all
too often been neglected because they don't have a big union
and they don't have a big lobby and they don't count in the
way people keep score nowadays, but, if you care about
knowledge, here is a place to spend more, not less, money
(p. 31). . . .

Newt Gingrich, [House Speaker], *Library of Congress Information Bulletin* (23 January 1995). [Speech, January 5, 1995
at the dedication of THOMAS, the Library of Congress World
Wide Web access for bills and laws as they are being considered in Congress.]

There has been growing support in recent years for the view
that the importance of the principal to school quality and improvement is great. Indeed, as with teachers, some people
have gone so far as to claim that "everything depends on the
principal." We found in the schools we studied a relationship between teacher satisfaction and strong leadership by
the principal. . . . Our data in fact show that the degree of staff
cohesiveness and the nature of the problem-solving and decision-making climates at schools were factors also highly related to teachers' satisfaction. The principal's role plays a part
(pp. 178–79).

John I. Goodlad, *A Place Called School: Prospects for the Future.* New York: McGraw-Hill, 1983.

Technology by itself changes very little. It works in tandem
with a whole variety of elements. If you're doing the same
old thing with the new technology, it's going to be pretty
much the same old thing. If you have actual changes going
on—in what people do, in the values, in the culture of the
classroom—computers can help support that change. So it's
this larger process of interrelated variables, as opposed to putting a computer in a classroom and hoping that magic is going to happen (p. 16).

David Goodrum, "Technology: It's Not Just for Hackers Any
More," *Indiana Alumni* (September–October 1995).

[I]magination and information resources in all formats are necessary for effective programs, and young people need to be
able to access them both physically and intellectually, through

the integration of information skills and literary appreciation with classroom programs and team teaching by classroom teachers and teacher-librarians (p. 7).

Ken Haycock, "Notebook," *Emergency Librarian* (January–February 1995).

What a school thinks about its library is a measure of what it thinks about education.

Harold Howe (former U.S. Commissioner of Education)

Success in education, employment and civic involvement increasingly demand the ability to use technology to access, process and communicate online information. Parents and citizens should insist that students at all grade levels have successful experiences with major technologies (p. 8).

Doug Johnson, "Student Access to Internet: Librarians and Teachers Working Together to Teach Higher Level Survival Skills," *Emergency Librarian* (January–February 1995).

The principal must see to it that the media specialist is involved with the staff in planning, in continuing staff development, and in evaluation (p. 40).

No in-depth planning occurs at afterschool or lunch hour staff meetings (p. 41).

Betty Martin, *Principal's Handbook on the School Library Media Center.* Hamden, Conn.: Library Professional Publication, 1981.

The notion that networks—including the Internet and digital libraries—will be critical features of all 21st century communities is becoming more of a certainty with each passing day. Networks and digital libraries will mean at least as much to the "life of the mind" in the knowledge communities of the 21st century as roads and energy sources have meant to the "life of the body" in the agricultural and industrial communities in the 19th and 20th centuries. We are now poised to change the ways in which we create, distribute, and use ideas and words at least as much as we have already changed the ways in which we create, distribute, and use goods and services (p. 32).

Paul Evan Peters, "Information Age Avatars," *Library Journal* (15 March 1995).

There are sharp dichotomies in the roles played by principals. Developmental leadership requires:

- vision,
- a willingness to experiment and change,
- the capacity to tolerate messiness,
- the ability to take the long-term view, and
- a willingness to revise systems.

Maintenance management, on the other hand, requires:

- oversight,
- the use of proven methods,
- orderliness, and
- daily attention (p. 301).

Sharon F. Rallis and Martha C. Highsmith, "The Myth of the 'Great Principal': Questions of School Management and Instructional Leadership," *Phi Delta Kappan* (December 1986).

The principal is the lead teacher and needs to be among colleagues and students, as that is where the most vital judgments in the life of a school must be made. . . . He or she is the school's primary "visitor," not in a destructive inspectorial sense, but in a collegial yet candid one (p. 198).

Theodore R. Sizer, *Horace's Compromise: The Dilemma of the American High School.* Boston: Houghton Mifflin, 1984.

Administrators, both in central office and in schools, have [a] more critical role to play than that involved in regulation and control. The importance of technical assistance, staff development responsive to identified needs within individual schools, and clear, on-going support for teachers in their efforts to enhance the educational experiences of students cannot be overstated. If the target of restructuring is improved student learning, all resources in a district must be directed toward achieving that goal (p. 20).

Dianne Taylor and Edward St. John, "Limitations of District Initiated Reform: A Study of a Major Urban Reform Initiative." Paper presented at the Annual Meeting of the Southwest Educational Research Association, Austin, Tex., 28–30 January 1993.

Information highways are emerging, but relatively few people know how to navigate and find what is there. By just moving their fingers, people can gather a great deal of information, but they typically do little synthesis (p. 54). . . . To work effectively with any tool requires more than simply having the tool. You must have the skill or technique to use the tool. You also need strategies or methods for working with it. In addition you need a goal or objective that provides a positive mutual attraction to open your mind to the possibilities the tool affords. Lacking any of these limits the benefits of the tool. As a result, the tool can even be a source of frustration. . . . Communication involves moving ideas and information (p. 55).

Mark Von Wodtke, "Thinking Skills for the Electronic Information Age," *School Library Media Annual.* Littleton, Colo.: Libraries Unlimited, 1994.

Physical access to Internet for both students and their teachers includes the availability of computer equipment at school and at home, adequate time online to learn and explore, and adequate skills instruction in using the basic tools of online research. These online tools include e-mail, file transfer, gopher menus and search programs like Archie, Veronica, WWW and WAIS. Physical access also includes the availability of online resources such as personal e-mail addresses and file space, access to listservs and news groups, the capability of telnetting to other computers, the capability to download files into personal file space and adequate print resources that can serve as skill and resource references.

While males and females do tend to see the computer differently, this could be interpreted as an opportunity to expand the uses of computers in educational settings rather than a barrier to female success (p. 10).

Karin Wiburg, "Gender Issues, Personal Characteristics, and Computing," *Computing Teacher* (December–January 1994–95).

More recent literature shows that along with advances in technology the role of the principal remains much the same. It determines the success or failure of the learning taking place within the school.

The principal is the key to the ET [Educational Technology] team's success. Building effective teams requires principals to encourage spirited debate and discussion among team members prior to the team's decision. The principal should lead through asking questions, nurturing and removing barriers for team members. Simply asking the right questions often increases the quality of decision making. The understated role of the principal actually increases the principal's power due to the support gleaned from team members. (p. 73 ff).

Van E. Coolely, "Empower Teachers, Power Up Technology," *Educational Horizons*, (Winter 1997).

What we did was not so difficult that any school staff, with the principal's leadership, could not do it as well. (p. 596 ff).

William Glasser, "Choice Theory and Student Success," *Phi Delta Kappan*, (April 1997).

Administrators must provide strong leadership. Leadership is important because teachers begin using technology in part because they choose to but also because they percieve their organization expects it of them. (p. 89 ff).

Bob Hoffman, "Integrating Technology Into Schools," *NASSP Bulletin* (October 1996).

Sadly, assessment has been horribly neglected in most places as schools have installed billions of dollars of computers and other technologies during the past two decades. Genuine assessment, skillfully applied, spurs growth, adaptation and enhancement. (http://fromnowon.org)

Jamie McKenzie. "Emerging from the Smog," *From Now On* (January 1998).

The principal is responsible for leading technological implementation by obtaining resources, buffering implementation from outside interference, encouraging teachers, and adapting current policies to meet new demands. (p. 23 ff).

Julie Meltzer and Thomas M. Sherman, "10 Commandments to Implement Technology," *NASSP Bulletin* (January 1997).

Instead of new technologies changing schools, the schools have adapted new technologies to their own way of operating. If computer technology is to have any impact on education, significant changes will have to be made in the way teachers [and administrators] are trained. (p. 12 ff).

John R. Mergendoller, "Technology and Learning: The Research," *Principal* (January 1997).

It is dangerous to assert . . . that all information is online, free, and easy to use. . . . A realistic perspective is that all information is not yet electronic and probably never will be; electronic information will not be less expensive than current printed information; and libraries—physical and virtual—will continue to be needed, along with the professionals who run them and facilitate access to them. (p. A44).

William Miller, "Online Lies We'd Better Face," The Chronicle of Higher Education (1 August 1997).Paul Evan Peters, "Information Age Avatars," *Library Journal* (15 March 1995).

[Stanton] Ching [having watched poor visual presentations] cautions: Everyone wanted to use their laptop computer plugged into a projector, when transparencies would have been as good or better. We have to be careful and use the best technology available, even if it's a chalkboard. (p. 18 ff).

Lisa Walls, "Technology and the Liberal Arts," *Connecticut College Magazine* (6 September 1996).

PART TWO
Evaluation Modules

Introduction: Use of Evaluation Modules

Although the primary use of evaluation modules, which follow, is to assist individual supervising administrators with evaluating the library media programs in their schools, there are additional uses that may be made of them. They may be used as a base for staff development workshops for principals or curriculum supervisors. They may form the base for a section or unit within college-level administration or curriculum courses. They may also serve as an evaluative tool for school library media teachers or supervisors who are looking for a checklist. And finally, parents and other interested citizens may find guidance in what to look for when they become interested in evaluating their children's school library media services.

The modules have been arranged alphabetically within four broad function headings: administration of program, collection management, instruction, and technology. Sometimes elements of a module fit into more than one function and cross-references are indicated. The index will also provide clues to where to look for specific information.

3. Administration of Program Modules

ATMOSPHERE

The ambience of the library media center immediately welcomes or repels, telegraphs to students the type of reception they are likely to receive, and even the amount of willing assistance they can expect from both the professional and nonprofessional staffs. The contributing factors range from the color scheme to the amount of red tape they encounter. Millions of dollars have been spent in research regarding the impact of color on human behavior. Body language, placement of furniture, the quality of the lighting, signage, and other graphics are among the many factors that experts on motivating buyers look for when advising commercial establishments on how to improve business. These elements are equally important to selling the use of the school library media center program.

Recognizing Positive Elements

- Smiles are seen regularly on professional and support staff, as well as on faculty and student faces. Library media professionals may be purposeful and intent, but without being taut and snappish.
- There is an observable service-oriented attitude exhibited by the staff, which with their choice of words, indicates that the center is not "theirs," run for their convenience, but "ours," belonging to and

being run for students, teachers, and learning.

- There is a flexibility of schedule or of task at hand that permits "interruption" in order to respond to user needs.
- Lighting is proper for each of the specific areas of usage. Carrels are individually lighted, stacks allow for clear vision and eliminate user shadows, and areas where screens are viewed are equipped with dimming possibilities.
- Glare from windows and heat from changing amounts of sunlight are controlled.
- Colors and decor are attractive and do not detract from the purpose of the school library media center.
- There are sufficient, clearly visible signs identifying parts of the collection and areas of use. Posted directions for use accompany computers, catalogs and indexes, the copy machine, the time clock, and other equipment used by the students.
- There are numerous bulletin boards of varying sizes and display cases that are always in use and changed frequently. These are not just eye-catching and decorative but are learning devices that are designed to further ongoing educational projects. They tie into current events and interests from the local community or the world at large.
- Ceilings and floors are covered with sound-deadening materials that permit individuals, small groups, and classroom size groups to work simultaneously and comfortably together. A pleasant hum composed of controlled voices and the movement caused by various learning activities usually characterizes the high-quality library media program.
- Plants, animals, toys, mobiles, pictures, and any other types of atmospheric conditioning that creates

a warm feeling and excites student interest are placed about the center.

Recognizing Negative Elements

- The offer of assistance by the staff is expressed in the right words but the tone used, facial expression, or body language convey a less helpful (perhaps even impatient) message.
- Students and faculty are made to feel they are interrupting the school library media teacher's primary function (paper work) when they seek help or direction.
- Rules are never broken or even bent.
- Staff constantly works with things rather than with people.
- Phone and computer abused for personal business.
- Time spent in the workroom by the professional is disproportionately greater than time spent on the floor working with students and teachers.
- Dust, stains, and marks on furniture indicate a poor job by custodial staff and inadequate surveillance by the head of the center. When graffiti or other marks have been made and not removed promptly, it encourages other students to add to the destruction.

Identifying Missing Elements

- There are no display cases or bulletin board areas.
- There are no attractive draperies or shades at the windows.
- There is no color—rugs, furniture, and walls are all monotonous, monochromatic neutral shades.

Possible Solutions

- A new coat of paint adding a stripe, border, graphics, or other tasteful touches of color.
- Look for previously unused areas for display such as ends of stacks, tops of book units, unused shelf areas, window ledges, and easels.
- Rearrange furniture to adapt to a growing collection that calls for additional stacks or just to create a new image.
- Create a class gift suggestion list that includes items for the school library media center.
- Invite the art teacher and students to use a wall space as a gallery for hanging superior drawings and paintings.
- Add tackboard to wall spaces above bookcases or carrels.
- Add locked doors to display cases so that museum-type items may be borrowed for display.

BUDGET

The community, school board, administrators, faculty, and students are all interested in getting the best education possible from monies expended. Among the techniques that have proven effective in maximizing the value received are program evaluation, continuous curriculum revision, staff development, and use of standardized tests and measurements to identify areas that need improvement. Such techniques can increase significantly the educational return on the investments already made, and those that continue to be made, in the school library media center and its programs. A library media center of good quality costs money, but the informed administrator knows that there are few elements of the instructional program overall that offer greater educational potential for students at all levels of ability. They support gifted and remedial programs, and contribute extensively to teaching excellence and independent learning.

When the entire community (school and town) supports user responsibility and materials security, there is minimal waste from negligence, misuse, or vandalism. When all of these considerations are provided for, the per capita expenditure for the school library media program is recognized as an educational bargain.

Among other important ingredients in annual budget planning are allowances for inflationary rises in the cost of materials, services, postage, shipping, equipment, and supplies. *A decrease in the number of students should not signal a proportionate curtailment of materials, since the range of students' abilities and interests is the same for 100 or 1,000 pupils in the same grade.* Another salient aspect is the success factor, namely, that when students and teachers learn to use the library media center well and make it a part of their usual learning/teaching day, per capita patron usage grows exponentially. Thus, even if only the very same number of students and teachers were to be in attendance the following year, the expanded usage rate would call for a budgetary increase. Students and faculty members new to the school and/or the school system also impact on the budget.

Recognizing Positive Elements

- The budget provides for regularly scheduled replacement of worn and outdated materials.
- Purchasing flexibility provides for ordering materials throughout the year as needed.
- Purchasing officers understand that the lowest bids for equipment and materials should be only *one*

consideration when contracting with vendors. The quality of service is important, too.

- The budget provides for annual acquisition of new materials in accordance with per capita formulas, special curricular needs, and a comparison with previous budgets. Many administrators appreciate the value of a zero-based budget built strictly on needs, but they fear that voters will not understand this form of budgeting and will take into account only the previous year's expenditures and possibly inflation allowances. PPBS, that is program budgeting, is also a difficult concept for the public-at-large to absorb in a budget-voting session. The commonly used line-item budget does not give an easily discernible total cost. For example, processing costs for preprocessed materials are listed with the purchase price of the items as contrasted with an in-house processing expense that may only identify costs of the supplies, and not account for the value of staff time. Neither the public nor the administration is able to perceive the actual costs of running the school library media program. With the use of computers for budgeting and accounting procedures, more itemizing can and should be done. This type of accountability will improve budgeting and evaluative measurements.

- Maintenance of equipment is provided for on an annual basis, thereby spreading costs more equitably over a period of years and tending to prevent times of high expenses.

- State and regional standards and professional guidelines are carefully considered when the budget is formulated.

Recognizing Negative Elements

- The school library media teacher has little or no input in formulating the annual budget.
- There is insufficient budget for support staff, causing professional school library media teachers to spend a disproportionate amount of time doing clerical and other noninstructional work.
- There are too few school library media teachers to permit adequate instructional activities and teacher consultations.
- The singleton library media teacher's salary is identifiable in the budget because it is listed separately from all other teachers' salaries, thus making it a possible target.

Identifying Missing Elements

- There are no short- or long-range plans for materials collection development, equipment acquisition, or staff-to-user ratio correction.
- There has been no recent evaluation of the school library media program to determine its match with the program required to achieve systemwide educational goals. The ten-year interval used for most association accreditation is too long, considering the acceleration of new information, change in instructional techniques, and the growing disparity between well- and ill-prepared students.
- The library media program's costs are so grouped that there is little or no accurate accounting for the various elements of the program.
- There is no library fund, separate from the budget, that allows for the deposit of the monies paid for

replacement of materials lost or irreparably damaged. If such fine monies revert to the general fund,
the collection suffers not only the loss of the materials but also all the monies paid to replace them.
The library fund is also used for gifts made by organizations or individuals, thus earmarking the money
to be spent for the library media center and its program.

Possible Solutions

- Schedule the budget formation process far enough
  in advance to share with the community what goes
  into the budget and to justify the needs as part of
  an ongoing developmental approach.
- Make certain that school library media teachers are
  involved in curriculum development committee
  work to ensure their awareness of impending curricular needs that must be translated into budgetary
  requests.
- Require short- and long-range plans for development of materials and equipment collections.
- Establish special build-up funding plans if severe
  program shortages exist.
- Establish special renovation funds to make major
  improvements, such as the creation of hubs and
  labs for computer use.
- Establish a library fund to accommodate the fines
  collected for replacement of lost or damaged materials and also gifts made for additions to the collection. The requirement of two signatures for dis-
  persal of these funds may be appropriate. In no
  way, however, is this fund to be misconstrued as a
  substitute for an adequate budget.

BUSINESS MANAGERS

School library media personnel, especially the department head, must work very closely with business managers. Sometimes business managers are well informed about the unique problems involved with the purchasing of books and learning materials, and sometimes they are not. A district business manager may believe these materials should be bought on bids the way paper, pencils, and chairs are purchased. Bids on library materials cannot be obtained with a uniform percentage discount. In book purchasing, the types of binding carry differing discounts; that is, trade, text, library, reinforced, paperbound. Some publishing or producing sources offer only a "short discount"—university presses, for example. Moreover, a single distributor will not be able to provide all materials needed. Requiring the use of a single supplier precludes access to many materials. On the other hand, business managers are right in wanting as few purchase orders to deal with as possible and in wanting the best value for expended public funds.

There needs to be a clear-cut understanding about retaining some portion of the budget allocation for use throughout the school year, so that needed and newly published materials may be obtained when they will do the most educational good. Requiring that orders be placed once or twice a year, or that the entire budget be encumbered early in the school year, presents an obstacle to the best use of the funds. When encumbered funds are released because items ordered cannot be provided, those monies should revert to the original account.

Recognizing Positive Elements

- There is a warm and friendly business relationship between the business manager and the school library media personnel.
- Careful records of encumbrances, receipts, acceptances, and returns are kept and the school library media staff has an up-to-date financial record for use in checking the business department's computerized printouts.
- There is an agreed-upon timetable for encumbering school library media funds, and it may be different from that of other departments in the school.
- Monies received for replacement of damaged or lost school library media items are deposited in the fund established for replacement purchases.
- Monies released from encumbrance because of suppliers' inability to fill school library media center orders are freed for reencumbrance for other items selected by the school library media center staff.
- There is some flexibility to transfer funds from one account to another within the budget allocation. If there is not, the result can be forced cancellation of a periodical, serials, or indexing service. These are costly but needed items that may be more expensive or forever unobtainable if their purchase is postponed.

Recognizing Negative Elements

- Bid lists are required for all purchases regardless of the inappropriateness of the system and its negative impact on the school library media program. Monies are removed from accounts unexpectedly without respecting retention within accounts, thereby forcing hurried or ill-conceived purchases just to use up funds so they will not be lost.

- There are restrictions established regarding purchasing procedures that are geared only to the convenience of the business department, not to the benefit of the school library media program or student learning opportunities.

Identifying Missing Elements

- There is no contact between the business manager and the school library media teachers. The business manager may not understand the uniqueness of each item of library material or that items often are not interchangeable so that one title may not be substituted for another.
- There is no coordinated budget development process that permits verification by the school library media teachers of what appears in the final budget request.
- There are no regular financial statements sent directly to the school library media teacher or through the principal's office by the business department.

Possible Solutions

- When problems are identified, it is good practice for the administrators and the business manager to meet with the school library media center personnel to discuss the problems and to work out agreeable and educationally sound solutions.
- There is always a priority order list ready for immediate purchase should unexpected funds become available to the school library media program.

- Clearly identified procedures are used to establish budgets and there is close cooperation between the administration and the school library media center personnel in developing the center's budget for the next year.
- Short- and long-range plans are developed for continued growth and upgrading of the school library media center program, collection, and equipment. Budgetary implications are a part of the planning.
- The principal meets with the business manager and explains the school's commitment to the library media program and its importance to the overall instructional program.

CENTRALIZED ORDERING AND PROCESSING

Some school systems provide for a systemwide director of school library media services. This makes it possible for these school systems to provide for centralized ordering and processing because it is cost-effective when there are three or more schools in the system. Administrators realize that there is no point in having each library media teacher in multiple elementary schools order and do original cataloging for the same title in every school. Orders are coordinated in a centralized service office so that there is less paperwork to be processed.

When materials are received, cataloging is reproduced if the title is already held by one school in the system. Or, it is created only once, with copies being made for all the schools ordering the item at that time. If the school system is a member of Online Computer Library Center (OCLC, a machine-readable database used for cataloging) or some other network, or if the centralized unit makes use of a computerized program to create master catalog and circulation discs (or produce catalog cards or other types of catalog entries), there is still a cost-effective saving of labor. Vendors are now providing computer discs to their customers that match each order and can be downloaded into the system, or individual building, computer catalog, and circulation equipment.

While the cataloging information is being prepared, the book or other item is also being "processed." This means that it is being marked with its call numbers, has a barcode or a transaction card and pocket pasted in or on it, has a protective plastic cover placed over the dust jacket, and all other precirculation procedures are completed to make the item ready for use.

The cataloging arrives with the processed materials in the individual schools, and the school library media center personnel have only to put everything in its place and start using it. Materials are made available to students and teachers much more quickly than when they are purchased and processed school-by-school.

By pooling the individual school orders throughout the system, larger discounts may be received. This method is sometimes available to the individual school that is a member of a library network that pools orders from the varying member institutions for greater benefits.

Recognizing Positive Elements

- There is no backlog of uncataloged and unprocessed materials.
- Needless duplication of effort going into the ordering and processing of school library media center materials is eliminated.
- School library media teachers have more time to teach when the typing, pasting, marking, covering,

and assembling jobs are done elsewhere and all materials are ready for shelving when they arrive.

- Building-level school library media aides can keep shelves and files in better order and mend or refurbish materials for improved use when they no longer have to take part in the processing.
- Since processing supplies are not bought for the building level, only mending supplies are required.

Recognizing Negative Elements

- Because cataloging is very time consuming, materials remain uncataloged for long periods of time depriving students of their use.
- When cataloging and processing in the building are kept up-to-date, it may mean that the school library media teacher is shorting teaching responsibilities in order to accomplish this work.
- Because centralization is more effective and efficient when procedures are uniform, there must be agreement reached among building-level library media teachers regarding cataloging and processing procedures. This may preclude some desirable individuality and create dissatisfaction among library media teachers who believe they do not have enough say in decision making. Often, however, once the standard systemwide computerized catalog is in place, individual library media centers have the opportunity to use specific coding on their own catalog to indicate special or reference collections.
- If, as part of operating a centralized processing unit, placement of orders with suppliers is restricted to only two or three times a year, the freedom of the school library media teacher to provide newly pub-

lished material immediately is curtailed. This method also makes more complex the placement of prepublication orders that are designed to provide greater than usual discounts.

Identifying Missing Elements

- The school library media center is part of a network offering services such as ordering, cataloging, or processing, but has yet to take advantage of these services.
- School library media centers belong to networks that do not offer centralized ordering, cataloging, or processing services and no request for these services to be offered has been initiated.
- There has been no consideration given to creating a centralized ordering and cataloging center for the school system or region.

Possible Solutions

- Investigate the desirability of centralized ordering and processing for your school library media centers, comparing costs and examining options. Remember to account for the value of staff time (multiplied by the number of schools in the system) when operations are conducted in each school building.
- Consider establishing a part-time independent service or a regional approach involving several school systems.
- Discover whether belonging to an available network would provide the service. Many regional networks include all types of libraries—public, community

college, university, and special libraries—and would probably consider including schools if requested to do so.

- Pay the extra money, doubtless with overall savings, to buy materials preprocessed and cataloged by the vendor in either computer or card format.

COMMUNITY SERVICES

The school library media center is often the most comfortable and attractive area of the school building and is therefore sought out for after-school meetings by adult and student groups. The community has a right to use tax-supported facilities.

The school library media teacher is in a position to assist with badge and project work for Boy and Girl Scouts, the 4H, Campfire, and other organizations. Sometimes, adults need materials that are found in the school library media center rather than in public libraries, and they should have access to these materials.

On occasion it is good public relations to permit use of graphics production equipment by the PTA or other school-related or -compatible groups, or even to enlist student aides to assist with the production. Cable TV programming or videotaping done by school personnel, often working out of or in conjunction with the school library media center, are frequently linked to community interests. Art exhibits may be held in school library media centers when there are enough wall or display areas to accommodate them.

Recognizing Positive Elements

- There is evidence of cooperation between community groups and the school library media center personnel. School library media teachers can be good advisers to youth agencies in the community that are dealing with adolescent problems—such as a shelter for unwed mothers or a drug rehabilitation program. School-owned materials are borrowed directly by citizens or on interschool loan plans.

- Meetings are held in the school library media center by groups such as PTAs or board of education committees.
- The school library media teacher is involved with school youth group clubs and programs, both in suggesting helpful resources and responding positively to requests for assistance.
- There is a close working relationship with the cable television system that serves the community. Requests (approved by the administration) for tapes of school activities are made available to the cable TV system, and local or regional TV stations for broadcast.

Recognizing Negative Elements

- There is resistance to encouraging or even allowing use of the school library media center after hours, for which there may be justifiable reasons involving visitor thoughtlessness. These could include coffee spilled on the carpet and not wiped up, chairs rarely returned to original positions, cigarette burns, materials taken without being signed out, equipment left broken, or plants, toys, or collections generally abused by unattended children.
- Meetings after hours may make it necessary to keep the entire school building open, requiring security measures and extra use of utilities.

- Community adults who come to meetings in the school library media center may possibly intend to use the time to search for evidence of materials in the collection against which they will institute censorship proceedings.

Identifying Missing Elements

- There are no requests made for meetings in the school library media center by community groups, PTA, Scouts, or even the board of education.
- There has been no effort to make groups welcome.
- There is no attempt to borrow materials, although other schools in the system do lend materials to community people.

Possible Solutions

- Establish a code of responsibility to be followed by groups using the school library media center for meetings after hours. This could recognize explicitly the rightful indignation of the school library media staff when it finds disorder, misuse, and damage the morning after, and express proper support for the staff.
- Encourage the school library media personnel to place a higher priority on public relations and to recognize the values that should accrue from greater public familiarity with and interest in the school library media center.
- A brief explanation of library media center programs and services, including those available to them, should be part of community affairs held in the school library media center. A reminder flyer with information could be prepared for distribution.

FACILITIES

The size, shape, and location of windows in the school library media center facility can cause problems related to comfort, security, fading, or personal injury. Glare or overheating from continuous direct sunlight prevents using portions of the area for people or machines. Large windows cause the air conditioning system to overwork, or conversely contribute to excessive heat loss. Unsecured windows permit the tossing of materials to the ground below. Should air conditioning fail, some effective method of ventilation must be provided for when all windows are sealed.

Careful consideration should be given to furniture to be used in the school library media center. The most desirable pieces may not necessarily be available from school or library furniture suppliers. Manufacturers of office, restaurant, and hotel furniture offer possibilities. Furniture should be evaluated in terms of suitability, comfort, and quality. It must be sturdily able to withstand typical student use. There are suitable substitutes for even such specialized furniture as the charge desk. It often takes up too much room, is too high for comfortable use by students or staff, and is costly. Moreover, computerized circulation systems have changed the requirements for storage and counter space at the charge desk.

The location of the school library media center within the school building is important. Placing the facility on the ground floor permits construction for the weight of stacks without involving costly steel reinforcements. It can also permit less costly contiguous expansion when program demands exceed available space. Advance planning is necessary to make sure that the original school library media center is not surrounded on all sides by areas that will not allow for expansion.

Space requirements are determined by the educational uses

made of the school library media center program. Because a successful program creates increased demands on the facility, no center has ever been built large enough in the first place to accommodate this increase in use. In addition, the information explosion and the changes in technology used in education require substantially increased as well as different uses of space. The educational goals of the school system impact on the provision of space as much as they do on the quantity of materials. The space allocated supports or stifles achievement of these goals.

The newer technologies and their software require temperature and humidity control. Static control is affected by choice of carpeting. Acoustical control becomes a greater consideration as more machinery is installed and large numbers of students make use of the center. All these considerations suggest the need for selecting an architectural firm that can translate educational specifications and program requirements into facilities that make them possible, both for the present and in the foreseeable future.

Recognizing Positive Elements

- The planning of the school library media center begins with the architect and the school library media teacher sitting down together to identify the ingredients of a superior library media program and its requirements.
- The school library media teacher is involved with the planning, designing, arranging, and installation of the library media center from this beginning to a final acceptance of the building.
- The authorities believe that it is important to provide space initially even if it is not completely outfitted and will be underused at opening.

Recognizing Negative Elements

- There is insufficient space allocated in the plans to allow for the program as envisioned.
- Disproportionately large cuts in the new school plans have been made in the library media center.
- There is not enough electric power or outlets provided for the amount of machinery that will be used.
- Plans call for installing stacks and other equipment in such a way that it is not easily moved to accommodate rearrangement associated with growth and change in program requirements.

Identifying Missing Elements

- No provision has been made for easy delivery of large or heavy cartons or equipment from the receiving department.
- The planning has been done for "what is" without anticipating what "will be."
- When budgetary cuts are made relative to facilities, the consequences of this action on other parts of the library media program are overlooked.
- Human needs usually provided for in other departments are overlooked in the school library media center; for example, places to secure coats and purses, to store lunches, to work unobserved by students.

Possible Solutions

- Believe the national guidelines; they are not "pie in the sky." They are geared to supporting a quality teaching/learning library media program.

- Seek the advice of the state department of education library media consultants.
- Visit installations with exemplary programs and ask for the advice and recommendations of the library media teachers who work there.
- Bring your own enthusiasm and beliefs to the task of convincing the board of education and the community of the educational necessity for a superior facility.

JOB DESCRIPTION DOCUMENTS

As a school library media center program develops and grows, the jobs and functions carried out by members of the staff change. For this reason job and function description documents should be revised frequently to keep the descriptions in line with the actual jobs. These documents are used to determine when additional staff is needed, the appropriateness of salary scales, and as a base for evaluation of the work being done. Function descriptions are also of significant value as guides to substitutes for school library media center teachers or support staff when they are needed.

The difference between the two documents is that the job description identifies areas of responsibility while the function description lists in detail, step by step, the method of carrying out the job. The function descriptions form the major portion of the code book that should be kept up-to-date. Every operational detail should be included in this manual to ensure consistency and, if needed, to facilitate the transfer of responsibility. (See Appendix B for sample job description documents for a circulation desk aide.)

Recognizing Positive Elements

- The school library media staff members are certain of the scope of their jobs and responsibilities.
- When jobs change and responsibilities are added or subtracted, job and function description documents are revised.
- The school library media program is administered smoothly and effectively with satisfaction expressed by students and teachers.
- There is a hierarchy of job levels so that personnel may aspire to advancement within the department.
- There is evident job satisfaction and a low rate of turnover.

Recognizing Negative Elements

- Unpopular functions are pushed aside by each member of the school library media staff so that some are left undone or allowed to build up large backlogs.
- The appearance of the school library media center is one of clutter and confusion. This may indicate need for additional staff rather than poor performance on the part of the existing staff.
- Rarely will any school library media teacher willingly work overtime or contribute more effort than the minimum required.

Identifying Missing Elements

- There is no, or insufficient, paid nonprofessional support staff in the school library media center.
- There is no long-range plan to deal with personnel shortages.

- There are no job or function descriptions and no goals statements to use for evaluative purposes.

Possible Solutions

- Have a capable parent volunteer or practice teacher assemble sample job descriptions, forms, and philosophical and procedural statements and organize them. A practice teacher can gain an overview of school library media center operation by preparing such a manual, but regardless of who collects the information, the final responsibility for its accuracy belongs to the school library media teacher.
- Inquire about staffing problems and, if any exist, include appropriate budgetary requests or shift assignments to alleviate the shortages.
- Make sure that job descriptions receive official approval, are carried out effectively, and are kept up-to-date in terms of library media program demands.

LEGALITIES

Whole courses are offered on school law as a part of preparation for administration. There is little doubt that unawareness and lack of information leads to difficult situations for school authorities. Just as with any other segment of the school's operation, there are potential legal pitfalls associated with the administration of the school library media center. Every means should be explored to avoid these eventualities.

Areas of concern include: censorship, contracts, previewing rights and responsibilities, theft or destruction of public properties, copyright restrictions and computer program piracy, personal privacy, access to information, handling of monies, drug use, prompt payments of bills, charges for materials or services, and negligence. Various insurances are carried including those offered by various professional associations for the protection of individual members.

There is a new element of copyright related to cyberspace. Keeping the balance between "fair use" and economic gain resulting from sale of intellectual property becomes difficult when there is uncontrolled access to material appearing on electronic networks. The networks are global, and copying from them is easy and basically inexpensive. Moreover, in the minds of many people the networks are probably unpoliceable. In the foreseeable future questions will continue to arise and school personnel will have to be alert to regulations and liabilities as they are developed.

Recognizing Positive Elements

- The school system, or the individual school, maintains written policy statements regarding legalities.
- The code book or operations manual addresses each of the legalities that applies to the running of the school library media center, and gives explicit instructions for legal operation.
- The student and teacher handbooks contain references and reminders that pertain to legalities.
- Regulations are posted, clearly visible to the user. For example, near the copying machine are reminders of copyright restrictions, and in the computer lab and near where computer software is signed out are reminders of piracy restrictions.
- Appropriate insurance policies are maintained by the school system protecting all school personnel.

Recognizing Negative Elements

- Notices are received from collection agencies or legal firms regarding failure to meet deadlines or payments, or discounts are unavailable to the school library media center because of delayed bill payments.
- Individuals threaten to or actually sue the school system or individual staff members over one cause or another.
- Students are denied access to certain materials because of objections by one or more parents, without proper process of a written complaint, hearings, and adjudication by the school board.

Identifying Missing Elements

- No discussions of legalities or responsibilities take place in teachers' meetings or orientation sessions.
- No guidelines regarding legalities appear in student or teacher handbooks.
- The extent of liability is not made clear to school personnel.

Possible Solutions

- Make certain school policies regarding all types of legal matters are available in writing.
- Include legal awareness as a part of staff development sessions.
- Inculcate in the staff a sense of responsibility for the elimination of potential for legal actions.
- Conduct safety inspections throughout the buildings regularly. In the school library media center faulty or trip-causing wiring, broken glass (light bulbs),

paper cutter blades, books falling from loose shelves, and tipping or broken chairs deserve special attention.

POLICIES

Clear-cut policies are essential for the smooth operation of any school and its library media center program. Effective ones are an expression of the officially approved philosophy of education and the goals and objectives statements. Policies are the overarching statements that emanate from the board of education, the policy-making body of a school system. Policies are in continuous revision and are responsive to community and educational changes.

Some of the areas of operation of the school library media center affected by policies include regulations regarding purchasing, selection of materials, interlibrary loans, after-hours and school holiday use, and discipline. In some instances policies affecting other parts of the school are counterproductive to effective management of the school library media center, and alternate policies need to be written and approved.

Library media teachers who sense needed changes or additions in policies that affect the school library media program should take the initiative in suggesting policy statements through established procedures. Discussions with administrators concerning the rationale behind the suggestions will help inform them and may gain their support.

Recognizing Positive Elements

- There are handbooks for students and for faculty that include the policies as well as the rules of the school library media center.

- There is regular reassessment of policies by the media center staff, the faculty, and the administration. Students may also contribute.
- Board of education members and administrators recognize the need for differences both in policies and their interpretation.

Recognizing Negative Elements

- The practice of carrying out detention policy by placing students in the school library media center is a misuse of the facility and extremely damaging to student and staff attitudes toward the center and its program.
- The policy of assigning search and written work as punishment is employed—a practice very detrimental to students and almost guaranteed to make life harder for teachers.

Identifying Missing Elements

- There is no library code book or handbook for students or faculty that explains policies affecting the school library media center and its program.
- No consideration has been given to the possibility that policies that affect the school library media center and its program may need to be tailored to its unique requirements.

Possible Solutions

- Institute annual or biennial opportunities for regular reevaluation of policies that affect the school library media center and its program.

- Encourage the school library media center staff to initiate suggestions for change and solicit rationales to be used when working with the board of education.

PUBLIC RELATIONS

Another name for some of these activities is "public information." "Public relations" is the somewhat broader term since it covers all relationships and contacts by school personnel with the help and reinforcement of every staff member and the students.

Information about the school library media program is less often included in routine school public relations efforts than many other aspects of school programs. There is a great need for increasing the awareness of the school library media program's function and value. The rationale, philosophy, and potential of the school library media program is not very well understood in the community and often even within the school. Unless a larger view of the total program is made evident, neither understanding nor support will result. When talking about the functions of the school library media center program, students, teachers, and administrators tend to answer in terms of personal experiences. While this is understandable, conclusions based on such narrow samples may lead to mistaken perceptions.

There are two communities to which information goes. One is the "internal" community of the school or school system; the other is "external"—the community-at-large.

There are similarities and differences in the approaches that prove effective. The channels through which the school community is informed include the public address system, notes in teachers' mailboxes, the school newspaper or magazine, talks to teacher groups, presentations to the school board, posters, bulletin boards, display cases, in-house TV programming, e-mail, home room or classroom announcements. Those by which the total community may be reached include presentations to the PTA, articles or columns in local newspapers, announcements over local radio or television, presentations on cable television, notices sent home to parents, parent newsletters, school newsletters mailed to the taxpayers, posters displayed in local business places, special promotional booths at a mall, church, or other community sites and functions. Not to be overlooked is the goodwill and good word of those who come in touch with the schools from day to day: the man at the nearby coffee shop, the youth agency counselors, the public library staff, and many others.

Recognizing Positive Elements

- The weekly, monthly, and annual reports from the school library media center contain good basic material for the administration and school board to use for public information. They are also spiced with examples, illustrations, and "human interest" stories.
- There is a local reporter assigned by the newspaper to cover regularly the activities of the school library media center. The activities of the school library media center are tied to events such as the issuing of a national report on education, literacy, or continuing training for jobs.
- The school library media center staff sends approved, double-spaced copy to newspapers, radio, and TV stations for inclusion in local reportage,
- National events such as School Library Media Month, National Library Week, and American Education Week are taken full advantage of by the school

system.

- Board of education members, administrators, teachers, and students take pride in awards and other recognitions of excellence accorded the school library media personnel and program.

Recognizing Negative Elements

- School library media activities are considered to be of interest only to school and parent groups.
- Insufficient advance time is allowed for articles or notices to be sent, or reporter coverage to be arranged for, when special events are planned.
- Misinformation about the school library media program is allowed to stand and remain uncorrected.

Identifying Missing Elements

- Information about the school library media program is never, or rarely, included in presentations to the school board, PTA, or community service groups.
- Displays throughout the school (other than in the school library media center itself) do not include or reflect the school library media center program.
- No mention is made of the school library media teachers' responsibilities to public information in their job descriptions.
- There is no regular column dealing with school library media center news in school publications.
- Captions or credits under newspaper photos taken in the school library media center do not acknowledge the setting.

Possible Solutions

- Encourage PTA program planners to include presentations that make use of media center program services, productions, and personnel. Of course, proper credits should be given.
- Celebrate ceremoniously the recognition and appreciation of volunteers and arrange to have reportage through all public information media.
- Hold annual legislative appreciation functions or ceremonies in the school library media center. Include state and national lawmakers as well as town officials.
- Encourage/initiate the inclusion of school library media teachers on conference programs for other educators.
- Designate a person on the school system staff to serve as public information officer.

REASSIGNMENT OF PERSONNEL

The argument is sometimes made that the school library media teacher, being a teacher and working under the teachers' contract, should assume all functions other teachers do and be assigned home room and study hall responsibilities as well as bus, cafeteria, and playground duties.

On the surface this looks fair, but when examined it is found to be far from logical. Over and above the questionable use of professional time (which applies to all teachers) for nonprofessional duties, when the school library media teacher is removed from the center to carry out noninstructional functions, the educational use of the school library media center program is diminished, and thereby the instructional program itself. An even more important argument against this misuse of the school library media teacher is the fact that lunch period and before- and after-school times (which coincide with bus times) are important *use* times for the school library media center. The school library media teacher is expected to serve the entire school for the entire day. If assigned these additional noninstructional duties, the school library media teachers have legitimate claim to release time equal to that given other teachers, thereby further diminishing the library media program and the use of the resources.

Sometimes, in emergency situations, a school library media teacher is asked to cover a classroom or the students are sent to the library for supervision. While acceptable as a solution to a genuine emergency, it is paid for through reduced services to the rest of the student body and faculty, and therefore should never become a routine practice.

In regard to nonprofessional personnel, it should be recognized that because of experience and special skills requirements, clerical help should not be deemed totally interchangeable between the school library media center and other offices. While school library media center support staff personnel may prove helpful answering phones, sorting mail, or typing and filing, the office personnel can contribute little to the operation of the school library media center without additional specialized training. This sort of reassignment or "detailing" is a one-way street and the school library media center program suffers from it.

Recognizing Positive Elements

- Administrators limit the reassignment of school library media center staff to only the rarest of emergencies.
- Administrators recognize the extra responsibilities

assumed by the school library media teachers in operating the center and withstand pressures that weaken the effectiveness of the school library media program. Most classroom teachers will recognize the unique elements of managing a school library media center program when the administration does—and says so.

Recognizing Negative Elements

- The school library media teacher demands a duty-free lunch period and a daily planning period provided contractually and in conformance with other teachers' assignments. Problems arise when the library media teacher is regularly scheduled, for example, to a planning period on third period Tuesdays, meaning that classes meeting at that time receive no services from the center or school library media teacher.
- Reassignments are frequent and without recognition of their true costs.
- No effort is made to provide compensatory assistance.

Identifying Missing Elements

- There are no job or function descriptions to substantiate position expectations of either professional or nonprofessional personnel.
- There is no recognition of either the differing performance requirements or the teacher status of the school library media teacher in the employment contract.

Possible Solutions

- The administrator might spend an entire day or two in the school library media center observing and experiencing the demands that lively use of an effective program makes on the professional and support staff.
- See that accurate job and function descriptions are maintained. For example, the job description for an aide may read, "responsible for circulation of materials," and the function statement(s) for that operation would describe the details of how the function is carried out, "remove the book card from the pocket. Insert it . . . ." Note: function descriptions are useful to substitutes who need assistance in doing the work. (See sample documents in Appendix B.)

RULES

Each rule should be thought through to determine its impact on all aspects of the program and student use. There should be as few as possible and they should be applied democratically and diplomatically. The purpose of these rules is to enable the center to serve the needs of the students and faculty, and they should be reevaluated periodically to ensure that that intent is being realized. Whenever there are frequent conflicts or evidence that the rules are not assisting student use they should be modified.

Student and teacher assessment of the effectiveness of the rules is welcomed. Their interpretation regarding fairness of application of rules is responded to. Methods used to acquire this information include the formation of a library media center advisory committee or the creation of a student council committee responsible for transmitting student and faculty opinions, the use of questionnaires, or the installation of a suggestion box or open-forum flipchart.

Recognizing Positive Elements

- There is a library codebook as well as a handbook for students and one for faculty that include the policies and rules of the school library media center.
- Rules pertinent to the use of specific equipment are posted adjacent to the equipment whenever feasible.
- The student council or individual students have opportunities to contribute to the formation or modification of these policies and rules.
- There is regular reassessment of library media center rules by the staff, the students, the faculty, and the administration.
- No other school rules are changed without considering the impact and implications of the change on the functioning of the school library media center and its program.
- New students receive orientation to the school library media center and its services. Handbooks are distributed and their contents explained.

Recognizing Negative Elements

- Students are forever complaining about the rules, calling them unfair, senseless, discriminatory, and there is some perceived justification for their reactions.
- Solutions are sought through punishment rather than constructive means.
- Rules are drawn up for the benefit and convenience

of the school library media staff and without input from students, faculty, or administration.

- Handbooks have not been revised in recent years, and there is no provision for replacement or updating of handbooks and codebooks.

Identifying Missing Elements

- There is no handbook for students or faculty.
- Rules are unwritten and interpreted verbally with variations and omissions leading to confusion and misunderstanding on the part of students and faculty.
- There are no additional copies of the student handbook available in the guidance offices, main office, classrooms, or media center.
- There is no mechanism providing for student input concerning changes in the regulations.

Possible Solutions

- Remember that inexpensively produced handbooks tend to be revised more frequently.
- Form an advisory committee of students and teachers to reevaluate school library media center rules, and then meet with both professional and nonprofessional library media staff to resolve problems.
- Consider using a questionnaire to identify student and faculty levels of satisfaction with school library media center operations and suggestions for facilitating its use.

SCHEDULING

Perhaps the most controversial, misunderstood, and misused aspect of the library media program is scheduling. In making the basic philosophical decisions regarding scheduling, the administrator determines the role of the school library media program. As with any other segment of the educational program, among the questions that must be answered are, "what is its purpose?" and "what are the desired educational outcomes for the students?"

Administrators who schedule every class in the building into the library media center weekly for "library skills instruction" have not thought through what impact this will have on the total library media program nor what kind of educational value will result from teaching this content out of context. Students learn their searching, viewing, and listening skills where and when they occur in the integrated curriculum. The enthusiasm, excitement, and enjoyment children brought to school as kindergartners can be retained in the library media center if children are not scheduled into a meaningless series of lectures and/or workbook sheets of drill on the Dewey decimal system and indexing. That original delight in learning must be nurtured if students are to become lifetime learners. (See "Integration of Library Media Skills into Curriculum" in chapter 5.)

Is student time in the center meant merely to provide weekly exchange of materials? If so, this is wasteful. There should be ample opportunity provided for this function before and after the school day, during the lunch break, and intermittently from classrooms for individual students to return and select a new book. A book return slot in the wall will enable students going by the library media center to drop off materials at any time. With flexible scheduling, individual or small groups of students can come from classrooms to exchange materials whenever ongoing classroom activity permits it. A pass makes clear what is to be done there and how long the student may stay in the center before returning to the classroom.

Is the scheduling meant to guarantee all students at least weekly entrance to the library media center, to listen to a story (but many classroom teachers read stories to students), to browse, to handle new materials and check out those that capture their interests? Regularly scheduled short periods of time can become the *only* time students go to the center. Unscheduled but frequent use of the center provides students with more meaningful opportunities to use the center. Making certain that all classroom teachers use the library media center materials as teaching tools, consult with the library media teachers, and schedule class workshops in the center so that they tie in with classroom activities, is the responsibility of the appropriate supervisor—in most cases, the principal.

The school library media center is a teaching station and not a place to be used to meet the contractual requirements of unscheduled time for classroom teachers. When the whole class is in the library media center so is the classroom teacher. At times, planned activities can be shared with part of the class working with their teacher in the classroom and another part working in the library media center with the library media teacher. Students know when they are being "dropped off" and may quickly adopt the wrong attitudes about the purpose of the school library media program.

The school library media teachers are there to provide reading guidance, suggest new topics to explore, assist in student use of equipment, explain production procedures, and reinforce classroom instruction with audiovisual or computer software or networks. This one-on-one or small-group instruction is direct, individually tailored, and relevant to student needs—thus leading to meaningful sustained learning. Teachers should be asked to make use of sign-up sheets and arrange for their classes to have specific instruction or introduction to materials pertaining to new curriculum units. They consult with the library media teachers about materials for classroom use and arrange for students who were absent to make up lost instruction time with materials for self-instruction. They decide when and for what lengths of time their students will make use of the library media center as a class or as individuals. Teachers who accompany their students to the library media center and who participate in their learning experiences there, also see them in revealingly different circumstances that can be very enlightening.

Recognizing Positive Elements

- Flexible, open scheduling is the basic operational philosophy of the school library media center.
- Classroom teachers use the school library media center effectively as a teaching/learning tool.
- Students are encouraged and expected to find a variety of ways and times to use the library media center individually, in small groups, and with classes—more so with block schedules.
- Student attitudes toward the center are positive and enthusiastic, and the center is seen as a necessary element in their instruction and learning.

Recognizing Negative Elements

- There is a rigid schedule that controls all student use of the library media center, giving essentially no consideration to the real value of an integrated school library media program.

- Time to browse and make suitable selections of materials is diminished by the inflexibility of the schedule.
- Book return and selection sessions are not separated from instructional or workshop sessions.

Identifying Missing Elements

- There is no teacher sign-up system to permit media center use to match ongoing classroom activities.
- Classroom and library media teachers do not plan together to create instructional units and opportunities.
- Students do not relate the library media center with either learning opportunities or pleasure.

Possible Solutions

- Support the concept of unscheduled but nonetheless frequent and regular use of the school library media center.
- Encourage classroom teachers to employ the resources (materials, personnel, and programs) of the library media center as a teaching/learning tool on a planned, day-to-day basis.
- Include recognition of such cooperative effort (or lack of it) on the teacher evaluation form.
- Work toward solving contractual requirements through the use of sufficient staff (full-time substitutes) to provide unscheduled time for classroom teachers.
- Make certain that the library media center facility has sufficient space, materials, and staff to fulfill its educational purpose.

- Make certain that all members of the school library media staff actively promote the educational potential of the library media program.
- Plan staff development opportunities that help classroom/subject teachers to work effectively with the library media center staff.

SCHOOL–PUBLIC LIBRARY COOPERATION

Communities do not wish to engage in expensive duplication when it comes to supplying information resources. Since the beginning of networking there has been consideration of ways to share by means of technology. Unfortunately, the lesser endowed partner often seemed to be ready to "take" without contributing to the exchange. A better balance must be established for sharing to work. Schools and public libraries have the opportunity to engage in cost cutting through reduction of duplication of holdings, especially when they are linked electronically.

There will be as many different approaches to cooperation as there are communities wanting to engage in sharing. What can be done depends upon starting small, finding that some things work and some do not, making adjustments, and going on. Obviously, the technology that is in place determines much of what can be done.

Identifying Positive Elements

- Personnel in both institutions want to cooperate.
- E-mail for quick exchanges of information and faxing for sending document pages permit cooperative selection of periodicals and references.
- Hours for use of facilities are staggered, giving consideration to adult and student users' demands. Af-

ter-school and weekend hours can be assigned differently from those during the school day.

Identifying Negative Elements

- There is jealousy and competition among agencies indicating a disregard for the needs and overall good of the community.
- There is little evidence that the adults involved accept responsibility for reaching out and learning together.
- Suggestions for cooperation from either side are ignored by the other.

Identifying Missing Elements

- There is no suggestion or attempt made to cooperate at any level for any purpose.

Possible Solutions

- Initiate a discussion with concrete ideas that call for a reaction. "Why don't we . . . ?" without specifics seldom brings results.
- Fill in the missing pieces of technology needed to make electronic exchanges possible; e.g., additional phone lines, a fax machine, e-mail capabilities.
- Possibly change staffing hours or extend coverage to evenings.
- Establish a homework hotline that leads to facilities located in the public library as well as in the school library media centers.
- When initial sharing has been successful, add other community agencies such as community colleges,

universities, and special libraries located in hospitals, industries, or churches to enlarge the community's information bank.

SECURITY SYSTEMS

There are varying approaches to the school library media center security problem. What is done depends largely upon the nature of the community and the attitudes of the students in the school. Where there is a high respect for public property and shared facilities, losses will be low enough so that the installation of mechanical security systems will not be required. Where the percentage of losses is high and rising every year, no valuable materials collection can be established and maintained without a security system.

There are two basic mechanical approaches in use. With one, materials are desensitized at the charge desk and resensitized upon their return. In the other, materials cannot be desensitized at all. The impact of this difference is felt most when students need to bring previously checked-out materials back into the school library media center repeatedly, for example, when they are working on extended tasks such as term papers. High school students tend to carry materials from classroom to classroom throughout the school day because they are limited in the number of times they may return to their lockers. When materials cannot be desensitized, a library media center staff person must be stationed at the exit to manually hand materials around the sensing area. This is the procedure used in most university settings, because there, students do not tend to bring materials back to the library until they are being returned for good. Most K-12 installations use the system that permits desensitizing the borrowed item when it is checked out at the circulation desk, thereby permitting the student to bring the item in and out repeatedly until it is resensitized when it is checked back in. This pass-around problem becomes more acute when at the end of a period many students leave the school library media center at the same time. The five-minute passing period does not allow enough time to deal with this problem.

Some security systems operate on a radio frequency and others use a magnetic system. It is advisable to examine a given system carefully to determine how it might be invalidated before making a selection for purchase. There is no known system that cannot be compromised by some method, and the security system does not operate by itself. However, the systems do permit the school library media center personnel to be much more in control, and security systems cut collection losses dramatically, often paying for themselves within a year or two. Another advantage to the mechanical systems is that they are impersonal. No monitor is peering into personal belongings.

Recognizing Positive Elements

- Losses are reduced to acceptable levels.
- Students realize that they do not have to steal materials in order to have them available for use.
- The collection is allowed to grow systematically and the funds allotted for purchase of materials are not used up buying needed replacements.

Recognizing Negative Elements

- The system offers a challenge to some students to circumvent it.
- The machinery complicates egress during rush periods.

- A negative reaction created by the school's need to use a security system is certainly present, even though it is recognized that not only libraries but stores and other institutions must protect valuables from the lamentable societal disease of theft.

Identifying Missing Elements

- There is a weak sense of responsibility on the part of the administration regarding protection of public property.
- There is no recognition of the rights denied to students by continued theft of materials.
- There has been little or no investigation of the benefits of a security system.

Possible Solutions

- Giving frank and open explanations about the workings of the newly installed system to curious students will gain their cooperation. One need not reveal information that compromises the operation of the system, but an honest admission of its vulnerability helps. It soon becomes apparent to students that most means of bypassing the system are visible acts of mischief.
- Cope with exit crowding at the end of the period by having those teachers accompanying classroom groups dismiss them from the library media center a minute or two ahead of the bell.
- Create a positive student feeling about the security system by emphasizing the increased availability of materials that its use makes possible.
- Explain to students that the security system enables

library media center personnel to identify each borrower and the date the material is due. The students can be assured that their needs will be met through cooperative means rather than by arbitrarily calling in materials. It makes no difference whether they need materials someone else has or whether they have materials someone else needs. It is the responsibility of the school library media teacher to help solve this dilemma satisfactorily. When plans for sharing can be worked out, materials may not need to be called in, which helps keep all students happier.

SELECTING SCHOOL LIBRARY MEDIA CENTER NONPROFESSIONAL SUPPORT STAFF

Nonprofessional support staff includes clerks, aides, technicians, and other assistants. The "library media technical assistant" (LMTA) is the term applied to individuals who have completed two years of technical training in an officially recognized community college program that grants the associate degree. While these persons are not professional teachers, they do hold certification for the nonprofessional technical level of service. Unlike other technical training programs, the LMTA programs are not accredited by the library profession. The American Library Association accredits only graduate programs for the education of fully professional librarians.

The school library media aide has unique competencies. These include all the competencies required of a classroom aide and in addition encompass the specialized clerical and technical tasks associated with the operation of the school library media program. The most experienced and clerically adept personnel will need additional training to function effectively. Since the LMTA degree prepares personnel to work in all types of libraries, the specialization required in a school setting must be acquired in the school itself.

Since the nonprofessional is often the initial contact that the user has with the program, it is mandatory that this person be aware of how critical this contact is. A knowledge of human behavior, the rules for operation of the school and the school library media center, and an ability to get on well with people are crucial. The disposition and personality of candidates for support staff positions are as critical as their technical capabilities. How they react to students, interruptions, periods of overcrowding and understaffing, doing several tasks simultaneously, and their ability to anticipate needs are equally important. Ability to tolerate ambiguities and to improvise appropriately when no professional is available to assist them is an invaluable trait to look for.

The attitudes of the staff create the atmosphere within the school library media center that enhances or inhibits the program. Unexpected circumstances, always around the corner in any school, make it likely that anyone on the staff may be called upon to substitute temporarily for someone else. In order to prevent damage to carefully built rapport with students and teachers, no staff persons should be hired with the view that they will not have to interact with library media center users.

Recognizing Positive Elements

- The nonprofessional is flexible. The average school day may call for adjustment to any plans that have been made. The ability to accept this fact of school life and adjust to its demands is essential.
- The nonprofessional is cheerful and has a sense of humor, achieving a high level of good interpersonal relations with faculty and students.

- The nonprofessional is service-oriented and recognizes that the clerical tasks are secondary to users' immediate needs.
- The nonprofessional feels a part of the team and on occasion makes suggestions for improving service or solving problems.
- The nonprofessional is prompt, gives full measure, is not a clock-watcher.

Recognizing Negative Elements

- The nonprofessional has had experience in some other library and is unwilling or unable to accept the directions and methods of the school library media center director.
- The nonprofessional resists change.
- The nonprofessional does not understand, respect, or accept the limitations of nonprofessional service.
- The nonprofessional is left alone in charge of the school library media center.
- The nonprofessional provides service but in a manner that makes users feel that they are interrupting or are burdensome.

Identifying Missing Elements

- There is no paid support staff provided in the school library media center.
- A volunteer program is expected to take the place of paid support staff.
- Clerical personnel from other departments of the school are assigned on an irregular basis to the school library media center with no knowledge of its operations.

- No consideration is given to potential incompatibility among department personnel.

Possible Solutions

- A thorough needs assessment should be made and accurate job and function descriptions written for each position of the nonprofessional support staff.
- Interviewing and hiring should be done in terms of approved job descriptions.
- Recognize the differences in demands made by the school library media center program on the skills of clerical staff; for example, accuracy over speed in keyboard skills or unique filing rules used.
- Do not allow personnel who exhibit marginal or questionable performance to be retained in the hope that they may improve.

SELECTING SCHOOL LIBRARY MEDIA CENTER PROFESSIONAL STAFF

School library media teachers, like classroom teachers, are certified teachers. In addition, they are librarians, media specialists, materials experts, and middle-level administrators. They have expertise in library media center program creation, development, and growth. They keep up with current educational theory and practice and respond to the changes in student and faculty needs. They are experts in the materials of learning and serve as resource persons on curriculum development committees.

Their appearance and demeanor portray an attitude that affects the success of the entire school library media program. Too often the stereotype is that the "librarian" is mean, scowling, and obsessed with order over service, use, or enjoyment. Of course, a pleasant manner is not to be equated with competence, but neither need be sacrificed for the other; both are required.

Because of the difficulties involved in dismissing less than adequate personnel, it is essential to evaluate candidates carefully. In addition to their credentials on paper, the candidates should be observed working with teachers and students. Checklists matching job descriptions and requirements should be updated continuously, not only for hiring purposes, but also for ongoing evaluations. Permanent job status should not be given automatically.

Recognizing Positive Elements

- The school library media teachers operate as members of a team. They exhibit mutual respect and show an appreciation for the skills and performances of each member of the staff.
- School library media teachers are actively involved in faculty activities.
- School library media teachers are active members of state, regional, and national professional associations.
- They regularly attend conferences and workshops, sometimes making presentations or writing for professional journals.
- They are constantly sharpening their own professional skills.
- They provide faculty and administration with current sources of information.
- They see themselves as part of the instructional team in the school and as a part of the service team in the school library media center.
- School library media teachers are considered neces-

sary by the classroom teachers as materials resource experts. They serve on curriculum development committees.

Recognizing Negative Elements

- The school library media teacher is rigid, resists change, and is convinced that old ways are always best.
- The center is operated for the convenience of the school library media staff rather than for the educational benefit of the users.
- There is no leadership for change evidenced; there is minimal acceptance of newer technologies or practices.
- Students and faculty tend to avoid using the school library media center and express negative attitudes toward the school library media teachers.
- The school library media teachers have little or no input regarding selection of additional professional or nonprofessional staff.
- Inexperienced personnel are selected to gain budgetary benefits.

Identifying Missing Elements

- There is little pleasure taken by students or faculty in using the school library media center.
- Teachers make assignments that eliminate the participation of the school library media teacher or that obviate the use of the center by students.
- The school library media center is run by nonprofessionals.
- There is no teaching/learning school library media program in place.

- Insufficient professional and nonprofessional staff are hired to permit quality service.
- Little or no investigation is made regarding the relative quality of the preparation program of certificated candidates for professional positions.

Possible Solutions

- A thorough needs assessment and evaluation of the existing school library media program should be undertaken, and proficient staff selected to fit needs as exactly as possible.
- Goals and directions for the desired school library media program should be established.
- Short- and long-range plans should be formulated with budgetary implications applied.
- Examine the credentials of professional applicants for evidence of sensitivity in interpersonal relations, people dynamics training, successful experience with children, and above all, enthusiasm.
- Do not allow personnel who exhibit marginal or questionable performance to be retained in the hope that they may improve.
- Recognize that when the wrong person has been hired, that person must be removed, and the best way is never to have granted tenure in the first place.

STANDARDS AND GUIDELINES

There is a tradition of referring to the national school library media program guidelines promulgated by the profession as "standards." The term appeared in the titles of the 1960 (*Standards for School Library Programs*) and 1969

(*Standards for School Media Programs*) documents, but not in the 1975 (*Media Programs: District and School*) nor the 1988 (*Information Power: Guidelines for School Library Media Programs*) documents. (Note: At the time of writing, the latter is in the process of revision and it is not known which form will be used.) The term *standards*, however, implies that there are mechanisms for their enforcement, and when there are no means of enforcing compliance with the specifications or procedures that are recommended, they cannot truly be considered "standards." Some local education authorities and state departments of education have set enforceable standards, but many of them use only goals and guidelines. In all cases these are much lower and less precisely stated than those of the professional group or groups.

Many guidelines have been stated quantitatively. It is easy to count the numbers and types of items that should be purchased, measure square footage, or check copyright dates. It is simple to determine the ratio of professional and nonprofessional staff to faculty or students served. It is far more difficult to evaluate the uses made of the materials and staff, but if a program is to be evaluated for its quality, a way must be found to determine uses made and resulting effectiveness.

Recognizing Positive Elements

- The school system has determined the quality level of the school library media program required to foster the educational achievement of its students.
- Guidelines established by local, state, regional, and/ or national agencies to achieve this level of program are applied.
- Adequate budgeting and financial support are provided to achieve and maintain the desired quality level.

- The school system applies for awards, enters competitions, and accepts visitors as further evidence of the quality of the school library media program and its compliance with guidelines.

Recognizing Negative Elements

- Little regard is given to meeting and maintaining standards or guidelines, least of all surpassing them.
- Regional or state accrediting team reports are negative regarding the school library media program. These reports make little impact.
- Students' scores on the search and study skills parts of standardized tests are below average.
- No visits are made by administrators to schools identified as having excellent school library media programs.

Identifying Missing Elements

- There are no philosophy, goals, objectives, or standards/guidelines statements written or in use by the school library media center or school system.
- No plan for evaluation of the school library media program exists.
- Administrators are unfamiliar with state, regional, or national standards and guidelines. There are no copies of these documents in the schools.

Possible Solutions

- Use self-evaluation forms (such as those provided by accrediting agencies) to evaluate the school library media program.

- Consult with school system and state department of education consultants for help in evaluating the school library media program.
- Plan and develop staff development to upgrade educational use made of facilities to meet guideline expectations.
- Revise curricular documents to upgrade educational use (and value received) of the school library media program to meet guideline expectations.
- Launch a campaign to educate the community regarding the educational and instructional role of the school library media program and to gain financial support needed to meet guideline recommendations.

STUDENT ASSISTANTS

The concept of students helping students is attractive. Those who support the idea of using students as school library media center assistants may be partially motivated by this concept. They may also believe that student assistants learn "something about the library" by working in it, which surely is good for them, and quite possibly the activity serves a dual purpose and provides career aspirations as well. Those who concur with the latter notion often suggest the assignment of workstudy program students to the library media center. When large numbers of students volunteer their unassigned time to work in the center, it is logical to create a student association or club and provide a special extracurricular program for them. At times, local clubs have belonged to state and national associations of library student assistants.

In general, however, when students are assigned to the school library media center to "assist" with its operation, an underlying thought is that it will save the library media teachers' time. This is fallacious thinking. Recognition must be given to the added responsibilities and demands for library media teachers' time that this plan demands, if it is to be done well. If it cannot be a beneficial learning experience for the students, it ought not be done at all.

First, the students should not be taken advantage of, expected to serve as cheap labor, or be left undirected and unattended. Students will need training to learn to do the jobs they are assigned properly and accurately. This requires library media teacher time to plan the instruction, carry it out, and continually verify that student work is done as expected throughout the term. It becomes debatable how much "help" these programs provide the school library media center. In all likelihood, the program costs more professional time than it saves.

A significant problem arises for student assistants when their friends put pressure on them for special favors that sometimes break the rules. Others use their position at the desk to wield "power" and to intimidate other students. Students should not be put into either position.

When students are part of a workstudy or for-credit course, demands increase. Actual classes must be taught, work graded, and marks filed and placed on report cards. Most of the urgent housekeeping chores that the assistant is assigned to do have little to do with research techniques, information use skills, or giving a sense of the professional side of a career in library information service. At best, the students' experience equates only with that of the lowest paid nonprofessional worker, for they rarely do more than shelve, correct the shelving of others, and paste, stamp, and cover books. Sometimes students from the business classes have used keyboard skills to produce catalog cards (if the system is still used in the library) through typing or through use of computerized card-producing programs. In either instance, the student is making only routine use of machinery. Even if the student were using a computer to enter cataloging and indexing information into the online databank, it is still largely routine number punching—scarcely an accurate picture of the work of the professional working in library and information sciences.

Sometimes students from business classes are asked to file cards for the school library media center. These students have been taught filing rules that are used in general office procedures. The old filing rules used for card catalogs in libraries are different. Even when newer rules that match those used on computerized indexes are followed to file the cards, the students who are expected to do library filing must still receive additional instruction beforehand.

Many times, because the student's counselor does not truly understand the functions of the school library media center, a marginal student who does not have the academic skills needed to function as a "library aide" is put into the program. These students often have problems with reading, decimals, and sequencing. Therefore they make mistakes in shelving, checking records, and filing periodicals and transaction cards. These mistakes must be undone by professionals, which takes additional time. These students are often embarrassed by their shortcomings and the school library media teacher is not able to spend enough individualized time with them to correct their deficiencies.

On the other hand, when it is realized that a student assistants organization is an additional school club assignment for the library media teacher, and there are sufficient staff members to permit providing the advising library media teacher to accept the responsibility properly, then there can be much value for the students. As a club activity, going on trips, sponsoring a visit from an author for the school, and learning something of the history and future of the field of information retrieval can be beneficial.

At the secondary level students have study hall assignments, have unassigned time, or are in workstudy programs. At the elementary level the students' time is entirely assigned. Recess provides social learning experiences and necessary physical activity. The lunch period is barely adequate for food consumption. The elementary child is in school to learn, not to provide extra hands as a substitute for staff.

Recognizing Positive Elements

- Sufficient paid nonprofessional services are provided.
- The students who contribute to the operation of the school library media center are provided with genuine educational experiences.
- Sufficient professional staff time is provided to carry out the program.

Recognizing Negative Elements

- Students are assigned as "library aides," expected to work with minimal supervision routinely and monotonously at the same task all year long.
- The curriculum for the student assistants' library media center course is not up to other academic course standards.
- Workstudy students are assigned to the center without consideration of the need to match the student's ability with the requirements and demands of the work.

Identifying Missing Elements

- No policy exists detailing the use of volunteer or course credit student programs.

Possible Solutions

- Establish a student volunteer assistants program within the school that serves the community and permits students to elect the school library media center as one of the agencies to be served.
- Retain the supervision of the program and the follow-up activities as a part of the schoolwide program.

SUBLETTING THE RESPONSIBILITY FOR MATERIALS

School library media teachers usually develop a high sense of responsibility. They place priority on having materials well marked, well organized for ready accessibility, and easily checked in and out. They believe in the importance of inventorying both for preservation of the collection and for control over the individual items. They are not opposed to the use of security systems when losses have gotten out of hand.

Unfortunately, not all borrowers (students and teachers both) share a similar sense of responsibility for the security of materials entrusted to their care. They see no reason not to help fellow students and teachers by subletting materials borrowed in their names to others without first returning the materials to the school library media center so that the borrowing responsibility may be reassigned to the person who has the material. Equally unfortunate is that administrators often choose to follow a double standard regarding lost materials: Students pay for replacement but classroom teachers are immune to penalty. When these situations exist, there can only be friction and bitter feelings. Costly, often irreplaceable materials have disappeared. Students and teachers alike suffer the loss.

Recognizing Positive Elements

- There exists a written policy concerning lost materials that applies to both students and faculty.
- Nonprint materials purchased in sets of multiple independent parts are separated, cataloged, and stored in hang-up plastic bags making it possible to borrow only the part or parts needed. Also, less storage space is required with this system.
- There is a policy that forbids subletting materials borrowed or borrowing for others to use.

Recognizing Negative Elements

- Borrowers frequently claim that they have not taken materials for which they are charged.
- Material sets containing multiple parts are returned with missing portions.
- Teachers help themselves to materials outside the school library media center (that is, in the workrooms or offices) when they are already signed out to someone else.
- Borrowers "lose" library media center materials in classrooms, gymnasium, cafeteria, or corridors, or someplace outside the school.

Identifying Missing Elements

- The impact of the problem has not been thought through and there are no written policy and procedure statements available.
- There are no sections in the teachers' or students' handbooks with responsibility statements.

Possible Solutions

- Form a committee to examine the ramifications of the problem and to suggest possible actions.
- Recognize that adults as well as students have responsibilities for materials borrowed.
- Provide workroom facilities that permit individually secured teacher areas.
- Include topics such as sharing, taking responsibility for public properties, and valuing common properties in the values instruction within the school.
- Publish statements concerning responsibilities and the impact on borrowers in both student and teacher handbooks.

SUBSTITUTE TEACHERS

Substitute teachers are an obvious necessity. Most school systems try to make their job descriptions as effective and simple as possible. However, the role of the substitute teacher in relation to the school library media center is often omitted from the guidelines or manual prepared for substitute teachers.

To find a successful substitute to function in the school library media center is a more difficult matter than finding one for the classroom. When one is found, that substitute should be highly prized and insofar as possible be reserved for that function.

Recognizing Positive Elements

- The substitute is aware of the many functions of the school library media center, and perhaps has served as a volunteer, acquiring special skills.

- The substitute works well with students and is one step ahead of their "testings."
- There is a procedures statement given all classroom substitutes that calls attention to matters regarding the use of the school library media center. This includes pass-writing, "dumping" the class into the center without a specific academic purpose (especially when no lesson plans have been left), and being alert to students' "goofing off" when a visit to the library media center has been planned.

Recognizing Negative Elements

- Teachers' lesson plans left for substitutes indicate taking the class to the library media center but give no directions regarding the purpose or intended accomplishment expected.
- Other teachers advise substitutes, "when you don't know what else to do with them, send students to the library media center."

Identifying Missing Elements

- There is no lesson plan, so the classroom substitute takes the class to the library media center.
- There are no substitutes available for the school library media teacher who are capable of administering the library media program. Either the center is closed for the day or lack of proper supervision results in chaos or destruction of materials and equipment.

Possible Solutions

- Require that assignments to be completed during the period spent in the school library media center are handed in to the library media teacher at the end of the period. This accounts for both presence and performance.
- Make certain that a handbook or set of guidelines developed for use by substitute teachers is revised to include a section addressing potential problems or concerns when using the school library media center and computers.
- Provide special training to prepare a group of suitable substitutes to be school library media center substitutes.
- Limit admission to the center to only classroom teacher-accompanied groups when the school library media teacher must be absent and no suitable substitute is available.
- Institute a program of responsibility awareness and consciousness-raising for both students and teachers.

TEACHER MONOPOLY OF MATERIALS

A few classroom teachers may acquire a reputation for attempting to check out all the materials useful for a specific topic (such as an upcoming holiday) well in advance to ensure having the materials when they need them. Such teachers also exhibit a preference for maintaining classroom and privately owned materials collections. They are the ones who probably protested the establishment of a unified print and nonprint materials collection in the school library media center in the first place. They may also show a tendency toward wanting exclusive use of computer lab space or equipment. They resist coordinating when specific units will be taught through departmental planning and scheduling. The bad feelings these teachers create within the school library media center and among other classroom teachers can only be controlled through administrative intervention.

Recognizing Positive Elements

- All print and nonprint materials owned by the school, regardless of where they are housed, are identified in the school library media center shelf-list and catalog. This does not mean that all materials must also be stored in the school library media center. For example, microscopic slides may be stored in the science department and cookery film-strips may be considered more useful in the home economics wing. Nonetheless, anyone has access to these materials through the library media center.

- Written policy statements concerning the use of reserve and classroom collections are enforced.

- The use of school library media center materials as teaching tools is a part of classroom teacher evaluations.

- The administration gives strong support to, and interpretation of, the benefits of a unified collection being equitably shared.

Recognizing Negative Elements

- Not all materials owned by the school are cataloged and listed in the school library media center catalog so that everyone may be aware of their existence. Classroom closets and teachers' desk drawers contain uncataloged and/or unreturned library media center materials.

- There is a "me first" rather than a cooperative and sharing attitude exhibited by classroom teachers.

Identifying Missing Elements

- There is little or no visible administrative support for the unified school library media center system of circulating and inventorying school-owned print and nonprint educational materials.
- There is no section of the official evaluation form that addresses the manner in which classroom teachers use or abuse materials.
- The school library media teacher does not employ a reserve or other type of sharing system to ensure fairness of materials' availability during periods of concentrated use.

Possible Solutions

- Have private conversations with the school library media teachers and representative classroom teachers to determine whether the problem exists in the school.
- If it does, take steps to develop measures such as those described as positive elements above.
- Establish a library media commission made up of classroom and subject teachers, administrators, students, and library media personnel to discuss and propose controls for these and other usage problems.

TESTING

Certain segments of California, Iowa, or other standardized tests address study and search skills. When the scores on these tests are examined, it becomes possible to determine how well students are doing in these specific areas as compared to overall achievement. There is a small number of standardized tests entirely concerned with library media skills. However, these do not always fit the local situation in terms of curriculum or library media holdings, making it desirable to construct tests in-house that address desired emphases on study and search skills or use of specific search tools. Few of the new state assessment tools address information acquisition, analysis, and reapplied uses.

The varying subject matter departments can be made aware of the desire to include, on major tests and semester examinations, some questions that call for the application of search skills. This is especially worthwhile when a significant amount of time has been spent in search; for example, for the junior year term paper in social studies or in English classes.

Skillfully constructed tests can be of a short-answer or multiple-choice type and still incorporate higher-order thought requirements—especially when asked to explain why the choice was made. Essay answers and open-ended questions may do the job more extensively, but they may not always be a desirable testing format. Teachers may need some guidance and practice to learn to create and verify that their test questions call for a range of taxonomy-level applications among their answers.

When the school has begun using performance-based assessment as a part of its multidimensional reform, much attention will need to be given to the construction of suitable tests. Just as multiple-choice type tests are less frequently used, the variety of assessments that will be used must support an educational environment in which students think, develop, and use scientific habits of mind. The goal is to nurture students who are mentally fit for the opportunities of the future.[14]

Recognizing Positive Elements

- Department heads include discussion of test construction guidance in departmental meetings.
- There has been a gradual change in schools' approach to testing relying less on multiple-choice and more on performance-based assessment.

Recognizing Negative Elements

- Teachers tend to use prepared tests simply because it is easy to do.
- Teachers retain old tests using them year after year.
- Teachers fail to upgrade questions they previously entered into their test question files.

Identifying Missing Elements

- No diagnostic or performance-based tests are used to determine student study and search skills.

Possible Solutions

- Decide that school testing will include verifying student ability to locate and *use* information in a wide range of formats.
- Develop a committee of teachers interested in the challenge of test construction to make a plan for improving tests used in the school.

- Send one or more representatives to workshops dealing with the topic.
- Develop a plan and a testing calendar so that student progress can be properly monitored and compared with national norms.

VOLUNTEERS

Volunteers are respected members of the school library media center team. However, they should not be used in lieu of basic paid personnel. Their value lies in their being able to supply "extras" upon which the school library media program does not rely on a daily basis. They work on special projects such as acquiring cushions for sit-upons or arranging an art show. They may assist with processing, mending, shelving, inventorying, and the like, but they should not become the sole source of labor for these functions. A few may be trained to work in a one-on-one mentoring capacity with students.

Volunteers' education, background, talents, interests, and physical conditions all vary. Their assignments must take into account these variables if they are to retain enthusiasm and interest in the school library media program.

Some administrators hesitate to make use of volunteers fearing they may misinterpret what they observe and pass unfair criticisms on to the community. On the other hand, as members of the community, they can be the most effective promoters of the school library media program and the school itself. They may even organize a friends or boosters club in the community to help keep the school library media program supported and in the public eye. A greater danger to be solidly "response-blocked" is that some officials may believe that volunteer help can be substituted for paid support staff.

Recognizing Positive Elements

- Volunteers are numerous and they tend to remain after their children have left the school.
- There is a coordinator of volunteers who is also a volunteer. This person administers the schedule set by the school library media teacher and is responsible for obtaining substitute volunteers as needed.
- Each of the volunteers is an enthusiastic booster of the school library media program and of the school.
- Volunteers provide leads to resource materials and people available in the community and may sometimes themselves offer unique talents, experiences, and skills to enhance the program and share with students and teachers.
- There is an annual celebration to acknowledge the value of the volunteers' services that is attended by administrators and members of the school board as well as by local and state officials.

Recognizing Negative Elements

- There is only token and infrequent acknowledgment of volunteer services.
- Students show little or no respect for volunteers when they are working in the school library media center.
- Volunteers are provided with little direction or training, leading them to wonder if their work is meeting expectations and often leading them to believe that their work is of dubious value.
- Volunteers are assigned tasks that do not match either their interests or abilities.

Identifying Missing Elements

- There is no volunteer program, either student or adult.
- Volunteers are recruited without any information about tasks or projects that would benefit from their efforts.
- There is no orientation or training program provided for volunteers.

Possible Solutions

- An organized systemwide volunteer program serving the entire school system could be put in place.
- Recruitment of volunteers for the school library media program should highlight the goals and functions of the program and list the range of areas in which volunteer efforts can be effective.
- Handbooks for volunteers should delineate the specifics for each task in a graphic, step-by-step, and easily understood manner.
- The accomplishments of volunteers, including the annual acknowledgment function, should be well publicized with length of service being recognized in some visible manner.
- Student volunteer and community service programs include the school library media center among agencies approved for service points.

4. Collection Management Modules

COLLECTION DEVELOPMENT

Collection development, whether starting with bare walls or upgrading an existing collection, requires good planning and in-depth curricular awareness. When starting from scratch to stock a new school library media center, there are things to be leery of. For example, it is not usually a good idea to purchase a preselected, preprocessed, basic collection package. Although a number of basic references and popular titles will undoubtedly be included, there could be a large number of titles that do not match the needs of the curriculum or the interests of the student body. The fact that all of the books will be there on opening day is of little value if they are not particularly useful and the monies could have provided more suitable selections. A far better plan is to hire the certified school library media teacher some months in advance of the opening of the new school to select, process, and build the collection in accordance with the curriculum and the characteristics of the students and the community.

Reference collections are designed to cover the entire scope of the curriculum, of information in general, so that students can expect to have something on the topic they seek in the school library media center whenever they need it. The size of the reference collection will reflect the emphasis placed on search for and use of information in the curriculum, as well as the size of the student body. Nonreference titles will also be used for information, and these will often be placed on reserve for a period of peak use, creating a type of temporary reserve reference collection. When demand for a title leads to purchasing multiple copies, some limit (such as six) should be placed on the number to be bought with library funds. Further copies of the title should be purchased from the textbook account.

When budgets are too small to permit making necessary acquisitions, a decision must be made on how to proceed. Some professionals believe it is wise to concentrate in a particular area of the collection, such as that needed to support a single unit of study, and stock it well. Students of differing abilities who will be assigned a topic in that area will then be able to find needed information. This single area saturation technique makes it possible for at least one teacher at one grade level and in one subject area to prepare exemplary projects. Having experienced the satisfaction of teaching with sufficient materials in one situation, this teacher should become a champion for providing materials needed for the same quality teaching and learning in all areas. Others believe that it is fairer to use a "shotgun" approach and try to include something for as many areas of the curriculum as possible. It is common, when this plan is used, to divide the budget equally among departments without regard for use made of the collection. However, this approach often provides so little in any given area that no unit has sufficient materials for the students. In this situation, trying to incorporate use of the school library media program becomes discouraging. The goal is to have a collection that supports all areas of the curriculum and all student ability levels. The problem is greatest when new schools are opened with inadequate collections, and yearly budgets rarely allow them to catch up with the goal. The decision about which method to use should be made cooperatively among faculty, administrators, and school library media teachers, and contain a reasonable timeline to effect the goal.

Recognizing Positive Elements

- A multiyear, formal collection development design is compiled and maintained, with clearly thought out long- and short-range plans for evaluation, selection, and acquisition of resources.
- Budget formulations are coordinated with long- and short-range plans to realistically meet acquisition goals for both print and computer software.
- School library media teachers are involved in departmental and curricular meetings so that they may keep informed about teachers' and students' materials needs.
- Formally developed and school board-approved policies and procedures are instituted for the reconsideration of challenged school library media center materials.

Recognizing Negative Elements

- A flat percentage (as for inflation) increase is budgeted annually without careful consideration of change/growth in curricular needs.
- There are areas in the curriculum where no assignments are made that require students to use school library media materials because the collection does not contain appropriate materials in those areas.
- The collection tends to reflect teacher assignments. Materials are often not added to the collection for subjects in which few or no assignments are made.

Where there are many assignments made, new and up-to-date materials are purchased. In examining the collection, recognize that worn out, outdated, and unused portions of the collection indicate the need for changed evaluation and/or staff development programs.

- The library media collection does not correlate with current curricular topics, subject areas, or classroom assignments.

Identifying Missing Elements

- There are no guidelines, recommendations, or standards adopted by the school system projecting a minimum or desired number of holdings per student, teacher, or subject area.
- There is no developmental plan in place to support selection and acquisition of materials.
- There is no conscious linking of the budget to curricular material needs when allocations are being recommended.

Possible Solutions

- Establish a committee made up of students and faculty to help recommend materials for purchase.
- Devise and conduct a student questionnaire survey to identify specific areas or topics needed for assignments that are insufficiently covered in the collection and purchase to fill the holes.
- Evaluate the collection for usefulness (see "Weeding" in this chapter and in the glossary), and if it is found to need a degree of upgrading that exceeds the annual budgeting potential, work for special

build-up appropriations (one or more years) to deal with the problem.

- Recognize that it is appropriate to allow for variation in the amount and types of materials provided for subjects or departments. For example, certain textbook series include audiovisual materials, models, and other needed instructional materials to implement the lessons as part of a total package. In these instances, the need may be only for current journals and a limited number of other materials. In other instances, a course may function with little use of text materials and great dependence is placed on library media center materials.

- Recognize that each year a new formula must be devised based on average daily attendance, curriculum changes, collection weaknesses, student and faculty recommendations, and other considerations for budget preparation.

CONTROVERSIAL TOPICS AND CENSORSHIP

The school library media center collection is expected to reflect many viewpoints, including the works of acknowledged experts or leaders. As a result, controversial topics, both of a personal and a societal nature, will be represented. Interests of the community, the faculty, and the students, which vary from school to school, should also be reflected in the collections.

Copies of the American Library Association Bill of Rights and Freedom to Read Statement, an interpretation of the Bill of Rights for school library media programs, the statement of ethics of the American Library Association Reference and Adult Services Division, and the National Council of Teachers of English Right to Read statement should all be used to support the school system's student rights policy (see Appendix E). The business of the school is to educate children to become responsible citizens. To do this, students need to learn about cultures, viewpoints, and lifestyles other than their own, and not only those of fellow Americans, but of the other peoples of the world.

Recognizing Positive Elements

- Controversial topics are routinely represented as are the works of significant writers, artists, or political figures, for example, regardless of their personal lifestyles, backgrounds, ideologies, or reputations.
- There exists a printed, school board-approved document that outlines the procedure for handling challenged materials. This document also addresses the intellectual freedom of teachers and students.
- All materials appear in the school library media center catalog and they are readily available to students.

Recognizing Negative Elements

- Complicated rules and procedures serve as obstacles to student use of controversial materials.
- Challenges often result in materials arbitrarily being withdrawn from the collection or filtered.
- The school library media teachers maintain a narrow view in their selection of materials for fear of creating problems and effect censorship through nonpurchase.
- Unnecessary delays in purchasing materials are effected through requirements of too large a number of favorable reviews.

Identifying Missing Elements

- While the community viewpoints on controversial issues are in evidence in the collection, opposing viewpoints are not represented.
- There are no intellectual freedom or bills of usage statements adopted by the school.
- All controversial topics have been deliberately removed from the curriculum, making both the curriculum and the school library media collection inadequate for the job of helping students to make independent critical judgments and develop a working set of values of their own.

Possible Solutions

- Establish a committee composed of parents, other community members, administrators, faculty, school library media teachers, and students to examine the relevancy of the collection to the curriculum, and social and political issues that impact both the curriculum and the community life in general.
- Reexamine the selection criteria used by the school library media teachers.
- Ask faculty and students their opinions about the adequacy of the controversial topics coverage to be found in the school library media collection.
- Make certain that the school's own bill of rights is current and reflects the school system's educational philosophies.
- Include student use of Internet in statements addressing controversial materials and censorship.

GIFTS

No one would suggest basing the school lunch program on leftover food sent in by members of the community after they have cleaned out their refrigerators. However, all too often the school library media center materials collection is stocked in part with books cleaned out of attics and bookshelves. This is usually a mistake. Individual items may occasionally have value, but most do not. It is important that the community understand that the budget is the source of obtaining specifically selected books, but that on the other hand, appropriate gifts are most welcome. Contributions to a gift fund, used to purchase expensive special items, make a very welcome gift indeed.

A written board of education policy concerning gifts is essential and applies to the school system as a whole. This policy assures the school system that it will have final jurisdiction over disposition of all gifts. Those that are suitable for use will be retained; those that are not will be disposed of in any appropriate manner. No gift is entirely gratuitous. A good film on driver education may not include direct advertising, but all the cars pictured as being driven correctly will be products of one manufacturer. This subtle influence does not detract from the educational value of the film, but it exists and should be recognized. This aspect may be used by classes studying propaganda, and it can be discussed and pointed out. Even with the best written policy statements, individual decisions must be made on each item.

When industry offers support or gifts for particular curricular areas, these are frequently presented as complete packages. The software programs are included with the computers, thereby committing the school, if it accepts the package, to a particular brand, point of view, and future purchases of compatible materials. The decision to accept or not must be made at the onset with full understanding of the implications for future purchases and use. There is also a decision here about just how much control may be appropriately exerted over school curricula by particular outside interests. For this reason, the current trend of industries to "adopt" a school program or curriculum area (almost always one in which upgrading is seen as being beneficial to the industry's interests) must be viewed with great caution.

Gifts of money earmarked for a discipline or topic must leave the choice of materials to the school. Bequests for materials on the American Civil War, for example, may not dictate the political point of view to be portrayed.

When class gifts are being planned, administrators can suggest suitable items. Too often the school library media center has not been considered as a recipient. Successful solicitations of gifts depend upon specificity. To suggest that the "library needs more books" does not bring the results that presenting a list of wanted titles does. Any gift must be acknowledged with both a letter of appreciation to the donor and an indication of its source on the item itself. These indicators may be bookplates, plaques, or other types of labeling.

Recognizing Positive Elements

- There is good community support for the budget.
- Service organizations and community members are regular contributors to a special gift fund.
- Senior class and activity clubs that traditionally make gifts to the school, quite regularly favor the school library media center.
- There is an active PTA and various parent booster clubs; they also regularly include the school library media center in their giving programs.

Recognizing Negative Elements

- Materials have been accepted as gifts that should never have been accepted, but the library media teacher and principal, having no policy on the matter, feel "stuck" with them.
- There is a prevailing attitude in the community that anything one wants to get rid of can be dumped on the school—especially books—for tax write-offs.
- The community believes that bestowing cast-off materials lessens the obligation for budget support.

Identifying Missing Elements

- The question of accepting gifts has not even been considered.
- No policy regarding gifts has been written or accepted by the board of education.
- Donors are not properly thanked and discontinue their interest.

Possible Solutions

- All offers of gifts are met with obvious and sincere appreciation.
- Gifts that are accepted are acknowledged in writing and the items given or purchased are identified.
- Bookplates for gift books have been designed by students.
- Students, faculty, and the community are routinely apprised of gifts through assemblies, newspaper articles, columns in the school paper, and other media.
- Make certain that there is general understanding that

gifts do not supplant budgetary support, but that they can provide extras that the budget may not cover.

- Publicize by way of interviews on radio and TV, in newspaper articles, and community speeches, that today's students require the most up-to-date books and other materials. Emphasize that the attractive condition of new books is often a great motivator and that most "hand-me-downs"—worn, out-of-date, and possibly never interesting anyway—do not fill the bill.

INTEGRATED PRINT AND NONPRINT COLLECTIONS

The collection of the school library media center consists of a wide variety of materials in many formats. Print formats include books, pamphlets, microforms, newspapers, periodicals, maps, pictures, charts, and databases. Nonprint formats include film, filmstrips, video and sound recordings, transparencies, slides, and computer software. All of these materials are chosen for their curricular use and the abilities and interest levels of the student body.

Since the use of many of these materials requires specific hardware, it is important to maintain the proper ratio between software and hardware to ensure effective use. Too little hardware prohibits flexible use of materials; too few materials causes the hardware to be underutilized.

As we have come to recognize that the textbook alone is inadequate to meet all the teaching/learning aspects of education, so too we realize that the differing student learning styles mandate a range and variety of materials. Each format has unique qualities and strengths and the matching of these characteristics with student needs makes for effective learning. It is crucial in this information age that students acquire while in school sufficient familiarity and competence for using the types of information carriers that they will continue to encounter in their postschool lives.

In 1960, 1969, 1975, and again in 1988 national guidelines have recommended collection sizes by types of materials. However, these are minimal guidelines to be built upon in response to the demands of such variables as nontextbook programs, ethnic populations, changes in curricular emphases, mandated special education programs, gifted and talented programs, or just plain excellence.

Communities with limited public library service, with few museums, art centers, and other cultural opportunities, of necessity place greater reliance on the school library media collections than do some other communities even when networking is practical. In rural areas and in places where climate restricts travel, there is further impact on school library media collections. School systems cannot expect local colleges, whose responsibilities are to their own students and faculty, to provide for local school students.

Recognizing Positive Elements

- Using national guidelines, state standards, and the recommendations of regional accrediting agencies, make a checklist of holdings by format, by subject content, and by recency of publication. Note, however, that in instances where primary sources or materials of historical significance are concerned, the recent copyright date is of no importance.

- Look for the match between curricular coverage, the numbers of students taking the course work, and the ability range of these students. For example, one honors, one top level, three average, and two low level sections in biology with assignments geared to specific topics will not have their needs met with a formula such as one book per student per year per subject. Six sections, with 30 students each, by such a formula, would equal 180 titles. A filmstrip on the life cycle of the frog will not serve the student who needs information on fiddle ferns. The student with reading difficulties will not be able to use the highly technical botanical reference that the honors student will require. Because the student body and faculty of any school are unique, the evaluator should not gauge the adequacy of a collection's match to that school's needs by comparing it with holdings in another school system. This applies equally to assessing schools within the same system inasmuch as demographics also impact on the collection match equation.

Recognizing Negative Elements

- The physical condition of the collection is an important factor. Worn, ragged, dirty, torn, yellowed, scratched, materials with missing parts should be replaced on a routine basis. They cannot be used with enthusiasm, if at all, and they discourage the student's desire to pursue the subject. There is no justification for keeping this material. Hardware that breaks down, chews up film, distorts the image or sound, or is eons behind current availability, is valueless. It is as necessary to have continuous maintenance and replacement of hardware as it is of software.

- List areas, formats, and levels that call for replacement or additional materials.

Identifying Missing Elements

- List those curriculum areas, topics, and levels with insufficient coverage. Recognize that every subject area in the curriculum brings with it a potential for resource materials, as do student interests and concerns.
- List upcoming curriculum changes and their requirements.
- List increases and changes in the make-up of the student body.
- List increases and changes in the faculty and their assignments.

Possible Solutions

- When there are shifts in grade levels within a school system, it may be possible to transfer some of the school library media collection from one school to another. Care must be taken, however, not to strip a collection of materials that would still be needed by students remaining in the building.
- Change policy and change plans for annual purchases to respond to immediate needs. A five-year plan to bring the collection up to adequacy will not help the students enrolled during that interim. A school library media center that was started without a sound basic collection needs a massive infusion that annual purchasing budgets seldom cover. A determination to make up the deficit through augmented annual budgets needs to be made.
- Care must be taken when engaging in build-up programs to maintain careful selection practices and not to fall prey to quick fixes, package deals, publisher

closeouts, or other nonquality "solutions." Many bargains turn out to be extremely costly.

- Sometimes special programs are instituted that augment the school library media collection, but these are not substitutes for adequate budgetary support. Citizens who contribute materials or funds gain a proprietary interest in the center. Students who engage in activities to raise funds for special purchases, or make individual, group, or class gifts, often develop an intensified pride in both the collection and the program (see "Gifts" in this chapter and in the glossary).

INTERSHELVING

Intershelving refers to the placement of print and nonprint materials (software) together on open shelves according to their content classification. This means that a filmstrip, a computer program, a recording, and book on blue jays will sit next to one another. While the concept appears to be the fulfillment of the educational objective of having all the materials dealing with a subject together for easy access, in reality severe storage, loss, and cost problems are posed.

The single filmstrip on the subject will have to be placed in a specialized container either allowing it to sit on the shelf like a book or be hung from a rod in a plastic bag known as a "hang-up." Spacing between shelves will have to be a minimum of twelve inches to accommodate phono discs or boxed items. The logical outcome of all of this is the need for between two and three times the linear feet of shelving that a nonintershelved collection would require. Space is costly. Not only the additional shelving but the square footage of the facility, the additional heat, light, cooling, and custodial services must be figured into the actual cost.

Increased damage occurs to nonprint materials stored on open shelves rather than in units especially designed for their storage. Loss and vandalism are additional factors to be considered.

If there is sufficient space, enough specially designed carriers, and adequate staffing to supervise the use of these materials, many of the negatives can be minimized. In school library media programs where intershelving has been successful, these conditions have been met, and student attitudes and sense of responsibility permit teachers and students to enjoy the proximity of materials. More often, however, the negative elements lead to dissatisfaction and eventual abandonment of the intershelving plan.

Another consideration is the use of listening and viewing machines or computers that should be kept adjacent to the software used on them. When materials are shelved according to their format there is space conservation, protection of the medium by its housing, and the related software and hardware can be kept next to one another.

Recognizing Positive Elements

- If intershelving is practiced, there is ample space allocation for future growth and sufficient listening and viewing machines are stationed at intervals throughout the entire collection.
- When evaluations are made regarding the effectiveness of intershelving, the user response is positive, the materials remain in good repair, and mischievous switching of contents has not occurred.

Recognizing Negative Elements

- Because of the amount of damage occurring in specific areas, these materials are removed for security purposes or are off the shelves because of needed repairs.

- The library media center staff tend to want to keep the materials in the boxes in which they were shipped. This, however, reduces the use of the individual parts of the set. Required circulation of an entire set for staff convenience is not desirable.
- Restrictive rules are applied to software in an attempt to control loss and damage, often resulting in less use or, what is worse, negative student behavior.

Identifying Missing Elements

- There has been no consideration given to the merits and drawbacks of the two shelving plans.
- There has been no contact made with library media teachers who have had experience with intershelving to elicit their advice and gain the benefit of their experience.

Possible Solutions

- Plan visits to several schools serving a comparable student body to see firsthand the pros and cons of the different systems.
- Discuss at length the ramifications of the system with library media staff experienced in the problems of intershelving.
- Make sure that budgetary considerations, both annual and long term, provide for the space, personnel, shelving, and carriers required before electing the intershelving alternative.

INVENTORY AND FOLLOW-UP

Inventory is a time-consuming job, but it contributes immeasurably to the smooth and effective operation of the school library media center program. It does not have to be done all at once, and in large collections there may not be sufficient time and personnel to do a complete inventory all at once. Whenever it is done, cooperative planning is needed to provide sufficient personnel to do the work, as well as to establish temporarily unused areas of the collection to work on without disturbing use of the collection or ongoing classroom activities.

Some places have called in a large group of volunteers to work on a Saturday or after hours in a concerted effort that has permitted the inventorying of large portions or of the entire collection in one session. Others have split the job between mid-terms and the year end when exams take place and classroom needs are temporarily suspended. Still others hire special crews to come in and do the inventory in the summertime. The job is somewhat simplified by the use of computerized circulation systems that permit the use of an inventory program as well, but even with the use of computers, barcodes, and light wands, a substantial number of people hours are required. Moreover, the really time-consuming functions begin when the shelf count is completed.

The purposes of inventorying are most important to the users. Only frustration can come from trying to work with an index (in this case, a catalog) that is too filled with error to be dependable. To the uninformed, the many housekeeping chores that are a part of inventory follow-up may seem unnecessarily nit-picky, but they are functions urgently needed to ensure the availability of resources as shown in the catalog. The computer (or other type) catalog must match the actual collection. Adjustments for missing irreplaceable materials, inconsistencies, outright cataloging errors, and problems of classification resulting from growth of a collection must be corrected once they are identified. This involves ordering replacement items, altering shelflist and/or accession records, and removing or correcting catalog records to maintain overall accuracy. Nothing is more frustrating than to try to use a catalog that does not include materials held or has numerous records referring to items removed or lost from the collection. User satisfaction, and even instruction in the use of the catalog, depends on an accurate match of the collection and its catalog-index.

Materials are called in from borrowers when an inventory is to be done. These items are placed in their proper shelf locations (a process known as "shelf-reading"). Since they may have been out in circulation for some time, and because there have been additions to the collection throughout the school year, a space problem may be created. There just is not enough space in certain sections to permit the shelving of all the materials that belong there. Because of normal growth, an inventory and shifting of large sections of the collection needs to be done annually, at least.

Recognizing Positive Elements

- Complete inventory is taken annually of both print and nonprint materials and the attendant hardware. Some parts of the collection may be inventoried more frequently.
- The follow-up clerical functions are completed so that the catalog is updated.
- Replacement copies or new titles dealing with the same content are purchased to replace lost materials.

- Materials that need rebinding or repairing, or should be discarded, are removed from the shelves in the process of inventorying the collection.

Recognizing Negative Elements

- Users complain that they cannot find materials that are listed in the catalog.
- The same title may be found under two (or more) different classifications because the copies have been ordered at different times and the difference in placement was not detected at the time they were initially processed and shelved.
- Without the occasion of an inventory the shelves are not read and needed rearrangement of the collection to reflect growth is not accomplished. Poor shelf arrangement contributes to uninviting and ineffective use of the collection.

Identifying Missing Elements

- A complete inventory is not taken annually.
- If inventory is taken, the follow-up processes are not carried out.
- There is no annual report made of holdings and losses.
- When materials are sublet to departments on long-term borrowing plans, these items may not continue to be inventoried.

Possible Solutions

- Check to determine when the last complete inventory was done.

- Check to determine if the follow-up clerical work was completed and over what period of time.
- Install a computerized circulation system to aid with inventorying.
- Create a computerized form of the card catalog that requires an overall inspection of the collection and the shelflist as well as providing for upgrading the cataloging of the collection.
- Develop plans for instituting an annual inventory of both print and nonprint collections, and budget appropriately for this function.

LAYOUT AND ARRANGEMENT

The arrangement of the collection on the shelves has impact on its use. Consideration should be given to placing the most vulnerable sections of the collection where they are most visible and supervised. The numerical starting point may be anywhere, but the collection should progress in uninterrupted numerical order from that point. Sometimes exceptions are made based on curricular needs or class size functions. These should be done thoughtfully and not just because some other school library media center does it that way. Areas for consideration include individual and collected biography, fiction and short stories, or, in large collections, the grouping of related classifications into physical areas; e.g., the 300s and 900s together as social studies, the 500s and 600s together as pure and applied science, and the 400s and 800s for language and literature. These arrangements tend to cut down on traffic and the scattering of materials when they are used by classroom groups. Student groups can be assigned seating in the areas that house the materials they are working with.

When laying out the arrangement of materials initially or

when making a major rearrangement of the available space, care should be taken to leave room for expansion. Shelves should be filled no more than two-thirds across, and top and bottom shelves should be left empty, if at all possible. Bottom shelves can be reserved for outsized materials within that number span. This eliminates the need for a special section for outsized materials which often leads to their being missed by someone looking for them. Additional space should be left open between Dewey categories. This is for growth. If one calculates the number of shelves available for use, the number of items in the collection, and notes the least desirable locations, a shelving plan can be worked out. A filled case houses approximately 100 books, figuring 25–30 books to the shelf. Most school buildings need more storage than was provided in the architect's plans, and this applies even more to school library media centers. A growing collection must be housed.

Nonprint materials require considerable space (one reason for repackaging them) and specialized storage as well. Hardware on movable carts also requires space to be used effectively and to be protected from damage. Periodicals, of significant value for search activities, are often the first casualty of cramped quarters. Back issues of periodicals can be retained on microform to reduce space requirements. CD-ROM discs are offered that provide partial text of articles in periodicals they index, and some provide full text. Obviously this plan reduces the storage space needed, but the computers needed to read the discs require space. Existing space guidelines and standards are at best realistic; they are certainly not overly generous.

Cumbersome materials such as large atlases and unabridged dictionaries should have usage areas that allow them to be opened with space allocated on both sides for writing by left-handed as well as right-handed students. The specialized and expensive furniture sold for housing atlases and dictionaries often does not fulfill the users' needs. Monies saved on these specific furnishings can be used to buy the materials, while nonspecialized furniture serves the needs better anyway.

Traffic flow impacts on layout. The book return should be as close to the door as possible, preferably through a wall slot. Consideration in laying out use areas should be given to separating activities that require quiet from activities that involve discussion, such as group workshops. Consideration should also be given to special traffic patterns that are caused by checkout, copying, browsing, periodical usage, and other functions.

Recognizing Positive Elements

- The center is laid out so that there is a variety of uses possible at the same time: for example, two or three classroom groups in large areas; individuals at computers, carrels, and reading machines; small groups in discussion or involved in viewing or listening activities.
- There is easy access to the center and materials may be returned without entering more than a lobby area.
- The circulation function is carried out close to the door, but the desk clerk has a view of a large portion of the facility.
- Sufficient space has been allocated to the charge desk and catalog areas so that the large numbers of students using these facilities during peak periods do not interfere with other center users.
- The technical processing function is carried out in an area secluded from the students. There is ample

space for workers to engage in a variety of procedures, both seated and standing.

- Deliveries may be made directly to the technical
processing area without disturbing the reading and
learning areas.

- The school library media teachers have office space
in which to hold conferences with students, teachers, or school visitors.

- The materials are shelved in a sequential order and
are clearly marked to match cataloging.

- There is clear, abundant, and attractive signage.

Recognizing Negative Elements

- Students from one classroom group must cross
through where other classroom groups are working.

- Because of illogical progression, quirks, and too
many special locations, students have difficulty locating materials cited in the catalog or index.

- Library media staff discussions and consultations,
and teacher conversations, can be heard throughout
the center.

- Books and other materials used by students are left
all over the center because there is inadequate seating and writing space available adjacent to where
they are shelved.

- There is insufficient light to see shelf markings,
book labels, or to read comfortably in various sections of the stacks and reading or viewing areas.

Identifying Missing Elements

- There are no "quiet" areas for students to use when
needed.

- There are no booktrucks on which to leave materials after use, or when a student does not have time to reshelve materials accurately. Many staffs prefer that students not reshelve because of their high incidence of misshelving.
- There are no waste containers except at the front desk area.
- No consideration has been given to the writing and seating space needed near often-used materials such as dictionaries, atlases, the reference collection, and catalogs and other indexes.
- Software and the machinery needed for its use are not within reasonable proximity of each other.

Possible Solutions

- Make a careful usage study to determine what is needed by the students and teachers.
- Design the layout so that it gives priority to the needs of the users.
- Provide time and assistance annually so that at least once a year the collection can be adjusted or moved to ensure adequate shelf space and accurate positioning of materials. The materials that are purchased during any school year may create a "bulge" that must be fitted in and often requires shifting large sections of the collection.
- Hire sufficient staff to deal with instructional and disciplinary problems that arise when the structural design of the center creates blind spots. When placing equipment try to avoid creating other blind spots.

MENDING, REBINDING, AND
PREVENTION PROCEDURES

The old adage about a "stitch in time" is manifest in the arrangements for upkeep of school library media materials. New acquisitions are examined, whether a gift or a purchase, with an eye to possible sources of deteriorating physical condition. Faulty materials or equipment should be returned at once to the jobber or other supplier for replacement. School closings and the resulting consolidation of collections make for longer use, so simple mending and other precautionary measures are vital.

Materials that are in the workroom to be mended are for all practical purposes not available to the students or teachers, so mending must not be allowed to pile up.

Appearance is an important factor in protecting the taxpayers' investment in school library media materials. Torn jackets, dull bindings with rubbed out embossing, weakened spines, and loose pages destroy users' interest. Such conditions invite careless use if not outright vandalism. Films and filmstrips with torn sprocket holes, stuck audiotapes, gummed-up videos, and scratched or mishandled CDs frustrate users. The message is that no one cares and the students, teachers, and administrators take their cues accordingly. If school personnel hope to train students to be citizens who respect public property, they must see to it that the property appears respected by those responsible for it.

Publishers invest time and money on providing paper dust jackets or covers that will attract readers. What these covers do best is what they were designed for—they catch the eyes of potential readers and users and tell them something about what is inside. When dust jackets are removed before books are placed on shelves, the most effective, individually designed promotional material has been cast aside. No display, booktalk, or required reading list can match this selling power. Plastic covers for these dust jackets not only intensify the colors, graphics, and artwork, they also protect the book and give it a longer circulation life. The publishers' blurbs cannot be cribbed for book reports if the teachers know anything about their students' writing, or if they construct report requirements in terms of thought to which the blurb does not contribute.

The decision to rebind should be based on the cost of rebinding, the length of time the book will be out of the building, and its subsequent appearance. A book that has a moldy smell, is water-stained, or has yellow pages will not be appealing to the browser just because the binding is new. On the other hand, valuable materials that cannot be replaced, such as works on local history, will profit greatly from rebinding. Tired paper and narrow margins, however, will not survive the normal rebinding process. If the material is valuable, other conservation measures might be considered.

Preventive procedures and mending skills need to be learned from impartial experts, not library supply company sales representatives interested in selling products. Many products have specific uses and should not be used indiscriminately or interchangeably. If the persons who are selected to receive mending training enjoy this type of challenge and opportunity, the results of their work can be very pleasing to the eye and of excellent quality.

Recognizing Positive Elements

- The shelved materials, as well as those on the book trucks, in the return slot, and in the students' possession, are attractive, reasonably clean, and in good repair.

- Students, teachers, and administrators are aware of the mending skills of the library media staff and are respectful of their work and of the materials.

- There are periodic workshops in mending techniques offered to all school personnel and the community. Increased awareness and skill, at least for those interested in the workshops, tends to be reflected in greater care of public and private materials.

- There is a sufficient supply of mending materials in the workroom for the wide variety of needs.

- Most hardbound books have plastic-covered dust jackets.

- Covers of paperbound books have been treated inside and out to protect them, improve their appearance, and prolong their circulation life.

- Audio tape and cassette copies (rather than phonodiscs or the original tapes and cassettes) are circulated and periodically evaluated for sound quality. Because copies are returned and blanked, the original serves as a master copy without proliferation.

- All visual materials are examined when returned and mended as needed.

- Books that have been vandalized or abused are attended to immediately upon return and the extent and responsibility for damages assessed and the offender charged.

Recognizing Negative Elements

- The impression conveyed of the library media collection is that it is consistently messy and not well cared for. (This is not to be confused with a tempo-

rary disarray following heavy classroom group usage.)

- Materials go into circulation with torn pages, loose
  hinges, or weakened spines.
- Ordinary transparent tape, masking tape, or package
  wrap (instead of products designed especially for
  mending purposes) are used to mend inside and
  outside of books and periodicals.
- Books are placed on the shelves without jackets
  and their colorful coverings kept for bulletin board
  use or to give to classroom teachers.
- Worn or torn plastic covers for dust jackets are not
  replaced as needed.

Identifying Missing Elements

- Library media center support staff are not encouraged to attend system-level workshops, conferences,
  or minicourses in repair or maintenance techniques.
- There are no in-house workshops for training volunteers, support staff, teachers, or community members interested in learning these techniques.

Possible Solutions

- Situate at the charge desk a tray of most often used
  repair materials, as well as a moist sponge and a
  gum eraser for cleaning smudges and smears from
  exteriors, so that items being returned (or charged
  out) can be given immediate attention.
- Institute a set of routine procedures for examining
  all materials being returned to the collection so that
  appropriate action regarding physical repairs can be
  applied.

- Encourage students to go to the library media center with all materials including textbooks that are in need of even minor attention. Most students welcome the opportunity to have them mended—especially when they know that should the damage become severe they will be charged for a replacement copy.

- Deal with much needed mending of textbooks at year or semester end by budgeting for mending materials and personnel to do the repairing. This task must be provided for, unless the storage, supervision, and care of textbooks is already a part of the school library media responsibilities. There should not be end-of-year "dumping" on the school library media center staff.

OVERDUES, FINES, AND LOSSES

The larger the student body the more overdues become a problem. Materials are unavailable to others if one person keeps them too long and the effort to retrieve them requires inordinate amounts of clerical and professional time that could be used more productively in other functions.

The charging of fines, regardless of their size, tends to legitimize in the students' minds the keeping of materials overtime. When items have been kept overdue a long time and the fines become exorbitant, the student either cannot afford to pay the fine or becomes too embarrassed to return the material. Students may keep materials out hoping for an "Amnesty Day" to be declared, miss returning items on that day, and just wait for another to come along. Too many such days defeat the reason for charging of fines.

Students have the idea that losses are of little concern, especially if they are willing and able to pay for them. They do not realize (nor do most adults, either) that many titles of book and other materials are not available from publishers or producers for very long periods of time. Publishers now print fewer copies of a title (because of changes in taxes on inventories) and often a title is out of print within a few months of publication.

Recognizing Positive Elements

- When a computer control system reduces the time spent in preparing overdue notices, more time is made available for other program activities, and more productive results occur.
- Students accept more personal responsibility and are challenged to "play fair" with other students and the school library media center. Peer expectations of proper borrowing (and returning) habits are a powerful motivation to do it properly.
- There are relatively few overdue materials.
- Overdue materials are sought for return to the school library media center in a considerate but effective way.

Recognizing Negative Elements

- Systems that restrict borrowing because of overdues encourage subletting or borrowing for someone else. Students who are bad risks are not likely to return sublet materials on time either, so the benefactors are punished by having borrowing restrictions or replacement costs charged to them. Friendships can be damaged and the library media center staff members, not the culprits, are blamed.
- Distributing overdue notices to classrooms or mail-

ing them to students' homes is time-consuming and costly. Parents, as well as teachers, resent being made the school library media center's collection agents, and should not be asked to be except in extreme cases,

Identifying Missing Elements

- There is no evidence that classroom teachers show any concern over their students' having accumulated overdues at the school library media center.
- There is no clearly defined policy regarding tracing losses related to families moving out of town.
- There is no cooperation from the administration such as withholding report cards or diplomas to encourage the clearing up of school library media center obligations.
- There is no attempt to find better methods to cut down on overdues.

Possible Solutions

- Charge no fines and point out to students that no amount of money can make up for keeping someone else from having needed materials. The next time it could be the offending student who is inconvenienced or frustrated.
- Use a system of flagging students' borrowing cards when they have overdues and curtail the amount of their additional borrowing until the overdues are cleared up.
- Consider using computer-prepared overdues which seem to be more effective than handwritten notices that may or may not be distributed by homeroom or

classroom teachers. Perhaps it is because they are impersonal and businesslike.

- Provide commercially available computer software programs for circulation management (e.g., at time of writing, Overdue Writer or Overdue Collector), which make the process of managing overdue books and other materials much more efficient and productive.
- Best, of course, is the overdue services provided in online circulation systems that identify borrowers' overdues and restrict further borrowing until records are cleared.

PHILOSOPHY, GOALS, AND OBJECTIVES

The statements of educational philosophy adopted by the board of education for the school system provide the rationale for the entire school program. Individual schools may have additional statements on which particular parts of their programs are based, but they complement the basic philosophy of the school system.

The school library media program translates the philosophy-based goals statements of the school system and the individual school into the specific goals and objectives that will guide its program.

Every aspect of the school library media program—its organization, selection of materials, budget, scheduling, program, policies, and use of volunteers—is influenced by these goals. Each revision or addition to the program should be planned in terms of moving toward the goals and objectives. Evaluation of the program's success must be in terms of these goals and objectives in order to judge effectiveness. Policies, rules, and regulations concerned with the operation of the school library media center must all be aligned with system, school, and media center philosophies and goals in order to be successful.

Just as curriculum should be in continuous revision and be reexamined in light of societal changes and present and future educational needs, so should these statements of philosophy, goals, and objectives be reevaluated and improved.

Recognizing Positive Elements

- There is a systemwide philosophy and set of goals adopted by the board of education.
- There are statements regarding goals and objectives for the individual schools as well as areas of instruction.
- There is a school library media center program philosophy with specific goals and objectives clearly defined and aligned with those for the system and building.
- The student handbook carries these statements on its first page as does the faculty handbook.
- The manual used by support staff and volunteers also begins with these statements.

Recognizing Negative Elements

- These statements, if they exist, are outdated, unused, unlocatable, meaningless.
- There is no recognition of the importance of the relationship between statements of philosophy and goals and policies.
- Student rules and regulations in regard to the use of the school library media center are drawn up without any references to philosophies, goals, or objectives.

Identifying Missing Elements

- There are no statements of philosophy, goals, or objectives at the system, building, or school library media center level.
- There is no recognition of the need for such statements or their impact.
- There are no printed student rules and regulations that interpret the goals and objectives of the school library media center, school, or system.

Possible Solutions

- Encourage the formulation and adoption of a system philosophy of education and the goals and objectives geared to carrying it out by the board of education.
- Appoint a committee to formulate or reevaluate a building-level statement of philosophy, goals, and objectives.
- Work with the school library media teachers to develop a statement of philosophy, goals, and objectives for the school library media center program. Make certain that all policies, rules, and regulations concerning the school library media program are in accord with these statements.

PREVIEWING MATERIALS

Because there is such a wide range of quality in educational materials and because they are increasingly costly and budgets tend to be small, the practice of previewing, always desirable, has gained importance. In the assessment of nonprint materials it has become mandatory. All previewing should be channeled through the school library media center. Both the responsibility for keeping track of materials and deadlines, and the authority to recall materials to meet these deadlines, need to be centralized for previewing to be effective and economical.

Publishers are in business to make money, and some have more integrity in the products they sell than others. It is the responsibility of the professional selector, the buyer, to ensure the quality of materials purchased. All too often, when a new topic becomes important, many items are presented for purchase that are not only inferior but erroneous. They may not be professionally reviewed at all, or they may be reviewed in the literature too late to be of assistance in the selection process.

For these reasons previewing is both wise and necessary. Reputable publishers and producers permit previewing and there are a number of previewing plans offered by them. When these plans are used by a school, there must be no illegal uses made of the preview materials. (See "Legalities" in chapter 3.)

Because of the tendency to pirate computer software, it has not been made freely available for preview. Perhaps this will change. Meanwhile, there are some jobbers who specialize in on-site previewing and sometimes private arrangements can be made with a distributor who has worked with your school long enough to have established a trusting relationship with the school library media personnel. It is sensible to seek out these opportunities for preview. Sometimes previewing can be done at a conference exhibit area.

Recognizing Positive Elements

- There is a written previewing policy that has official approval and is included in teacher handbooks. It is strictly enforced by the administration and the school library media personnel.

- Classroom teachers are cooperative about meeting deadlines and returning preview materials to the school library media center.
- There are few if any dunning letters received from publishers and producers regarding the return of preview materials.

Recognizing Negative Elements

- Collection agency letters are received regarding long overdue or lost preview materials traced to the school.
- Preview orders from departments for nonprint materials are not channeled through the school library media center. This can result in the acquisition of needless duplicate copies of materials or the purchase of inferior materials because all materials in the field have not been thoroughly canvassed.
- Preview materials are kept beyond return deadlines so that the school (system) is billed and the publishers paid regardless of the desire to reject the items.

Identifying Missing Elements

- Materials are purchased without previewing them.
- There are no written preview procedures, policies, or qualitative guidelines.
- There is no administrative directive to teachers or departments requiring previewing of materials they recommend for purchase by the school library media center and purchasing through the center for best price and efficiency.

Possible Solutions

- Insist that preview materials being requested by teachers using the name and address of the school do so only through the school library media center so that there is monitoring of return and due dates and reminders if necessary.
- Include the responsiveness of the classroom teacher to meeting preview deadlines on the classroom teacher evaluation form and offer praise when it is deserved.
- At back-to-school teacher meetings each year, explain the previewing system including procedures, forms, and deadlines.
- Use a computer database program to organize a record keeping system to monitor previewing procedures.

PRIMARY SOURCES AND GOVERNMENT DOCUMENTS

Reference publications are a chief source for locating information. They are sometimes identified by type, by their design, or purpose. Each type appears in most discipline content areas and therefore provides a suitable base for search procedure and instruction. Types include atlases, gazetteers, almanacs, yearbooks, directories, pictorial histories, handbooks, encyclopedias, dictionaries, indexes, and bibliographies, for example. These are all classified as "secondary sources."

Another type of information carrier is known as a "primary source" and is often not a book at all. The meaning of the term *primary* in this instance is "first-hand" or "original." The information is supplied or described by someone on the scene working with the person or event, and is not derived from or interpreted by others. For this reason diaries, letters, journals, logs, first-hand accounts (as in newspapers, on video clips, and e-mail), interviews, and the actual government documents themselves are considered primary sources.

Documents published by the government, whether local, state, or federal, are called "government documents." In most school library media center collections these printed documents are interfiled with the rest of the collection, although in large public and academic libraries they are often in a separate room with their own special indexing. The thin pamphlets are kept in vertical files, and subject listings for them should be included in the catalog. Currently, government documents are becoming available through computer use as well.

In many instances collections of the more important documents have been compiled and published. Supreme Court decisions, treaties, and the outstanding federal documents selected annually are examples of this kind of convenience collecting. These are usually sufficient for younger students.

Topics about which there may be controversy or divergent opinion are made more interesting through the use of primary sources. Students who are in the habit of believing everything they read without questioning need to experience differing points of view. Students also need to develop skill in defending and supporting positions taken. This calls for using primary sources as well as secondary interpretations and recognizing the differences.

Recognizing Positive Elements

- There are instructional units throughout the curriculum that identify and emphasize the use of primary sources and documents.

- There is sufficient access to primary sources and government documents in the school library media center to support the curriculum.
- Classroom teachers make full use of these materials in their teaching and assignments.

Recognizing Negative Elements

- Classroom teachers are unfamiliar with the contents of standard sources.
- The school library media center collection has too few primary sources to support curriculum needs.

Identifying Missing Elements

- There is no evidence that the use of government documents, as a type of reference, is included in bibliographic instruction.
- Classroom teachers do not require the use of primary sources in assignments.
- The curriculum does not include instruction in the use of primary and secondary sources, the differences between them, and the reasons for using both.

Possible Solutions

- Reexamine curriculum guides and make sure government documents and primary sources are topics included in instructional units.
- Reexamine the cataloging to make sure that there are references to primary sources in the subject indexing; e.g., UNITED STATES HISTORY—1860–1865—CIVIL WAR—SOURCES.

- If primary sources and government documents have not been provided in the school library media collection, establish a special effort and fund to correct the shortage.
- Provide for staff development sessions to assist classroom teachers in the use of these materials.

REFERENCE COLLECTION

While it is generally accepted that the reference section of the collection is important to students, teacher assignments may not reflect this view. Usually, reference sections in secondary school library media centers are extensive and include standard works in all disciplines. In elementary school library media centers the reference section is too often restricted to general encyclopedias, atlases, almanacs, and an abridged dictionary.

Today's educational requirements (at all grade levels) call for use of a wide range of specialized encyclopedias, dictionaries, handbooks, yearbooks, indexes, and periodicals. Unless these materials are readily available, they cannot be put to use in assignments that will enable students to gain the information management skills they must acquire. Granted, not all fact finding is done in reference materials. The entire collection should contain materials that will be useful.

While the reference section materials should be on hand throughout the school day, various plans can be developed to permit overnight borrowing. Reserve or "temporary" reference collections are established to make possible the use of the same materials by a large number of students. Another method of making restricted materials available for circulation is to provide for individual copying of selected pages (always within copyright regulations).

New reference books are continually being published. Although it is important that the students come to know the standard references in various fields, they should also have the opportunity to become acquainted with the best of the new ones. Sometimes it is said that there are limited reviews of reference materials, especially those for younger children. Part of the problem may be that there is poor recognition of what constitutes a suitable reference book for the elementary grades. Basic lists of recommended titles are proof of this view. The abilities of students in elementary grades are often underrated. It is up to the school library media teacher to select materials that will extend the range of student inquiry, whether they are placed in the reference section or not. Materials placed in the reference collection will need to be specially marked to make it possible to keep the collection together. A similar need is established when easy nonfiction is placed in the EASY area. When using an online catalog these markings may need to be added after the collection disc has been obtained. This is especially so if the library is a part of a network and these special collections will differ from those held by others in the network.

Recognizing Positive Elements

- There is a wide range of up-to-date materials in the reference section with all disciplines represented.
- New publications are available.
- A back file of periodicals and newspapers is related to the indexing available. This file may be hard copy, on microfilm, on microfiche, or CD-ROM in abstract or full-text format.

Recognizing Negative Elements

- Encyclopedias are exceedingly out-of-date (more than five years after copyright date).

- Science and technical materials are not kept current.
- Insufficient attention is given to developing search and information management skills throughout the curriculum, including use of CD-ROM, online networks, indexing, and databases.
- Classroom assignments do not reinforce practice of these skills even when they are in the curriculum.

Identifying Missing Elements

- There is no plan for systematic replacement of encyclopedic, scientific, and technical materials.
- The reference section is not evaluated or weeded annually.
- No reserve system is established.
- No use is made of government documents as reference materials,
- Print is the only format available.

Possible Solutions

- Insist on a lively skills instruction program that makes good use of the school library media center's reference collection both in print and in computerized formats.
- Make certain that the reference section adequately supports curricular and skills instruction programs.
- Encourage the acquisition and use of materials that are beyond traditional and limited expectations and are produced in more than print formats.
- Assume that students will have interests in new or esoteric subject areas and provide reference materials in support of such interests.

SELECTION OF MATERIALS

There should be a selections policy statement, together with a method for requesting reevaluation of an item, approved by the board of education. Administrators should be familiar with this procedure and use it consistently.

The school library media teacher selects materials for purchase in accordance with the selection policies and the plans established for collection development. Requests and suggestions are sought and welcomed from students, faculty, and administrators.

Recognizing Positive Elements

- Professionally recognized selection tools are purchased, subscribed to, and consulted in formulating orders for materials.
- Gifts of materials are subject to the same standards as purchased materials.
- Suggestions for purchase from students and staff are checked against holdings and on-order lists to avoid unwanted duplications.
- Students and classroom teachers find the materials that are needed to carry out assignments.
- When there are curricular changes, provisions have been made to support the change at the time it goes into effect.
- Titles found in standard bibliographies are available in the collection when they match curricular needs and grade levels.
- There is a policy followed for weeding the collection at regular intervals and for disposing of the discards. (See "Weeding" in this chapter.)
- There is a plan for collection development supported by the budget that keeps the collection current.

- The collection undergoes continuous evaluation. Inventory is part of this evaluation process. (See "Inventory and Follow-Up" in this chapter.)

Recognizing Negative Elements

- There is no "wish list" on hand because selections are not made continuously throughout the year.
- Should additional monies become available (gifts, year-end surpluses, etc.), purchases are made on a hurried rather than on a reasoned basis.
- Selection aids are few in number and out-of-date.
- The business manager does not permit the setting aside of some monies for second-semester purchases to respond to unanticipated curricular needs and newly available materials.
- Bids are mistakenly required to obtain jobbers as if the purchase of books equated with the purchase of supplies or furniture. (See "Business Managers" in chapter 3.)

Identifying Missing Elements

- Business managers and administrators show little or no understanding of the unique elements of school library media center management.
- There are no official written selection policies or plans for collection development. (See "Collection Development" in this chapter.)
- Library media teachers are not members of curriculum revision or development teams and therefore are not aware of impending curricular needs.
- There is no method made evident to faculty and students by which they can make requests or suggestions for purchases.

Possible Solutions

- Insist on having an officially approved selection policy that calls for the use of current material reviews and selection aids, includes a reconsideration procedure, and a plan for systematic collection development.
- Make certain that the school library media teachers have the opportunity to attend conferences and workshops at which new materials are examined.
- When appointing curriculum revision or development committees, be sure to include the school library media teachers.
- Encourage faculty to make recommendations for new purchases and to assist with the evaluation of the collection of materials in their discipline areas.

TEXTBOOKS AND TEXT MATERIALS

The school library media center collection should include all materials of learning in the school regardless of where they are housed. Thus there is one department in the school with an inventory of what is owned, where it is located, and what its condition is. This includes textbooks and other text materials—unless, of course, the school has abandoned textbooks and moved on to resource-based instruction.

In some schools the textbooks are in the custodian's charge. In others, individual teachers or department chairpersons have this responsibility. In some schools the principal's office is also the textbook repository. Textbook distribution as part of the school library media program requires additional storage area and clerical personnel to carry out the necessary tasks. The textbook clerk(s) will be totally involved in this operation at certain times of the year, but otherwise serves as support staff in the school library media center. When such a plan is in effect there is a marked decrease in damage, and repairing is an ongoing activity. Textbooks that are needed for only part of the school year are issued just before time of use and recalled immediately afterward. Losses and damage resulting from distribution in September with recall in June are greatly diminished.

Class size collections of paperbacks are texts whether they are novels for comparative literature courses or biographies for science or social studies classes. These materials need the application of special processing techniques to lengthen their term of usefulness.

While students are sometimes careless with school property, generally they appreciate having their texts in good condition. Knowing that the textbook clerks will repair loose bindings or torn pages, students are more likely to bring materials to them for repair before the damage is catastrophic. These habit patterns benefit the students and also cut replacement and rebinding expenses for the school.

Special text materials designed for teacher use are charged out for the time period they are needed and are returned afterward for inventory, evaluation, and repair. Thus, they clearly are the school's property, not the teachers'. The idea of "personal ownership" of school property often leads to its removal when the teacher is transferred to a different school or leaves the system.

Recognizing Positive Elements

- There is a continuous accurate accounting for all of the texts in the school. This includes complete bibliographic information, location, condition prior to circulation, and accession numbers for each item.
- There is an equitable distribution and sharing of text materials among teachers and students.

- Time text materials are not being used is minimized. When materials are returned to the center immediately after use by one class, they become available for other classes to use at once.
- Text materials are in good repair.
- Replacement and rebinding costs are low. New classroom sets bought one year remain intact for the following years.

Recognizing Negative Elements

- Replacement and rebinding costs are high.
- Textbooks carried by students are in poor repair.
- Textbooks sit in the bottom of school lockers or at the back of the classrooms until the end of the year even when they are no longer in use.
- School materials are referred to as "belonging to" a grade or a teacher.
- Students and parents resent unwarranted charges for textbook damage.

Identifying Missing Elements

- There is no mechanism for or persons assigned to repair text materials. Conscientious parents and students try to make their own repairs with the wrong kinds of glue and tape which further damages the item.
- There is little or no administrative displeasure expressed when teachers fail to be responsible for accurate textbook records for their own classes.
- There is no centralized plan for textbook and text materials control.

Possible Solutions

- When departments are responsible for their own textbooks, departments obtain specialized glue and tape supplies from their own budgets and designate and train personnel to make suitable repairs for students within their departments.
- When the school library media center is charged with the responsibility for textbook and text materials control, adequate nonprofessional staff is supplied to carry out the assignment.
- An informational program is developed, possibly by the student council and student publications staff jointly, to improve student attitude toward accepting responsibility for community property in their custody.
- Just as students are expected to clear their obligation records prior to the end of the year or graduation, so too are classroom teachers. Clear records (or obligations) are noted in evaluations. There are no double standards for students and teachers.

VERTICAL FILE

The vertical file can be either a blessing or an albatross. When out of control it eats up maintenance time out of proportion to its worth. When handled well its contributions are significant. No other place can house pamphlets, clippings, or flat pictures as well, or have them as readily available. While it is foolish to attempt to house all topics in the vertical file, judicious selection of topics pays off. Local history, government, and special events; clippings on a new topic until the publishers catch up; and esoteric material on standard or elusive curricular topics all prove useful and worth their investment of time.

A portrait file can be a part of the vertical file. Students use this type of material for reports and classroom teachers use them for bulletin boards and introductory instruction on that writer or historical figure.

Sets of flat pictures, art prints, and maps have long been used for curricular enhancement. Although some of these materials require flat storage drawers of deeper dimensions than a vertical file cabinet, they are handled the same way.

Travelers are a good source for esoteric pamphlets brought back from sites visited. For example, Stonehenge fits into a number of curricular topics. Pictures of homes of Scott or Wordsworth and scenes of Scotland or the Lake District enhance learning and comprehension in literature studies. Likewise pictures of Roman ruins will always have relevance to the curriculum. These materials will not need periodic weeding as contrasted with clippings of present but not lasting issues. Students who send for current materials when preparing for a report often give their "tested" materials to the library media center vertical file for use by others. They also help with weeding folders when they identify useless or outdated items as they use the file.

The dependence on the vertical file will vary from school to school. In some instances adult volunteers, especially those who do not wish to become involved with technology, enjoy clipping newspapers and periodicals for curriculum-pertinent pictures and text. Others will help with labeling new items and refiling ones that have circulated.

When the file folders are labeled by broad subject only and when the catalog carries an entry for each file, searchers are reminded of its existence and do not have to hunt through it to determine if there is anything on their topic.

When newspaper clippings are of lasting value, two methods for preservation, ease of use, and shelflife are lamination and photo reproduction. Lamination prevents yellowing and shredding and reproduction creates a uniform and more lasting document. Maps that have been laminated and are stored flat do not crack along fold lines.

Identifying Positive Elements

- A vertical file is an actively used information source.
- The topics addressed in the file are listed in the collection index thereby permitting the user to know of their existence without having to hunt through the folders to find information.
- The materials housed in the file are carefully selected for curricular value, thereby avoiding clutter and extensive need to weed.

Identifying Negative Elements

- The vertical file is overstuffed and contains many out-of-date items.
- There is no indexing to guide the potential user to help save time and avoid disarrangement.
- Too much paid staff or volunteer time is consumed in handling folders, sorting, and filing to justify the file's existence.

Identifying Missing Elements

- No vertical file is maintained.
- Curriculum in the school does not include visual literacy elements.
- The school has few sources for current information.
- The school has not considered the use of free and inexpensive materials.
- The school has some of these materials but they are not organized and made useful to students.

Possible Solutions

- Decide whether this type of material would be of value to the curriculum.
- Establish a committee to determine the scope of useful materials, their indexing, and the possibility of recruiting personnel to manage the project.
- When there is a decision made to maintain a vertical file make sure that there are limits established to keep it under control.

WEEDING

The materials collection, both print and nonprint, needs to be evaluated periodically for wear, compatibility with curriculum, currency, and overall usefulness. This function should be engaged in by classroom teachers as well as by school library media teachers. It is a function often coordinated with the inventory process, although the two procedures are distinct and may well be done more effectively at separate times. A thorough weeding should be an initial step in preparing to go online.

A formal written policy needs to be established which addresses mending, rebinding, discarding, replacing, and purchasing new or additional materials. There should be recognition of the demands made on personnel to accomplish this task and to do the follow-up clerical work related to ordering and adjusting the catalog records to reflect removals and additions.

There is wisdom in working with a collection a full year before attempting to weed it in order to learn which teachers use what materials, which "oldies" are considered curricular treasures, and to identify holes that will influence orders. There is also some merit in involving faculty in double-checking those items pulled for discard as a further help in avoiding making mistakes and creating unhappiness.

On occasion a decision to discard is made based on when the item was last circulated, i.e., used. One should remember that materials do not have to leave the library media center to have been used. Also, materials that go out to classrooms as booktruck collections for a type of reserve use may not have any indication of this function either. To counteract this problem Betty Dawn Hamilton's LM_NET suggestion is to place the rubber-stamped message RESEARCH (and date) on an inside cover either as the books are leaving or returning. This small effort can prevent a large mistake and much unhappiness.

Perhaps the most difficult part of weeding is what to do with the rejects. Sometimes they are offered to students and faculty after clearly being marked discarded and dated. This can have bad effects when citizens do not agree with their being discarded no matter how good your reasons. One of the worst things that can be done is to put these materials into the dump where they will be found and citizens will be enraged over waste. Nor is it ethical to send castoffs to impoverished communities. If the material is not suitable for use by the students in your school, it is most likely not suitable for use by anyone else—unless it is merely a mismatch of reading levels or curricular content. Even when discards have been deposited in a dumpster in another distant town they often are carefully returned to the library media center by mail. Perhaps the only sure way is to arrange for immediate (but legal) incineration.

Recognizing Positive Elements

- There is an established calendar for carrying out routine weeding.

- There is an established policy used as a base for making weeding decisions.
- The department heads or classroom teachers who are concerned with the subject matter appropriateness of these materials are involved in the weeding process, at least to the extent of examining pulled materials before they are discarded.
- There is an officially approved, clearly defined discarding procedure meticulously followed by all personnel involved.

Recognizing Negative Elements

- The materials on the shelves are dirty, torn, and unattractive.
- The collection materials are out-of-date, do not pertain to the curriculum, or are of little interest to faculty or students.
- Students and teachers do not make use of the collection, and circulation figures are low indicating that the collection does not fit the users' needs.

Identifying Missing Elements

- Neither professional time nor added clerical personnel are provided to permit carrying out periodic or comprehensive weeding activities.
- Classroom teachers are not involved in the weeding process.
- There is no policy regarding the weeding process or the disposition of the weeded materials.

Possible Solutions

- Make certain that the weeding function is included in operations manual write-ups.
- Budget for time and personnel to carry out the weeding function.
- Use a questionnaire with students and with faculty to gather opinions regarding the usefulness of the collection for assignments and for individual interests and needs.
- Develop a specially funded program to upgrade particular areas of the collection, if necessary.
- Create a clear, board-approved policy regarding what is to be done with discarded materials. Remember that if the material is not "good enough" for your students' use it is not appropriate to make a gift of it to less fortunate students. Dirty, ragged items are insulting, and the transmission of out-of-date misinformation is unforgivable.

5. Instructional Elements Modules

ACCESS

Without good access for would-be users there can be no genuine program. Students must be able to enter the school library media center as individuals, in small groups, and in classroom units. They need to be able to use it before and after school. During school sessions they must be provided with a means of entry from study halls, classes, or lunch rooms. If warranted, some hours during evenings, Saturdays, or school holiday times might be provided.

At the elementary level predetermined scheduling assures each child a guaranteed weekly session, but such scheduling should not limit the student or the class to that one weekly class visit. With flexible scheduling in place, the classes can be accommodated both by length and numbers of visits to fit the project they are working on. There must also be the opportunity for unscheduled use of the center. Individuals and small groups sent to the school library media center from the classroom should carry with them a pass that indicates to the library media teacher the type of materials they will use and the time allotted for the purpose.

Scheduled classes must never close the use of the library media center to others. Access is not just to the center itself, but to all its services. The scheduled visit should be more than a book exchange opportunity or a routine lesson in library skills unrelated to ongoing classroom activity.

Restrictions on use of materials take many forms. Items

set aside to be sent to the bindery next June are not in the collection so far as the student is concerned. Controversial materials that have been removed from the open shelves and require parental permission for use create a restriction on accessibility. The so-called EASY collection to which younger students are often limited must contain easy nonfiction as well as fiction, or else these students are denied the full range of materials at their level. Provisions must be made also for these younger students to have the use of needed materials in the collection which are not designated as EASY.

There ought not to be artificial barriers to learning and library usage such as not permitting use of nonprint media until fourth grade, not allowing kindergartners to take books home, limiting primary grade students to borrowing one book at a time, or insisting that a borrowed book be returned before another can be taken. Too many rules and regulations couched in negative terms can constitute a psychological barrier to access, as can brusque or insensitive staff in the center.

At the secondary level access to the school library media center usually is by a pass system. These passes, obtained from classroom teachers, differ in size, color, and format from other passes used in the building. They are issued by the school library media center, require minimal filling-in, and are designed for use with the school library media center time clock. Students are responsible for obtaining passes from classroom teachers, clearance from the study halls, stamping time in and out, and staying within the travel time constraints.

With the increase in numbers of handicapped students being mainstreamed, physical access also becomes an important consideration. Libraries are not always on the ground floor, so elevators become necessary. (Not a bad idea when delivery of heavy merchandise takes place, either.) When security systems are in place there must be an additional entrance or a so-called wide aisle version used to meet the handicapped's requirements.

Recognizing Positive Elements

- Standards call for 10 to 30 percent of the student body to be able to be seated at the same time in the school library media center reading area. Seeing all the chairs in the school library media center filled does not guarantee that the program is functioning adequately. Conversely, empty chairs do not indicate that it is not. Observations should be made on all days of the week and at all hours of the day to assess student flow in and out of the center and kinds of use taking place within it. It should be possible to ascertain that students at all levels of ability are finding satisfactory types and amounts of materials suited to their needs.
- Examine the sign-up sheets to discover whether there are any departments or classroom groups that are not being given sufficient opportunities for workshop use of the center.

Recognizing Negative Elements

- If students may use the school library media center only during their assigned study hall periods, those students without scheduled study halls are denied access.
- Insufficient seating space places unreasonable limits on student use.
- When use of the library media center by students is on a fixed schedule basis only, the children who are absent on that day are denied a week's access.

- When a school holiday eliminates a scheduled visit to the library media center and no replacement time is substituted, the students whose scheduled time is taken are denied access. The same applies to auditorium programs, pep rallies, guest speakers, and other activities that interfere with the master schedule as well as school closings for weather conditions or mechanical malfunctions.
- When a classroom group is in the center for a workshop or instruction, no individual, small group, or another classroom group may be admitted.
- If the school library media teacher is absent, the schedule is not followed because no substitute is hired.

Identifying Missing Elements

- There is no schedule, there are no sign-up sheets, there is no weekly and/or monthly report on classroom, small-group, or individual use of the center.

Possible Solutions

- Questionnaires to students may bring to light problems of access and suggestions for remedies.
- Extended hours, before and after school, with late bus service similar to that provided for participation in sports, are needed for students whose schedules do not allow for school day use of the library media center.
- Classroom teachers should be alerted to make arrangements for individuals or the entire class to have class time for workshops in the school library media center. Workshops need to be planned jointly

so that whatever skills need to be learned or practiced by the students, or whatever support needs to be provided to make the assignments successful experiences will be in place.

ASSESSMENT

This entire book is concerned with assessment—of the library media program, of the library media support staff and teachers, and of classroom teachers. It has been suggested that part of the evaluation of teachers' performance be concerned with the use those teachers make of the library media program themselves, as professional educators, in instruction for their students, and in giving assignments that require the use of the library media center and its varied materials. Sample teacher evaluation sheets are included in Appendix A, and, attributable to principal Carol McKenzie (Austin, Tex.), another effective method of evaluating teachers who are learning to use more advanced technology. This is to have them prepare portfolios of their technology work for her inspection and evaluation.

The assessment we are referring to here is that of *students*, whether in a format with predetermined rubrics or the authentic assessment that is seen continuously in the activities of students in the library media center. In reality, it begins in the classroom when the students depart for the library media center armed with clearly defined assignments, goals, and needed equipment in preparation for the effective use of time spent there.

Rubrics may be devised that alert all students to what procedures, routines, products, outcomes, time frames will be expected as a result of a particular assignment. Simple tasks and assessments for the primary grades should deal with more than expectations concerning behavior, locating materials, their care, checking them out and returning them. Not only will they be assessed regarding their comprehension of stories, finding main ideas, and supporting details, but they will become able to differentiate between fiction and nonfiction and know how to identify facts and relationships.

Authentic assessment of student behavior and search skills is easily made with a rudimentary checklist for the lower grades and added to in planned developmental increments allowing for the ages of the students and the sophistication of course content. Assessment of student search strategies and results, whether in the library media center or as a result of the information gathered there, will usually be done by classroom teachers. However, an occasional check by administrators (with shared evaluation of the observations) would be informative for students, faculty, and administration alike.

Recognizing Positive Elements

- Students arrive at the library media center with a clear understanding of what they are to accomplish while there: information to be found, notetaking including citations, browsing and selection of materials, equipment to be used, and in the case of group work, who is to do what.
- Students make effective use of the indexing and databases and can translate that information into finding materials wherever located.
- Students feel free to ask for help or clarification from library media staff.
- Students participate in a booktalk presentation, storytelling session, or information skills lesson with courtesy and decorum.
- Students are aware that excessive noise is disturbing to others and rarely need reminders.

Recognizing Negative Elements

- The library media center is used as detention for unruly students who then live up to that expectation. This is a terrible mistake that may have negative lifelong impact on library use.
- Students are aware that they have been sent or brought to the library media center by a substitute teacher without a lesson plan for what is to be accomplished.
- Students regard the visit to the library media center as the weekly death march and behave accordingly. This attitude is rooted in the behavior of adults and its source must be discovered and changed.
- The lesson, booktalk, or story planned by the library media teacher does not meet the needs, abilities, or interests of the students and little effort is made to respond to their reactions.
- Student-initiated activity appears to make use of the library media center only for social interaction.

Identifying Missing Elements

- Assessment methods and techniques are still in the discussion phase in the school.
- There has been no thought given to assessment of students in the library media program as a part of the total assessment plans of the school.
- In-house assessment is not done; state mastery tests are thought to suffice.
- There are no benchmarks for student accomplishments upon which to gauge assessments.

Possible Solutions

- As assessment procedures are developed make sure that the library media program is an integral part of the plans.
- View the library media center and what transpires there as an extension of the classroom.
- Involve students and teachers in the planning for assessment and the continuing evaluation of the assessment techniques to ensure fairness and equity.

CATALOG FORMATS

The catalog is the index to the collection. As simple as the concept is, variations in format and arrangement require considerable decision making on the part of the school library media teacher. Students are being taught to be confident and competent users of public, academic, and special libraries through their use of school library media centers. With the advent of computers, the catalog formerly only on cards, became available in book form (i.e., computer print-out) and ultimately in online formats. With the introduction of microforms, some cataloging still appears on microfiche. As librarians choose to use the online facilities, the catalogs of their own libraries may be augmented by joining networks or by purchasing database services. The degree of sophistication with which the students learn to cope has budgetary implications. It is difficult for more than one person to use a computerized catalog at one time. When an entire class is working at one time, as frequently happens in the school library media center, multiple computer stations are needed.

Regardless of the physical format chosen for the catalog, there are other considerations and decisions to be made regarding its organization. First, catalog records (i.e., entries) will have been arranged using word-by-word alphabetization. It is possible that the cards have been rearranged to make the catalog compatible with the "as is" letter-by-letter alphabetization used on computers. Word-by-word alphabetization is different from the letter-by-letter application used in dictionaries and some reference-book indexing. Students need to be proficient in both systems.

Then the decision must be made whether to construct a dictionary style or divided catalog. In the dictionary style, authors, titles, and subjects appear in a single alphabet. In the divided catalog the authors and titles may be filed in one run of the alphabet while the subjects are filed separately in another run of the alphabet. This is of no concern to the computer which creates its own divisions upon command when the user asks it to search by author, title, or subject.

Another decision to be made is whether print and nonprint references will be interfiled in the same catalog or whether the user will have to consult separate specialized print and nonprint catalogs. Note: The former choice is preferable regardless of catalog format.

Consideration will need to be given to the subject headings used. As use of computerized catalogs increases in school and small public libraries, and as these agencies join computerized networks, students will increasingly need to use Library of Congress (rather than Sears' List) terminology. A student will need instruction regarding use of subject heading terminology in catalogs and databases as well as in other indexing. In time, a more universally used list of subject heading terminology than now exists probably will be developed, but retrospective searching will still require broader awareness of subject options because it is not likely that older references will soon be restructured.

When a card catalog still serves as the index to the collection, care must be taken to clearly label drawer fronts using multiple letters to indicate breaks in the alphabetic string. Three or more letters may be needed to prevent omission of alphabetic coverage, depending on where drawer spacing forces a division. Abbreviations should not be used on drawer labels. In addition, it is helpful if the drawers are also numbered sequentially with this numbering being added apart from the alphabetic labels. The purpose is to quickly scan and correct misfiling of drawers. In the case of divided catalogs, it is sometimes helpful to use different color labels for author-title and subject catalogs to assist quick visual spotting of misplaced drawers.

Recognizing Positive Elements

- There is evidence that the school library media teachers have investigated options and are making thoughtful choices for their particular centers, with logical reasoning to support modifications and modernization of collection catalogs.
- There is a comprehensive program of instruction that enables students to use a wide range of indexing and cataloging formats within their ability levels.

Recognizing Negative Elements

- The card catalog's structure has not been reexamined in recent times to determine its relative merits, clarity, and completeness.
- Skills instruction stops with basic introductory use of the card catalog, neglecting the introduction of refinements or the use of other types and approaches to indexing.

Identifying Missing Elements

- Clear identification of catalog drawer contents is missing.
- There are no use guidelines posted.
- After the inventory count has identified missing titles, corrections needed in the catalog to reconcile the holdings with the indexing are not made. Records have not been corrected or removed (catalog cards or computer entries) as needed.
- The entering of records for acquisitions is not kept up-to-date, creating a sizable backlog. This keeps users from knowing about and gaining access to the newest materials available.

Possible Solutions

- Begin a campaign to update the catalog. Hire temporary clerks and schedule clerical personnel employed elsewhere in the school for as much time as possible until this priority task is completed.
- Recruit students and community members in addition to, but not in place of, the paid personnel working on catalog corrections. This task force must check all catalog corrections called for by the recently updated shelflist.
- Verify that there are sufficient "see" and "see also" cross-references.

CENTER USED AS STUDY HALL

Experience has shown that it is not advisable to use the school library media center as an assigned study hall area. Often the center facilities are not large enough physically to accommodate the classroom groups and individuals who wish to use them at the same time. Guidelines, recommendations, or standards regarding the number of seating accommodations for work in a school library have been revised upward. New guidelines to be published by AASL to replace *Information Power* (c1987) will doubtless follow this trend, which reflects greater use of the library media center for on-site reference as compared with circulation (taking out books).

When the instructional program is examined and it is found that three or four teachers usually sign up to bring classroom groups to the school library media center at the same time, this accounts for 90–120 of the available seats. Add to this number students from several study halls and small groups from classrooms, and many centers would be overcrowded. If entire study halls are assigned as well, it usually means curtailing the availability and services of the school library media center program during those periods.

Requiring the school library media teachers to supervise these study hall sessions diminishes their availability as consultants and instructors to the rest of the student body. Probably the most damaging element in putting study hall assignments into the school library media center is what it suggests to the students about the center program and the desired use of the materials located there.

Note: While it is not study hall use, even more disruptive to educational purposes is the use of the center for various nonacademic, non–media center associated uses. These include such things as conducting eye examinations, interviews of applicants, mass testing, or yearbook photographs. The message received by teachers and students is the same as that given out by any other "holding pen" type activity put into the school library media center; namely, there is little value to the school library media program.

Recognizing Positive Elements

- When the school organization permits it, students may be free to determine whether they will spend unassigned time in study halls, the school library media center, or in other areas of the school building.
- Small groups or individuals may come to the center from classrooms with teacher permission to pursue spontaneous investigations.
- There is sufficient space in the school library media center and teachers make ample use of opportunities to bring their classes there for instruction, workshops, finding information for a project or paper, and acquisition of materials.

Recognizing Negative Elements

- Limited numbers of passes are available for students who want to use the school library media center during their unassigned time.
- There are no facilities for classroom groups to use the school library media center as a workshop.
- If a classroom group is scheduled into the school library media center, no one else has permission to enter.

Identifying Missing Elements

- There are no scheduled study hall periods.
- Students have no unassigned time to use the media center.

Possible Solutions

- Undertake a remodeling program to enlarge the physical space devoted to the school library media center.
- Assign a classroom adjacent to the school library media center to be used for classroom workshops and library media skills instruction.
- Investigate the use of other areas in the school for study hall purposes, and hire aides to supervise these areas and to free classroom and library media teachers for additional instructional purposes.
- When the school is organized without study hall periods, teachers are encouraged to send students individually or in small groups from the classroom, or plan workshop time in the center for the entire class. Otherwise, students may not have adequate access to the school library media center to do their search projects and block schedule assignments.

COMMITTEE PARTICIPATION

Too often library media teachers are isolated within the school. They feel overwhelmed with the workload of the library media center and certainly are not looking for added jobs of any sort. This attitude is counterproductive. One of the best ways to promote the school library media program is to participate in curricular planning and share with classroom teachers the types of assistance they can receive through collaboration. This is also the best way for the school library media teacher to learn about current practice and what is being considered for future instruction. Teachers working on curriculum revision need the services and perspective of library media teachers to assess materials support for units being developed.

Being visible at faculty meetings and in the lunchroom helps, but in no way supplants working with other faculty in curriculum redesign. Making sure that needed materials are on hand for a new unit or course and avoiding the creation of bibliographies that list old and unavailable materials are helpful to the faculty, but do not replace face-to-face interaction.

Principals should make sure that library media teachers are participants, or assigned members, of all committees concerned with curriculum. Site-based management, curriculum redesign, long-range planning, school restructuring—any such committee—profit from considering the school library media program's role in its deliberations.

Identifying Positive Elements

- The school library media teachers are well informed about teaching/learning theory and current curricular issues.
- The school library media teachers seek participation in committees that influence the future of the school.
- The classroom teachers welcome the participation and contributions made by the school library media teachers to their classroom activities.

Identifying Negative Elements

- The library media teachers avoid participating in curricular redesign, school restructuring, or long-range planning committees because they do not see these topics as part of their jobs. Staff development to expand vision and understanding of mission is indicated.

- Classroom teachers and department heads do not see the point of including the school library media teachers in their deliberations. As above, staff development to expand vision and understanding of mission is indicated.

Identifying Missing Elements

- Library media teachers rarely participate in curricular committees.
- The classroom teachers do not look to the library media teacher for assistance with curriculum design.

Possible Solutions

- Make sure that library media teachers participate in all curricular development and educational restructuring.
- Make sure that department heads are expected to identify the linkages between their departments and the school library media program.
- Create staff development sessions that will expand vision and understanding of missions.

DISPLAYS AND EXHIBITS

Display space is as essential within a school library media center as it is throughout the school. An effective program makes use of display areas wherever they are located and as frequently as possible. Wall coverings, ends of stacks, and lockable, glass-enclosed display units are all necessary for the promotion of the program. Students' or adult citizens' creations or collectibles are displayed in locked cases. Wall space may be used to display artwork or coursework. Bulletin boards are suitable for the creation of learning stations or involvement bulletin boards that, in addition to being interesting and colorful, serve the purpose of promoting student learning.

Many collections include realia and reproductions, items that are cataloged and stored separately. Just as in a public museum or gallery, stored items are taken out for seasonal or topical exhibits and can be viewed by the students even though they may not have requested specific use of them. The awareness of their existence tends to encourage students to look for catalog listings of such items to use when making classroom presentations or when exploring the topic for personal interests.

It is rewarding to students and their teachers to have high-quality classroom work put on public display. There is no better place than in the school library media center. The library media teacher should capitalize on the opportunity to offer classroom teachers the space. This is an important service to teachers and students, whose need for recognition is not always met.

Displays done by adults, teachers, or volunteers are often more attractive and employ more sophisticated attention-getting techniques than those done by students. However, being responsible for setting up a display is an important learning experience.

To make interesting and eye-catching displays requires the availability of materials such as fabric and papers for backgrounds, lettering devices (including computer programs), colorful yarns and pushpins, pegboard, and the like. The acquisition of these is a continuing effort, and there must be space in which to store them for future use. The display designer needs to have access to an abundance of such materials which often suggest other ideas and uses.

Recognizing Positive Elements

- When architectural plans are drawn for building or remodeling the school library media center, attention is given to providing for storage, display, and exhibit areas.
- Bulletin boards, mobiles, and wall and case displays are filled interestingly and changed frequently.
- Students and faculty look forward to new exhibits and comments are heard throughout the school about newly posted or arranged displays.
- Parents comment favorably about exhibits of students' work at PTA meetings and conferences.
- Individuals whose collections were borrowed for display develop and maintain an interest in the library media center and school activities.
- When bulletin boards and display cases are routinely assigned to departments on an annual schedule and the departments do not make use of them, the school library media center takes the opportunity to do so.

Recognizing Negative Elements

- The same posters, decorations, and exhibits remain unchanged over long periods of time, losing their impact. This practice implants the impression that the library media center is stodgy, uninteresting, and dull.
- Students vandalize materials that have been displayed.
- There is seldom enough tie-in between displays and curriculum or library media center materials.
- The only time effort is made to put up exhibits or

display student work is for parents' conferences or back-to-school night.

Identifying Missing Elements

- No student work is ever on display in the center.
- No displays are borrowed from museums or individuals within the school or community.
- No lockable display areas are provided.

Possible Solutions

- When sufficient display cases have not been built into the facility, arrange for the installation of a free-standing, lockable glass display case to be placed on the floor.
- Consider purchasing cases from retail outlets that are closing or moving. Often stores will donate to the school cases no longer in use.
- Have bulletin boards made and fastened to the ends of stacks, or simply use the ends by taping materials, signs, and posters to them.
- Consider the use of easels to display framed art prints.
- Arrange for a volunteer committee or chairperson to be in charge of identifying, proposing, arranging for, and returning exhibits from the community.
- Have the student council form a committee to be responsible for creating displays and exhibits within the school, including the school library media center.

EVENTS AND SPECIAL PROGRAMS

Local, regional, state, and national celebrations are reflected in both displays and programming in the school library media program. When recognition is given to outstanding graduates, members of the community, or the person for whom the school was named, there is opportunity to take a leadership position in participation. Cataloged archives can be created from the promotional materials used and the photographs and audio and visual recordings made.

Informed planning for field trips influences the learning outcomes for the students. Information for making contacts and getting current details, as well as the evaluation and tips from field trip leaders, is kept in the school library media center for use by other classroom teachers. Place entries in the catalog or a database that list, under appropriate subject headings, places of interest for field trips. Classroom teachers new to the community or teaching courses new to them will benefit. So will students who want to make trips independently or with their parents.

The school library media center can be used for receptions honoring visiting authors or other notables. It is also suitable for an informal musical performance or recital presented by students from the music department after hours. Perhaps students can be invited to provide background information to go along with the performances. Recorded music might prove as interesting to listeners on occasion as live performances.

If space permits, display racks can be brought in for a special art exhibit, showing either student work or a traveling exhibit.

Recognizing Positive Elements

- Promotional materials arrive frequently from national TV networks, local theaters, museums and galleries, and the sponsors of public events, because the school library media center teachers have seen to it that they are on the appropriate mailing lists. Information about these and other presentations are routinely examined for curriculum tie-ins, and promoted. There is a calendar of such events displayed in the center and in a column in the newsletter.
- The school library media teacher encourages presenting programs in the center in cooperation with other departments or agencies.
- There is a specified location where the calendar and announcements of future events, maintained by the school library media center, is posted.

Recognizing Negative Elements

- The school library media teacher discourages any use of the center other than for traditional school day functions.
- The school library media teacher is unaware of events not directly tied to the school and does not see their educational value.
- The school library media teacher does not attend after-hours activity taking place in the center and misses the opportunity to promote the school library media program.

Identifying Missing Elements

- There are no after-hours or outreach programs presented in the center.

- There are no displays or promotional activities refer-ring to school or community events.
- The school library media center is rarely considered by planners as a site for holding special events or publicizing them.

Possible Solutions

- Form a student committee of representatives from the various school departments to plan programs that will highlight their interests and student accom-plishments.
- Form a PTA or other adult volunteer committee to plan programs that will broaden student experi-ences. Start small and when the center is outgrown, move the events that are likely to attract a large au-dience to the auditorium.
- Have the library media teacher, perhaps in conjunc-tion with other faculty, offer a book discussion pro-gram.
- Make sure that when plans are being formulated for special events, the school library media teacher is included in the planning and contributions are ac-knowledged in the printed program.

FACULTY USE OF THE LIBRARY
MEDIA CENTER PROGRAM

While most careful attention should be given to the stu-dents' use of the school library media center program, equal attention needs to be paid to faculty use. The school library media professionals' job descriptions include team teaching with classroom teachers, helping to develop units of study taught both in the classroom and in the school library media center, assisting with materials production, facilitating interlibrary loans, informing faculty about new devices and materials, cooperating with staff development programs, and more. Classroom teachers should learn to expect these services as part of normal working conditions.

Recognizing Positive Elements

- Examine weekly and/or monthly reports from the school library media center to learn what use was made of it by classroom teachers and their students.
- When meeting with teachers, individually or as segments of the faculty, inquire about current usage, types and amounts, made of the school library media center program.
- Look for exhibits and displays of classroom work in the school library media center. Conversely, notice which classrooms seem to be making good use of learning packages, materials, and equipment from the center, and books on classroom loan for a special unit, event, or reading corner.
- Ask classroom teachers for suggestions about augmenting the school library media program.
- Look for bibliographies and reading lists that have been prepared jointly by the classroom and school library media teachers.
- Look for evidence of school library media teachers having been called upon to introduce students to materials related to a new unit.
- Look for multiple short-term assignments, as well as occasional long-term papers, that require use of the school library media center materials.
- Note which teachers are inclined to send students to the school library media center to answer spur-of-

the-moment inquiries. This permits capitalizing on student interest that may be lost if there is needless delay. The younger students have shorter attention/ interest spans and if inquiry is to be meaningful for them, answers need to be found as quickly as possible.

- Be especially aware of unusual or steady progress by any student and how this correlates with that student's teacher's expected use of the library media center. (Remember to include such observations in teacher evaluation reports and conversations.)

Recognizing Negative Elements

- Look for classroom assignments that can be considered unreasonable: insufficient materials on hand, assignments given with such short notice additional materials cannot be obtained in time, materials available that are beyond the capabilities of the students, or materials based on textbook bibliographies which were already out-of-date when the textbook was published.
- Note assignments that have not been tried out or tested sufficiently to ensure that students can avail themselves of what is needed to complete them.
- Note assignments that have been made without the students' having been adequately prepared for the level of sophistication the assignments call for.
- Note teacher-generated reading lists that include many titles unavailable in the school library media center collection and/or are out-of-print.
- For the most part, classroom teachers see little need to use the school library media center either to prepare units or assignments or for their students' independent learning.

- Classroom teachers' ability to use the school library media center for search or as a teaching/learning tool is minimal.
- Teachers seem not to be aware that search and bibliographic skills instruction is essential for students and is most effectively taught through collaboration of classroom and library media teachers.
- A wide range of bibliographic formats is required by teachers rather than a common one agreed upon for the whole school and preferably for the entire system.
- Parent complaints are received frequently concerning students' inability to find materials or to get into the school library media center during the school day. (Remember to include such observations in teacher evaluation reports and conversations.)

Identifying Missing Elements

- Sign-up sheets indicate when classroom groups are brought to the school library media center for workshop time. When these are examined, it becomes possible to identify department or individual classroom teachers who are not making full use of the program in their teaching,
- There is no mention of use of the school library media program as a teaching/learning tool on the classroom teachers' evaluation forms.
- The curriculum guides do not offer teachers sufficient directions for integrating the use of the school library media program into their teaching and the students' learning.

Possible Solutions

- Student questionnaires or other surveys can indicate student opinion regarding expectations, opportunities, requirements, and quality of use of the school library media center indicated by their assignments.
- Query parents to learn whether they believe a student's complaints about access opportunities and materials are justified.
- Schedule new faculty for orientation sessions with the school library media teachers.
- Plan annual staff development sessions regarding the relationship of curriculum and the school library media center program for all the faculty. These are most satisfactorily held as departmental or grade-level meetings.
- Set standards for classroom teacher competency in library usage and offer instructional opportunities to improve their teaching/learning skills.
- Make certain that the evaluation forms used for classroom teachers include a section on their use of the school library media center and its programs.
- Make certain that the evaluation forms used for school library media teachers include a section on their collaboration with classroom teachers.
- Make certain that curriculum guides in all disciplines address the integration of school library media usage into instruction in all subject areas and for all grade levels.
- Appoint a school library media teacher to serve on any curriculum revision committee.
- Encourage the faculty to look upon the school library media teachers as learning resource specialists and make sure that they truly are.

INTEGRATION OF LIBRARY MEDIA
SKILLS INTO CURRICULUM

There should be a well thought out written curriculum of library skills ranging from search skills for locating information to the processing of the information found, including listening, viewing, observing, speaking, writing, and reading at all levels of the cognitive taxonomies. Being able to select from a wide variety of materials those that most nearly suit their specific needs, and becoming independent, clear thinking, self-motivated learners are the objectives for all students.

Library skills, which are for the most part reference, search, and using information skills, are learning skills common to all disciplines throughout the curriculum. As a classroom, the school library media center and its program identifies these learning skills and incorporates them into its own curriculum.

The skills curriculum taught by the school library media teachers must be integrated with the entire school curriculum to ensure that the skills are learned and practiced by the students in a wide variety of applications. This guarantees that the students' knowledge of such matters as footnoting and bibliography writing applies to all subject situations, not just in science, history, or English classes.

Recognizing Positive Elements

- There is a printed, well-delineated, board-approved library skills curriculum.
- This curriculum is prepared cooperatively by school library media teachers, classroom teachers, teacher specialists, and administrators.
- This curriculum covers pre-K through grade 12, relates to all disciplines, is revised frequently to en-

sure currency, and it incorporates new content, approaches, research, trends, and methods.

- The skills are developmental, being introduced, practiced, and mastered in incremental steps and successive grades.
- The skills curriculum is structured in such a way that classroom teachers make their own applications to fit specific classroom activities.
- Student projects are structured in such a way that the application of the skills calls for different and individualized answers for each student.
- There is a teachers' guide to assist in interpreting the library skills curriculum.
- There is a bibliographic format common to all grade levels and it is taught by all teachers for creating bibliographies and footnotes.
- Copies of these style sheets are distributed to all students to keep in notebooks and are made available to parents. Students are expected to use them in all classroom assignments.
- There is a collection of commercial and in-house-produced games that are made available to individual students and classrooms for skills reinforcement.
- Pleasurable activities are used for skills practice including schoolwide games or contests and classroom competitions.

Recognizing Negative Elements

- There is an approved printed library skills curriculum but it stands apart as being "what a library does" instead of being integrated into each of the other disciplines throughout the school's curriculum.

- Teachers use English textbook library skills units in which all students use and answer the same questions.
- Teachers incorporate skills teaching only in the traditional language arts and social studies curricula.
- There are interminable dittoed worksheets distributed, or computer drill and practice programs used, without observable application to ongoing classroom activities.
- Worksheets are taken from commercially prepared materials that have not been checked or adapted to suit either the library skills curriculum, the school library media center collection, or the students' needs.
- There are no materials and/or ideas emanating from the school library media center to assist teachers in making the library skills instruction meaningful.
- Teachers use the same lesson plans calling for the same topics, the same references, and the same answers year-in and year-out.
- The school library media center program, including instruction in skills, is administered by nonprofessional staff.

Identifying Missing Elements

- When classroom groups are scheduled into the school library media center, there is no requirement that the classroom teacher be present and assisting with the instruction.
- Students are not being prepared to know what they will be doing in the school library media center before going there as individuals or in classroom groups.

- There are no periodic workshops scheduled to acquaint teachers with new acquisitions in the collections.
- There is no orientation for new teachers to acquaint them with the library media center resources, program, services, or curricular expectations.
- Administrators do not verify that the library skills portion of each curriculum area is fully implemented.
- Administrators rarely spend sufficient time in the school library media center to observe student search activities or learning in progress.

Possible Solutions

- Form a committee to examine well-integrated library skills curriculum documents from other school systems or state departments of education, and revise or create suitable documents for your own situation.
- Inaugurate a staff development plan to introduce the integrated library skills portions of the new school curricula and to show how these portions may be taught effectively.
- Work at finding ways to provide for library media/classroom teacher planning sessions and cooperative efforts.
- Include library skills instruction and media center use in administrators' evaluations of both library media and classroom teachers.
- Results of standardized tests (California, Iowa, your own state, etc.) in areas using study and search skills will be examined, and when deficient scores are observed, administrators will make correction of these deficiencies a high priority.

- Routinely schedule sufficient time in the school library media center (at varying times of day and on different days of the week) to observe and evaluate the application of teaching/learning skills.
- When the school library media program is as effective as it can be, the administrator can expect to be kept up-to-date with schoolwide learning activities through the reading of weekly school library media center reports, by viewing teacher sign-up calendars, and by conferring with the classroom and school library media teachers about what is going on and what is being planned.

KEEPING CURRENT IN LEARNING THEORY

The work being done to integrate higher-order levels of thinking skills into the curriculum relies on the theories, taxonomies, beliefs, and concepts developed by a number of learning theorists. The school library media teachers need to keep up with educational research, be aware of these studies, and able to apply them to instructional design. In this way, the school library media center will be used to its greatest potential as a laboratory for finding and processing information.

Terminology, as is often the case in education, does not mean exactly the same thing when used by different researchers. Benjamin S. Bloom, whose taxonomy is one of the older works in use, provides the terms *analysis, synthesis, evaluation.*[15] Robert Marzano categorizes thinking skills as learning to learn skills, content thinking skills, and basic reasoning skills.[16] The term *metacognition* has come to mean thinking about thinking. There are references to problem finding versus problem solving, to creative thinking versus critical thinking. And in the midst of the literature addressing the teaching of thinking skills, there is the voice of Leslie Hart who emphasizes the need to make all teaching/learning brain-compatible.[17]

The range of opinion about how this is to be done is wide. Some educators urge the teaching of thinking skills in isolated units. Some believe that success is possible only when learning and practicing thought patterns are infused into the overall curriculum. A third group recommends using a combination of the two methods as the most efficient approach. This is confusing if one is trying to determine a single or best approach to use. On the other hand, the variety of approaches makes possible fitting the school's thinking skills goals to teaching styles and subjects more easily. This should make gaining teacher support for systemwide thinking skills instruction easier to achieve.

Additionally, when students are expected to enhance their thinking and problem-solving skills as a result of classroom experiences, there is need to assess how well they are doing. A whole new look is being taken at testing; reliance on multiple-choice type questions has been reduced. Opportunities are being increased to demonstrate how well newly acquired information can be integrated into that already known in order to create new knowledge. Performance testing and short-answer testing do not tap the same information or duplicate each other, but they do call for different ways of teaching to match the demands of the tests.[18]

All of this will work best when the school library media teachers are well-grounded in current literature and practices, and when they are accepted as instructional teammates who can help devise units, locate needed information, save the classroom teacher design time, and increase teaching satisfaction.

Recognizing Positive Elements

- School library media teachers are just as conversant with learning theory and thought research as are the administrators and classroom teachers—preferably more so, since they are resource specialists.
- The lessons designed by the school library media teachers incorporate these theories and include activities that permit and encourage students to apply them.
- The professional collection used by both the school library media teachers and classroom teachers contains standard references on the topic.

Recognizing Negative Elements

- Teachers' lesson plan designs do not indicate a high priority to giving students the opportunity to practice higher-order thinking skills.
- The search for and finding of information receives more attention than the *use* of information.
- Neither teachers nor administrators keep up with teaching/learning theories and current research.

Identifying Missing Elements

- The development of critical thinking and higher-order thought patterns is not included in all school curricular documents.
- Evaluation procedures do not include looking for maximum incorporation or application of thinking skills.
- Teachers' test questions are not examined to determine the taxonomy levels that should have been achieved in order to answer them.

Possible Solutions

- Provide for staff development sessions to help teachers learn to make the most of the school library media program in their teaching.
- Have a committee examine lesson plans and tests to ascertain needs or deficiencies.
- Make clear what is included in evaluation of teacher performance and explicitly state all areas on the evaluation form. Interpret performance criteria to teachers and make sure teachers understand them.

LEADERSHIP ROLE OF SCHOOL LIBRARY MEDIA CENTER

Since the school library media center is a kind of curricular workshop for the entire school, the center staff has an obligation to supply materials needed for the various units in which students have assignments. The extent to which the center can supply leisure reading materials, over and above those that also serve a curricular purpose, is a matter of budget, space, and other considerations. Remember, however, that the line between what is read for pure enjoyment and what is read for learning can and should be a very thin one. If a school is bent on developing the reading/learning habit, reading for enjoyment is a basic, essential part of this development.

What is often overlooked is that the school library media teacher, in the role of principal selector of materials for the collection, wields sizable influence as an instructional leader for the school overall. It is for this reason that the school library media teachers should be members of curriculum revision and design committees and keep abreast of what is taking place in the various departments. In this way, someone is definitely responsible for making certain that ample materials are available for the new course, for the new unit, for the new teachers' special emphases. That same someone, the school library media teacher, is also the one to be alert to new topics as they appear in the news and in publishing. Each topic must be analyzed for curricular tie-ins and potential use by teachers and students, and if it seems likely to be valuable, materials should be found and purchased in anticipation of use.

If the school library media teacher waits until requested to provide materials for a class unit, there will probably not be enough lead time to supply the need. If there has been a section of the collection developed sufficiently to meet class demand very satisfactorily, the school library media teacher may be able to suggest to the classroom teacher that the topic could serve as a curricular unit or as the base for search projects. This is the kind of service that is possible when a base of understanding and confidence has been built between classroom and library media teachers. It is an important one that should be looked for by administrators when evaluating the worth of the school library media program in building and enhancing curriculum design.

Recognizing Positive Elements

- A request for materials on a new topic can be filled at once.
- There are headings in the catalog that address the new topic content, or at least use the new terminology. These may be only "see" references.
- A pathfinder or similar branching or ladder device has been prepared for the new topic.
- The school library media teacher is a member of departmental, school, or systemwide curriculum revision committees.

Recognizing Negative Elements

- There are complaints from students or teachers that materials are not available on needed topics.
- Little, if any, change takes place from year to year in the topics assigned to students for search projects. The same tired topics are used over and over again.

Identifying Missing Elements

- "New" topics tend to receive initial coverage in periodicals or journals, but there is insufficient periodical indexing to identify information sources even though these would have to be secured through interlibrary loan services.
- No vertical file folder on the topic contains reprints of articles appearing in esoteric publications to which the school library media center would not be expected to subscribe, but which an alert and watchful eye would note.

Possible Solutions

- As part of the evaluation of classroom teachers recognize favorably the incorporation of up-to-the-minute topics in the curriculum. This could motivate classroom teachers to expect and accept more assistance from the school library media teacher.
- As part of the evaluation of the school library media teacher indicate that anticipating curricular needs successfully is a positive element.
- Make certain that some funds for collection building

be retained for use later in the school year without fear of loss. This allows for the purchase of newly published and timely curriculum-related choices.

- Use a student questionnaire survey to determine specific perceived areas of insufficient or omitted curricular coverage, and use the results, as appropriate, as a buying guide.

LEARNING USE OF INDEXES

This refers to the use of the index of a book, the cumulative index to a set of books, multiple indexes within a single reference, the catalog (dictionary or divided, card, microforms, in book form, or online), databases, special subject indexes to periodicals/books, union catalogs, newspapers. The index is the quick and efficient key to information whether it be contained in a book or a database. The skills needed to use an index effectively apply to indexes in any format. They include at least the following: understanding guide words or phrases, standard bibliographic abbreviations (such as "ff.," "5–15," "a,b,c,d" for quadrants, "passim," "vol.") page, publisher, date, illustrations and portraits, cross-references, by and about order, the two ways to alphabetize (letter-by-letter and word-by-word), catalog filing rules, descriptors, headings and subtopics, meaning of visual clues (bold print, indentions, etc.), using standard subject heading thesauruses, and substituting terminology (going from specific to general and back) both broadening and narrowing terminology as needed (see also "Skills" in this chapter).

Recognizing Positive Elements

- The students have not only learned these index-interpreting skills but know how to use them in other contexts. There are both immediate and long-term results to be observed from this teaching.

Recognizing Negative Elements

- List from the above skills those areas in which ineffective instruction was given and student learning was negligible and/or there was no carryover one week, one month, or one year following instruction.
- Instructional materials were of poor quality, inappropriate, and irrelevant to the curricular tasks at hand.
- Iowa, California, and other standardized tests show small retention of skill.

Identifying Missing Elements

- List from the above skills those areas in which no instruction was given and students had no other means of acquiring the skills.
- No pretesting or diagnostic testing is used resulting in assignments that are inappropriate because they are beyond students' comprehension or preparation, or are insulting to students' intelligence and achievement levels.

Possible Solutions

- Provide a wider variety of self-instructional materials and programmed learning (commercial or prepared in-house).
- Work to institute an officially approved scope and sequence search skills program for all grades kindergarten through high school systemwide. Mean-

while, establish such a program within your own school.

- Expect classroom teachers to introduce, provide practice in, and follow-up on these skills in each of the disciplines. Provide staff opportunities to help make this expectation realistic.

- Make certain that the school library media teacher gives instruction, participates in team teaching approach, assists with staff development, recommends auxiliary materials, and suggests new and innovative approaches.

OBSERVATIONS

Most evaluation is based on observation. Administrators responsible for evaluation of staff and program may experience difficulties if they have no clear concept of what they should be looking for. Circulation statistics do not reflect the in-center use of reference or other materials. Often informal observation can tell as much or more about the state of things as formal measures. The placement of materials or chairs may be more truly indicative of use than a statistical count of the number of persons or materials passing through the entryway. If the evaluator is checking on quantitative and qualitative student use made of the center, observation may elicit more accurate information than what is recorded in the teacher sign-up book. For example, say that chairs are normally placed four to a table; if two tables have had their chairs removed and a third has the dozen chairs clustered around it, the observer could interpret this placement to mean that a small group of students was engaged in purposeful activity, or they could have been socializing. Either conclusion may be valid. However, if the practice is to upend chairs onto tables at the close of the school day so that the custodians can vacuum the carpet and at eleven o'clock the following morning only the chairs around one table have been replaced in normal position, the conclusion has to be that very few users have needed table and chair space that morning.

Developing skill in asking open-ended questions can also lead the evaluator to useful information. The answers to the questions, "Can you describe a unit designed jointly with the school library media teacher this marking period" or "What made a successful library experience for your students successful?" indicate considerably more than the answer to "Do you include library usage in your lesson plans?"

Conversations with students regarding their assigned and leisure time use of the school library media center materials can be helpful in determining attitudes. Body language, tone of voice, and choice of language used when comments are made can be very revealing. These indicators are just as useful when evaluating library media center staff performance.

Analyzing scores on search and study skills segments of standardized and special purpose tests can give direction toward what to look for. The use of well-developed (but brief) questionnaires with faculty and students can also provide clues for directing evaluative observation (see Appendix C).

Recognizing Positive Elements

- Evaluators make frequent informal observations as well as formal planned visits to classrooms and the school library media center.
- Evaluators stay to the end of a formal lesson and pick up on follow-up activity as well. They should be concerned also with the preparation for the lesson.
- Evaluators are welcomed by the classroom and

school library media teachers at any time and are invited to visit when especially interesting or innovative programs are in progress.

Recognizing Negative Elements

- Classroom and school library media teachers are visibly tense when evaluators appear.
- Evaluator is uncertain about what to look for or the real meaning of what is observed.
- There is little discussion or give-and-take between the evaluators and teachers except for that which is required as a part of the formal evaluation process.
- Students are rarely permitted input into evaluation of their learning opportunities.

Identifying Missing Elements

- Evaluation of personnel is carried out but there is no similar scheme for evaluation of program effectiveness.
- An insufficient number of observations are made to convince the school library media teachers that the evaluators are truly aware of the program's successes and problems based on firsthand observation.
- There is insufficient or no space on classroom teachers' evaluation forms addressing their use of instructional materials, the school library media center, or its personnel. The evaluator can easily overlook that facet of teaching/learning unless there is a required section to be filled in.

Possible Solutions

- Read library media literature, especially that which deals with program integration.
- Attend conferences and workshops designed for school library media teachers and administrators jointly.
- Become increasingly alert to in-house attitudes toward the school library media program and look for verification of both positive and negative findings.
- Encourage administrators' associations to present conference sessions that address getting the most from the school library media center investment, or that deal with a specific aspect of the topic that causes the evaluator concern.

PLAGIARISM

It is imperative that students be taught that plagiarism is not only frowned upon but, like copyright infringement, is illegal. Taking notes from the monitor screen *is* tedious, even when the CD-ROM disc program has a "notebook" capability. This notetaking device built into the program allows the students to excerpt passages and put them into a file which can later be downloaded to their own data discs and/or printed out. It is all too easy for the students to feel this compendium is their own "work" but is no different than reproduced material which has been cut and pasted and handed in as a report. Even more regrettable is the encouragement by teachers for individual students or cooperating groups to take bits and pieces from films, videos, CD-ROMS, and print media and put them together with a similarly purloined music background and then show it off to other students, parents, and the community. Most of this is copyright material; some is not. The ethics are questionable even where the legality may or may not be. Sources must be cited.

The real question is "What are we teaching our students?" If we simply want them to learn the techniques involved, let them do it as classroom exercises. Projects and reports should be original work with only an occasional quote or picture included and with acknowledgements made as to their source. (See "Legalities" in chapter 3.)

We must also teach selectivity. It is all too common for students to guess at a general keyword heading in the database which might, or might not, lead to any information on their topic and then (without even scanning the screen) press the print command. Often pages of printout are produced with nothing students can use. This indiscriminate use of the database and profligate waste of paper is very bad procedure.

Identifying Positive Elements

- There are printed policy statements regarding the legalities of using information and these are enforced.
- These policies are posted in areas where copying is done and interpretive training is provided.
- Teachers do not get taken in by glitzy plagiarized student presentations. Grades reflect originality of content and thinking skills rather than packaging.
- Teachers design papers so that students have difficulty resusing, purchasing, or taking them off computer networks.

Identifying Negative Elements

- There is a cavalier attitude toward plagiarism and theft in general throughout the school or within specific departments.

Identifying Missing Elements

- The topic and ramifications of plagiarism are unaddressed throughout the school.
- The element of misuse of time, supplies, and equipment is unaddressed throughout the school.
- No codebook of citations is in use across curricula.

Possible Solutions

- Mount an "integrity" campaign throughout the school.
- Classroom teacher evaluations recognize attention given to the prevention and unacceptability of problems associated with plagiarism in their classes.
- The habit and practice of citing sources begins early in primary grades.

PLANNING TIME

Classroom and school library media teachers need designated times when they can plan together. While each has separate contributions, it is their collective and collaborative thinking that produces the most effective results. Often planning time for the individual teacher is guaranteed by contract, but unless the school library media teachers' time is flexible, cooperative planning sessions are difficult to arrange.

It is common practice, especially in elementary schools, to assign students to art, music, and physical education classes with special teachers but without their classroom teachers in order to provide for contractually guaranteed classroom teacher planning periods. This practice causes no problems for students since these are nonacademic subjects with little carryover to the classroom. Occasionally, however, administrators who are not fully aware of the academic instructional functions of the school library media center will "stash" students in the center for the same purpose—release time for classroom teachers. This is a bad practice for three reasons. It ties up the center and its staff and prevents them from working with classroom teachers who are on planning periods. It negates the possibility of team instruction and two-way reinforcement of instruction between classroom and library media teachers. Perhaps most serious of all, such action trivializes the act of going to the library media center by projecting the visit as a detached interlude rather than part of a seamless continuum of learning.

Unless classroom teachers participate in their classes' learning activities that take place in the school library media center, they will not know exactly how to relate this learning to classroom instruction. Students' attitudes may be markedly different, depending upon whether the classroom teacher participates in the library-centered learning. When the classroom teacher is absent, students tend to believe there is no relationship between classroom learning experiences and those taking place in the school library media center, and no accountability for the latter. The center and its staff and materials may bring out an astonishingly different facet of a student's personality and ability from the one the classroom teacher usually sees.

When the classroom and the school library media teachers have planned the units together, "library skills instruction" not only relates in timing and content to ongoing classroom learning, but the classroom teacher will probably be able to conduct the valuable follow-up reinforcement that fosters mastery and varied application of skills.

Recognizing Positive Elements

- The school library media center schedule is flexible and not developed on a "scheduled only" basis.
- More than one classroom group (whole or partial) may use the school library media center at the same time, making possible both scheduled and spur-of-the-moment use for all.
- Two or more school library media teachers on staff permit one to be available for planning purposes with individual classroom teachers or grade-level or departmental groups, while the other instructs or assists students.
- There is evidence of joint planning in ongoing classroom activities.
- School library media teachers are encouraged to attend conferences with classroom teachers as a means of extending teaming and planning.

Recognizing Negative Elements

- Only noncertified staffperson(s) monitor the school library media center when the school library media teachers are meeting with classroom, department, or grade-level teachers.
- Valuable team planning experiences are at the cost of access by other classes or individual students to the school library media center when the only library media teacher is thus engaged.
- The administration advocates locking the school library media center in order to provide planning time.

Identifying Missing Elements

- Substitute teachers are assigned to cover the school library media center (as a means of allowing for planning time) even though they may not have sufficient background in school library media instruction, management, or supervision to make this useful.
- No encouragement has been given to joint planning.
- No alternative means of scheduling class groups have been considered or attempted so that classroom teachers can plan cooperatively with school library media teachers.

Possible Solutions

- Work with classroom teachers to find the means by which continuous joint planning becomes possible.
- Make sure that one of the permanent substitutes in the building has sufficient background to serve effectively when needed in the school library media center.
- Mandate that the school library media center operate on an open (not scheduled only) use plan.
- Recognize that when contract negotiations are taking place, it is the time to address the issue of team planning.
- Recognize that provision of sufficient personnel to provide for planning time has budgetary implications.
- Be committed to expanding school library media center staff (both professional and nonprofessional) sufficiently to provide the curriculum and teaming

services that should be an expected part of classroom teachers' working conditions.

PRODUCTION FUNCTIONS

One of the useful services and instructional programs associated with the school library media center is that of in-house production of learning materials. Many skills on scope and sequence charts include learning to make transparencies, audio tapes, laminations, photographs, film strips, videotapes, and other such audiovisual media. Currently, classroom projects are enhanced by computer-produced graphics and sound and film clips taken from CD-ROM and other databases. Desktop publishing is only the beginning of computer-produced items. There will be a continual stream of production enhancements made available by the industry that will need to be evaluated and considered for adoption.

Some schools enter student-produced materials in state and national competitions. Increasingly, schools are involved in cable TV programming and students learn and accept responsibility for various creative and production functions.

Here again, there are budgetary implications to recognize if these programs are to be encouraged and adequate supplies of materials and equipment are to be made available to students. Care must be taken to protect equal opportunity for learning experiences; this can be destroyed when students must pay for needed materials themselves and some cannot afford it. The materials for these programs tend to be costly and when there is inadequate instruction and supervision, equipment is ruined and materials are wasted. These programs should be undertaken only with careful planning.

Recognizing Positive Elements

- Clearly defined policy statements are available concerning the use of production equipment and materials both within and outside of the school.
- Classroom teachers plan production programs cooperatively with the school library media teachers, and amounts of materials are budgeted for use throughout the year rather than being used up by the first classes engaging in production experiences.
- Learning to use equipment to produce materials is made a part of the skills scope and sequence schedule.
- Adequate budgets are provided to support the level of student production experience the school system desires.
- Clearly defined policies cover teacher production; for example, if more than ten copies are to be made they will be done using fluid (i.e., less costly) duplication systems, or workbooks may not be reproduced for classroom use (i.e., legalities).

Recognizing Negative Elements

- Supplies in teacher workrooms or production centers are exhausted weeks or months before the end of the school year.
- There is evident belief on the part of teachers and/ or students that use of equipment for private personal purposes is acceptable.
- Teachers expect the school library media staff to produce unique teaching/learning materials for their classrooms without having discussed their needs or objectives with the school library media teachers. They merely say, "I need something on hurricanes."

Identifying Missing Elements

- No production materials budgeting plan is in evidence.
- No security is provided for storage of materials and equipment.
- No use responsibility policy statements are available for either student or teacher use of equipment in or outside of school.
- Teachers are unaware of what in-house production facilities and assistance are available to them or what this service could mean to the teaching/learning in their classrooms.

Possible Solutions

- Examine thoroughly the extent of a production program slated for the school library media center. Photography, for example, may be taught in the vocational arts program and not need to be duplicated in the school library media center program.
- Provide for adequate instruction and supervision of production areas.
- Budget appropriately for the level of production desired to ensure effective and equitable use of the program.
- Include production skills in the curriculum documents if production is a learning experience subscribed to by the school system.
- Conduct staff development sessions that enable teachers to see examples of the school library media production services that have enhanced teaching/learning experiences in a variety of subjects and grade levels.

PROFESSIONAL DEVELOPMENT

Most states have requirements for professional development for certified teachers. Some demand a requisite number of courses, hours, or CEUs for continued employment, retained certification, and/or advancement. In many cases schools or school systems are required to offer a minimal number of hours or CEUs at the school or district level to satisfy the state's mandate. Library media teachers have a double set of professional development needs. First, they need to keep abreast of what is going on in the grade-level classrooms as well as the content area or special classrooms. Second, they need to meet with other library media teachers from other schools and other systems. The first need can be met in the school or school district, but providing for the second need is often very difficult. Neighboring school systems may have staff development dates that do not match. Exemplary programs in schools that are within possible travel range may not be able to offer accommodation. Cursory visits to other schools will not improve teacher performance, the avowed purpose of professional development activities. A lengthy visit (with prepared questions to be answered and a report expected from the visitor) probably cannot often be arranged during school sessions.

Monthly afterschool meetings of library media teachers have proven effective, whether to swap duplicate materials or ideas. Such an arrangement may have to be voluntary if there are contractual time constraints. When the distances are not too great, other systems' personnel may be invited as well. Meeting places should rotate so the various library media centers will serve as hosts and, over time, all attendees will get to see the other facilities. Sharing experiences has come to be recognized as more valuable to professional development than listening to lectures from imported gurus.

Just as hands-on experiences and cooperative learning have proved effective for students, so, too, are these methods superior when teachers are the learners.

Library media teachers should be encouraged to attend workshops, continuing education programs, and state, regional, and national meetings of library media professional associations. Release time should be provided, substitutes hired, and credit given according to the time spent in meaningful activities. Among the latter are the opportunities available at the biannual national conferences of the American Association of School Librarians (AASL) to visit exemplary public and private schools. These visits are very well organized and extremely informative, but the visitor with prepared questions who takes notes and requests school brochures, fact sheets, and floorplans will maximize the experience. The attendee should provide a written report to the administration and share same with colleagues.

Identifying Positive Elements

- Faculty who attend conferences bring back new information which they share in staff and departmental meetings.
- There is a warm and friendly collegial attitude shared by faculty who are quick to help one another with professional problems.
- Provisions are made for library media teachers to attend staff development sessions within the school system and also programs designed for library media professionals at other school systems.
- Library media teachers are encouraged to attend workshops, continuing education programs, and state, regional, and national professional association conferences. Release time, substitutes, and professional development credits are all provided.

- Written reports are read by the administration and follow-up discussions with the attendee reinforce the benefits of the experience.

Identifying Negative Elements

- Little or no instructional help is provided for faculty or support staff, and that which is, is geared only to the needs of classroom teachers.
- Staff development sessions are all lectures by outside experts, some of whom are enlightening, while many are not.
- There are no opportunities provided for library media teachers (frequently only one in the building) to share ideas and experiences or to brainstorm with other library media teachers.
- No provision has been made for library media teachers to attend sessions geared to their needs and interests within the school system or at another system.
- Opportunities to attend workshops, continuing education programs, and state, regional, and national library media professional conferences are denied to all but one attendee from the school system, whose second-hand impressions are supposed to be widely shared but seldom are.
- Districtwide efforts to attempt staff development workshops are rejected by those for whom they are intended.
- Poor attendance, uncooperative and cynical attitudes, and little evidence of changed attitudes or behavior result from what is tried.
- No follow-up system is in place identifying or evaluating change in classrooms.

Identifying Missing Elements

- The little training that is done is devised by supervision without willing and interested input by the recipients.
- The special needs of library media teachers have not been considered.
- Possible shared staff development programs with other school systems has not been explored.
- There is no provision for giving professional development credit for professional growth experiences other than those provided in-house.
- Classroom teachers are not expected to keep up with the advance of technology in instruction; library media teachers are not expected to keep up with education research.

Possible Solutions

- Administrators should meet with library media teachers to assess needs and gain suggestions for possible programs.
- Administrators should contact adjacent or neighboring school system administrators about possible shared staff development offerings.
- Needed changes in the rules concerning professional development credit should be made to acknowledge participation in workshops, continuing education programs, and attendance at library media professional conferences at the state, regional, and national levels.
- Library media teachers participant in LM_NET.

RESOURCE-BASED LEARNING

Resource-based learning and resource-based teaching are *not* the same thing. Most teachers will state that they teach with many resources other than the textbook and some of them truly do. Resource-based learning refers to a nontextbook program in which there is a curriculum selected by the school or the district, not the textbook publisher. The curriculum consists of many topics and the library media center's collection of print and nonprint media covers those topics with material geared to a wide range of reading levels and comprehension abilities matching those of the students enrolled in the school. Literature-based reading programs and whole language programs are two subsets of resource-based learning. They deal with reading programs that do not use basals and have students use whole stories or read entire books instead. Some schools with these advanced reading programs still have textbooks for other disciplines, but as they begin to use interdisciplinary or topical approaches to teaching/learning they soon see the validity and superiority of abandoning the "everybody is the same" mindset in favor of serving all the students according to their needs. Even states that had textbook adoption rules for many years have seen the efficacy of hands-on approaches to the teaching of science and relinquished science textbooks.

In resource-based learning the role of the library media program is central and quintessential. The library books that will be used in the classrooms for reading and language arts instruction are bought, processed, housed, and distributed from the library media center complex. Classroom lots of paperback atlases will be loaned for social studies units as needed. The money previously spent on costly textbooks buys a multitude of trade and paperback books, videos, laser discs, CD-ROMS, computer programs, and more. These materials are loaned to students and teachers for the time period that the theme or topic will last, and/or as long as the students are given to complete assignments, projects, or reports. Another cost-cutting feature is that books that are no longer needed in one class will be used by another instead of sitting on the first classroom's shelves for the rest of the year. Yet another benefit is the myriad of uses the same materials will have in other parts of the curriculum or geared to a youngster of another grade level or with a different need. For example, books depicting the parts of the human body with simple language and labels will serve many preschool or first graders; older students for whom English is a second language; the visually impaired; or sixth graders who need to be able to draw body systems and find that these books have illustrations they can use as models.

In the nontextbook school the library media center is the true hub or heart of the curriculum and its services must be efficient, speedy, anticipatory, and as omniscient as possible. The library media teachers serve on all curriculum committees, participate in curriculum revision, and serve as materials experts to the students, faculty, administration, and staff. They must also have expertise in reading guidance to be able to advise the individual student looking for an exciting mystery or the teacher who wants a good book dealing with prejudice to read aloud. The library media teachers are aware of what is going on in all classrooms, understand differences in teaching styles as well as learning styles, and know how to cater to them.

The resource-based learning program with its emphasis on the individual learner requires a substantial collection and an enlarged facility. The augmented space is necessary not just to house the varied materials but also to accommodate individual students as well as whole classes and small groups, all of whom may need to use the library media center at the same time. Methods of serving multiple classes studying the same topics simultaneously must be encouraged. Assignments can be staggered and/or materials can be put on overnight or noncirculating status during crunch periods of great demand. Cooperation with other schools in the system may lead to certain topics being taught in the autumn in one school and in the spring in another, while the larger amount of materials from the collections of both schools accompanies the seasonal needs of each.

Identifying Positive Elements

- There are no sets of textbooks used in the teaching/ learning program of the school.
- The library media program adequately serves curriculum needs.
- Classroom and library media teachers regularly evaluate curriculum and topical areas.
- Materials are bought throughout the year.
- Students, teachers, administrators, staff, and parents feel free to make recommendations for additions to the collection.
- The budget reflects the changing needs and requirements of the curriculum, the students, and the faculty.
- There is adequate space to house and use all types of materials.
- There is sufficient space and furniture for 10–20 percent of the students to use the library media center at the same time.

Identifying Negative Elements

- Neither teachers nor administrators are willing to give up textbooks.

- Teachers and administrators see the library media program only as necessary for covering release time for teachers.
- The library media teachers do not attend any curriculum meetings or work with curriculum revision.
- Library media teachers are not considered resource materials experts.
- Library media services are considered ancillary, not integral, to classroom activities and instruction.

Identifying Missing Elements

- There has been no interest in hands-on science teaching.
- There has been no interest in literature-based or whole language reading programs.
- There has been no interest in topical or thematic approaches to teaching.
- There is neither full-time professional nor support staff assigned to the library media center program.
- Reference materials are neither current nor plentiful.

Possible Solutions

- Teachers, administrators, and parents need to visit schools where hands-on approaches to teaching/learning and whole language- or literature-based reading programs have been in place for some time.
- There needs to be proper planning and a guarantee that there will be sufficient and varied materials for all students to match their needs, interests, and abilities when there are no textbooks. It may be a weaning process for some teachers; others will see the advantages immediately.

- Classroom and library media teachers must be selected who are capable of and interested in promoting and supporting this type of program.

RUBRICS

"Eby and Hunt (p. 94) consider the major reason for failure in school to be that students do not know what they are expected to do in order to succeed. Unclear and vague expectations lead students to get discouraged and fearful of turning in end products, giving speeches, or taking a test."[19] Realization that multichoice standardized tests rarely measure thinking skills or the ability to synthesize content or solve problems, has led to the use of rubrics for both student assignments and teacher assessments. They are especially valuable when more than one person evaluates a student's end product. "The selection of different rubrics for multitiers of evaluators provides the student with feedback from varying activities."[20]

Doyle points out that accompanying the societal shift from an economy based on capital goods (industrial) to an economy based on services (information) there has been a corresponding shift in what is expected from education.[21] As classrooms have responded and students are asked to turn more information from a wider range of sources into knowledge, library media centers and library media teachers become increasingly involved in the process. Wiggins believes that "typical tests, even demanding ones, tend to overassess student 'knowledge' and underassess student 'knowhow with knowledge'—that is, intellectual performance. . . . We want to know: Can the student use knowledge and resources effectively to achieve a desired effect? This is the question Bloom and his colleagues argued was at the heart of synthesis. These tasks should only be judged well done to the extent that the content is well used. For this the student needs to know details of context."[22] From this need, both in learning and teaching, the use of rubrics has arisen. (See sample rubrics in the glossary.)

Identifying Positive Elements

- Students and teachers both know at the beginning of an assignment the criteria that will be used for evaluation.
- Students exhibit the ability to self-evaluate their work.
- Teachers will have reasoned thoroughly and stated exactly what it is that they want students to do to demonstrate mastery or learning.
- Students are involved with developing rubrics for evaluating their finished products.
- The rubrics in use tend to indicate use of open-ended, creative assignments.
- The way the rubrics are designed identifies for students what must be accomplished to attain top level results.
- Teachers also use rubrics to keep their evaluations even-handed and focused.

Identifying Negative Elements

- Students don't know what is expected in order to fulfill an assignment successfully.
- Teachers don't know what they want students to be able to do to demonstrate learning.
- Lack of use of rubrics tends to indicate dependence on assignments that emphasize rote, recall, and single correct response types of answers.

- Students tend to choose to function at the minimal level within the rubric.

Identifying Missing Elements

- Rubrics are not employed by the teachers and students.
- Rubrics that are used do not identify criteria for multiple levels of grading.
- No training has been given to teachers on how to develop and use rubrics.

Possible Solutions

- Explore how the use of rubrics might provide differentiation when working with students of varying abilities.
- Begin by applying the use of rubrics to a specific unit or assignment. As with any other technique, constant use leads to boredom.
- Initially design rubrics for recurring assignments such as sharing of current events articles, book reports, writing assignments, or the search process.
- Expand checklists or mastery learning criteria into multilevel rubrics.
- Involve students in designing rubrics. They relate closely to top-level performance.

SCHOOL HOLIDAYS AND SUMMERS

That school is not in session does not have to mean that its materials cannot be used. Reserve systems allow instructional materials in high demand to be taken from the center for overnight use. Many items in reference collections are regularly borrowed at the end of the school day for overnight use. This is done even when there may be extended after-school hours provided for students to use the center. Since a reference item can be used by only one student at a time, it makes little difference where it is used. Methods must be created whereby more students can use materials when school is closed. School library media centers should permit the borrowing of materials for weekends and week-long school holidays. Also, plans are needed for extended summer use of materials. Students can prepare request lists giving call numbers and full bibliographic information. Parents then sign a responsibility form guaranteeing replacement if materials are lost or damaged, as well as the return of these materials by the opening day of the next school year.

Because there may be clerical personnel working throughout the summer at housekeeping and technical tasks in preparation for the next school year, it should not be assumed that the school library media center is open for use. These employees are nonprofessionals who are not equipped to provide students with reading or study guidance. Summer programs are made possible through the use of the building for summer school, or through a supply of extra funds to hire a school library media teacher to keep the center open some days and hours during the vacation. A PTA may be able to provide these extra funds.

Sometimes townspeople will also want to make use of school library media center materials. During school time, townspeople may borrow materials with the understanding that should assignments create an unexpected need for the materials, they may be called in at once. Students must have primary consideration.

Recognizing Positive Elements

- Reference and reserve materials are circulated overnight.
- Reference and reserve materials are circulated over school holidays.
- Non–summer school students have access to the properly staffed library media center during summer school hours and may borrow materials the same as summer school students.
- Special funding is provided so that school libraries may be kept open during the summer.
- There is a plan by which students may borrow materials for extended summertime use, returning them for the reopening of the school in September.

Recognizing Negative Elements

- All reference and reserve materials must remain in the school library media center at all times.
- Rules are rarely bent in favor of instructional needs.

Identifying Missing Elements

- There are no plans made for use of materials during the summer or other closed-school periods.

Possible Solutions

- Investigate plans used by schools that do engage in extended summer and holiday time borrowing.
- Institute a borrowing plan more responsive to student needs than the present one.
- Encourage parent and community groups to support funding for summer school library media programs.

- Develop a cooperative summer and holiday use plan with the local public library that might provide for supervised use of the school library media center's materials when the school building is closed.

- At the very least, develop a cooperative summer reading plan in which students read books from the public library. Student participation in summer public library reading programs can be recognized with an in-school assembly at the beginning of the school year. By posting a sign-up sheet in the public library's children's area inviting students to add their names to the list of summer library users, record keeping is simplified. Students whose names appear on the list receive a bookmark, stickers, or other small token.

SKILLS

There is a wide range of interpretation given to the word *skills* when applied to those that should be learned and practiced within school library media centers. The shift in curricular emphases and the advance in technological information retrieval have influenced educators' thinking. Just as nonprint carriers of information have become standard along with books in school library media centers, print format microformed and on acetate is common. Computers used for word processing have replaced typewriters and they have produced a different technique for storing information, replacing the card catalog with databases and making it practical for schools to become parts of regional, state, national, and international information retrieval networks. The ability to locate information through the use of a card catalog alone is no longer sufficient for the student.

The curricular shift requiring students to use, evaluate, synthesize, and reapply information, not just find it, ties in with the development of thinking skills. The school library media center program is now recognized as a true partner of the classroom program in training students not only to retrieve but also to use information.

One of the purposes of the school library media program is to make students competent users of any type of library. The skills learned, therefore, must address systems of alphabetizing, organization of information, indexing, and the use of subject terminology and controlled vocabulary. Skills also include the ability to substitute alternative terminology or that which is broader or narrower in scope, all of which is necessary whether the search for information is done manually or through the use of a database.

To use the information located, the student must become able to evaluate the content of the material. This means recognizing propaganda, bias, authority, the disagreements among both primary and secondary sources, and the frequent differences of opinion between retrospective and current coverage of a topic. The notetaking and organizational skills that are required to manage selected information become increasingly important. Visual literacy must not be neglected because much of modern information transmittal is visual, and an unwary viewer is every bit as vulnerable as a reader or listener who is unaware of persuasion techniques.

Clear thought processes involving fact recognition, analysis, comparison, sequencing, evaluation, synthesis, and ultimately valuing, must be acquired in order to process information. These same skills are basic to effective writing and communication, and involve listening and viewing as well as reading and writing. For these reasons thinking skills have received curricular attention throughout the nation. Library media teachers team with classroom teachers in providing opportunities for students to engage in a developmental skills program that follows a defined scope and sequence and is integrated into ongoing classroom activities.

Modules in this book on integration of library skills into curriculum, learning use of indexes, primary sources and government documents, and resource-based learning relate closely and address specific skills in more detail.

Recognizing Positive Elements

- The broader interpretation of library skills as inquiry and independent learning is in place in the school.
- Curriculum documents include library skills integrated throughout prescribed units.
- Classroom teachers make assignments that require student use of library media center materials and services.
- Faculty are evaluated on their ability to use and integrate into teaching/learning activities the broad scope and sequence of library skills.
- In addition to classroom instruction, students have the opportunity to use computerized programs to learn and practice a variety of library skills with a variety of formats.

Recognizing Negative Elements

- Library skills instruction stops with finding materials through use of the card catalog.
- Little attention is given to student competency in viewing and listening skills.
- Classroom and library media teachers do not work together to produce instructional activities for students.

- Classroom teachers do not accept responsibility for teaching library skills.
- Library skills are part of only the Language Arts or English curriculum instead of being integrated into the entire curriculum.
- In the attempt to have all students learn library skills, the administration has scheduled classes into the media center leaving no time or space for any other aspects of the library media center program.

Identifying Missing Elements

- There is no scope and sequence curriculum document identifying library skills, and indicating joint responsibility to provide the students with instruction and practice in using them.
- Administrators have no clearly defined documentation verifying that every student is experiencing a full school library media program.
- Some members of the faculty remain unconvinced that they need to use the facilities of the school library media center in order to teach well.

Possible Solutions

- Work to provide the library media staff, materials, space, and accessibility within the school that are needed to establish a superior school library media program for all students.
- Use standardized tests and in-house tests to evaluate students' ability to use a library media center facility.
- Visit schools that have exemplary school library media programs to look for ways to improve skills instruction and learning.

- Encourage classroom teachers, as well as library media teachers, to attend conferences and workshops to learn additional techniques for improving skills instruction and learning.

STUDENT USE

Every student in the school, regardless of ability, motivation, achievement, attitude, or plans for the future, requires full usage of the school library media program to progress at an optimum rate. The school library media program exemplifies very well the effort of a school or a school district and provides equality of educational opportunity.

School library media teachers are often in a better position to approach students and work with them toward their learning goals than classroom teachers who give grades. Because they know the whole curriculum of the school and evaluate student abilities only for the purpose of matching those abilities to appropriate materials, their assistance tends to be just as supportive and less judgmental.

The incidence of students' success can be higher in the library media teacher relationship because the feeling of accomplishment is not diminished by whether they are reading "on grade level" or not. Because of the range of curriculum materials at hand, the library media teacher can better guide the students from what they feel comfortable with into new and untried areas that are not so great a challenge as to be frightening. Also, the wide range of formats in materials provides the school library media teacher with options that make possible bypassing roadblocks to learning.

The properly integrated school library media program crosses all subject areas, grade and ability levels, and learning styles. Probably the most valuable skills students can acquire in school to equip them for the future is to learn how to find and use information. To the extent that this is true, the school library media center becomes a laboratory for learning and polishing these skills. The classroom teachers, following the school curricula, design lessons that call for the application of all levels of higher-order thought when locating, applying, analyzing, synthesizing, and evaluating information.

Recognizing Positive Elements

- Students recognize the value of the school library media center program in their educational experiences. They feel at ease in the center and have learned the rudiments of information retrieval well enough to feel comfortable in using many kinds of tools.
- There is an official developmental library media skills curriculum totally integrated with all subject areas that introduces skills, provides for their practice, and leads to mastery in grades K through 12.
- Students, teachers, and parents are familiar with this incremental library media skills curriculum and see evidence of its value as it progresses.
- Segments of standardized tests show students' achievements to be high in those skills directly related to library media center usage.
- A distinct carryover can be seen in the use made by students of public and academic libraries available to them.
- Reports from high school graduates who go on to advanced studies indicate that their school library media training has contributed positively to their success.

- Students consider the school library media center as a place to go for serious or purposeful leisure reading, viewing, or listening.
- Students solicit the school library media teachers' advice concerning both curricular and leisure use of materials.

Recognizing Negative Elements

- Students consider the school library media center as a place to socialize, an escape from study hall, and an indoor recess area.
- Students see little value in library media skills instruction because it is out of sync with their studies—taught out of context with the subject content with which it should be allied.
- Students believe that their curricular needs can seldom be met in the school library media center setting.
- There is a high level of theft as well as a high incidence of petty vandalism.
- Discipline is a problem.
- Students show little respect for the school library media center, its program, or its personnel.

Identifying Missing Elements

- The library rarely shows signs of use.
- The school library media program is considered to be a support service rather than an indispensable, integrated element of instruction.

Possible Solutions

- Faculty who are skillful in using the school library media center program as a teaching/learning tool cause greater use of the center program by students through assignments and example. This may call for staff development sessions, and even some mandate on the subject by administrators.
- Initiate a series of special programs related to literature, illustrators, and authors; book and film discussions; story telling; photography and/or video production; book talks.
- Conduct schoolwide contests that require use of the school library media center to win.
- Provide learning centers in the school library media center so that students may explore independently and at their own rate.
- Provide experiences which give insight into the delight of discovery.

6. Technology Modules

CD-ROM (COMPACT DISC—READ ONLY MEMORY)

The general public is no longer surprised that a single disc holds the contents of a complete encyclopedia and more. They have become familiar with and accept musical recordings that are contained in such a disc, so it is no wonder that CDs have become popular in the school library media center. The CD-ROM is simple enough for young students to operate and suitable for adults to use. The tremendous storage capacity of the CD-ROM, its informative material accompanied by sound and motion picture or video clips, makes it a favored source of information for students of all ages. It has been shown that this combination of visual and audio, along with print, is especially useful in helping students learn who cannot (or will not) learn from print media alone. However, since a single CD-ROM holds the equivalent of 300,000 printed sheets, 10,000 image pages, 1,200 microfiche sheets, and 1,800 floppy discs, the user must become adept at finding what is wanted from so much information.

The computer (with built-in or added-on sound board) needs a great deal of memory, mouse, keyboard, and CD-ROM drive for the disc to be used. Only one CD-ROM disc can be used at a time and, unless there is a multidisc drive (jukebox style) or a network supported by a multi CD-ROM server, each disc has to be removed from the drive and another inserted and started up by the user. Another approach is to set up CD-ROM stations for each CD-ROM, or the most used ones. Thus, when students wish to use a particular disc, they go to the station where it is installed, sometimes encountering a wait if that station is in use. Another method is to put popular CD-ROM discs on the network so that larger numbers of students can have simultaneous access. This access might be at several of the stations in the library media center or in the classrooms throughout the school.

When workstations are limited, the CD-ROM can be a useful learning tool inasmuch as several students can use a CD-ROM together and apply critical thinking to establishing search strategies. No learning takes place when students print out information, take it home, and copy word for word. This is plagiarism, not original work. Students must acquire skills in sorting out what type of data is wanted out of the large amount available, learn to select precisely what material is needed, and then be selective in using what they have retrieved. (See "Plagiarism" in chapter 5.)

Some CD-ROMs are relatively inexpensive, others are more costly or are obtained by annual subscriptions such as periodical citations, whether whole text or abstracts. Unlike online searching, the cost of a CD-ROM is merely the purchase price or the annual update subscription fee. This assumes that the necessary hardware is already in place. If a new CD-ROM will require another workstation, the additional hardware must be figured into the cost. Because this compact disc is small and relatively unbreakable, there is increased possibility of theft as compared to larger volumes of encyclopedias or other reference tomes. It is unwise to leave the discs lying about or in an open file next to the computers.

CD-ROM discs cannot obviate the need to purchase new encyclopedias or other reference tools on a regular basis. A whole encyclopedia can be put on a CD-ROM disc, but more students can use the many volumes of an encyclopedia set at the same time. Better yet, they can choose from among the many and *varied* sets of encyclopedias in the library media center. Unless students own laptops with built-in CD-ROM drives, books are still the most portable sources of information. At this writing, there is no easy or inexpensive way to copy CD-ROM discs. Unwarranted or excessive numbers of printouts must be monitored for plagiarism.

Identifying Positive Elements

- There are ample workstations with CD-ROM drives to satisfy student needs.
- Workstations are placed near electrical outlets and within sight of an adult who can see the monitor.
- Workstation is spacious enough to accommodate more than one student at a time thereby promoting cooperative learning.
- Teachers' assignments require making use of CD-ROM technology, and teachers are insistent on accepting only original, properly cited work.

Identifying Negative Elements

- Many extension cords provide possibility of tripping.
- Long lines of waiting students at each CD-ROM workstation.
- Discs are left in machines after hours at night posing potential problems if space is used by the public.
- There is a high rate of loss of CD-ROM discs.
- Potential users have not received adequate instruction.

- Students generate reams of printouts, much of which ends up in wastebaskets.
- Teachers neither insist on nor check for original work on projects, reports, or term papers and seem impressed by glitz rather than content in student submissions.

Identifying Missing Elements

- There are no CD-ROM discs, drives, or workstations in the school.
- Plans to acquire CD-ROM discs do not include proportionate workstation purchases.
- Student access to CD-ROM use has not been adequately thought through from budget implications to changed instruction requirements.
- Computers in the school are used mostly for programmed instruction and drill.
- No surge protectors are used.
- There is no system of allotting usage time.
- No clear instructions are visible regarding printing regulations, economic use of materials, or fees.

Possible solutions

- Decide who (and under what conditions) may change program discs or network access.
- Try to keep one network or program up and running at all times, such as an encyclopedia in elementary grades or indexes in secondary school.
- Use a color LCD or TV for large-group instruction, and provide one-on-one instruction as needed.
- Train capable students to assist peers.
- Initiate staff development programs to facilitate

proper use of CD-ROM references by both teachers and students.

COMPUTER MANAGEMENT FOR EDUCATIONAL USE

Computers have five purposes within the school library media center. The first is for the administrative functions of circulation, overdues, inventory, ordering, and cataloging. This calls for dedicated use of at least one, and perhaps more, computers.

The second purpose is to provide access to on-line catalogs for the school collection, regional networks, and/or fee-based databases. This function will require multiple terminals to replace the card style catalog and allow members of classroom groups to have simultaneous access to the indexing. The actual number of computers needed will depend on the extent and sophistication of the programs. If the collection index is an online catalog containing only the in-house collection, the decision will be determined by the number of students to have access at the same time, since each will need a terminal. If the collection index covers a number of collections, as in a regional network, the same access problem exists, but the capacity of the computer will have to be greater because of the greater number of entries. If the on-line index is that of a database such as Wilsonline, The Source, OCLC, or New York Times Information Bank, the decision will be based to a large extent on economics. How much of the subscription and use costs will the user be charged? Will a professional do the search for the student, to make more cost-effective use of computer time? In the latter instance, probably one terminal is all that would be used for each on-line service purchased.

The third computer-related task of the school library media center is to house computers and distribute them to individual classrooms in the same manner in which other pieces of hardware and equipment are handled. The machines are serviced, the users are instructed in their care and operation, and software is cataloged and circulated as needed by the school library media center staff.

The fourth purpose is to provide a computer lab in which a variety of computers and printers are available to students for use independently or in small groups from a classroom. The school library media teachers will be responsible for managing student use by supplying instruction, troubleshooting during use, controlling software used, and cooperating with classroom teachers to make certain that students are scheduled and receive the materials, practice, or instruction that the classroom teacher has prescribed for them. Sometimes a nonnprofessional or additional teacher has supervisory responsibilities for the lab.

A fifth computer function arises out of research requirements. The research hub contains not only CD-ROM-housed information but is also linked to informational networks around the world. (See modules on CD-ROMs and Networks in this chapter.)

Recognizing Positive Elements

- The school library media teachers have taken the lead in developing the computer program in the school, recognizing that the computer is simply one more aid to learning and, as such, should be available in and dispatched from the school library media center.
- There is a sign-up schedule for the use of the computers in the school library media center by teachers, classroom groups, or individual students.
- There is a pass form, used by teachers when send-

ing an individual or a small group of students to the school library media center to use computers. This includes directions to the school library media teacher regarding what software is needed and how long the student(s) may stay before returning to the classroom.

Recognizing Negative Elements

- Teachers do not feel comfortable using the equipment or making assignments for student use of computers.
- Computers remain unused in the school library media center being neither sent out to classrooms for use there nor used within the center under the school library media teachers' supervision.
- Students think of the computer only for playing recreational (as opposed to instructional) games.

Identifying Missing Elements

- There has been little or insufficient instruction of classroom teachers regarding the use of the computer as a learning or teaching tool.
- There has been little or insufficient instruction of classroom teachers regarding the use of the computer as an administrative tool to help them with records and grades.
- There has been no integration of computer use into the students' curricular activities.
- There has been insufficient purchase of computer programs to permit using the machines as learning tools for an entire class or for a range of subject areas and abilities.

Possible Solutions

- See to it that interested, skillful teachers who exhibit leadership potential are trained to use the computer creatively as a learning/teaching tool.
- Carry out staff development workshops until the entire staff is comfortable using computers for instructional purposes.
- Integrate the purchase of computer software into formal procedures for collection development and make plans to emphasize application of this medium for individualized instruction in higher-order cognitive skills and in given curricular areas.
- Encourage PTAs to raise funds for software or hardware in addition to what the system can budget.
- Develop a plan whereby volunteers can use computers to produce overdue lists, charts of math skills accomplished by students, or other management programs that aid education.

COMPUTER VIRUSES

Much is written on computer viruses, their different types, and the damage they can produce. Doubtless, new ones will be developed, because these viruses are created by human minds, as are the means of combating them. What is important for the administrator to know is that viruses exist, cause damage, and that steps must be taken to protect against virus damage. It is advisable to examine the avenues by which viruses can enter your computers and know that even brand-new programs are not immune.

Identifying Positive Elements

- Automatic virus checkers have been installed.
- Computers that contain highly important data are protected by having them programmed to save only to a disc rather than to the hard drive.
- Only authorized persons have access to the hard drive in school machines.
- All floppy discs are write-protected.
- A single computer serves solely for antivirus checking.
- All students use it before inserting their discs into any computer.

Identifying Negative Elements

- The practice of making and maintaining backup files is neither consistent nor current.
- Attitudes of personnel using school computers is uninformed or negligent.
- There is no computer setup to do antivirus protection.

Identifying Missing Elements

- Software is not run through a series of antivirus checkers before installation.
- No procedure has been designed to control haphazard use of unknown floppy software on school computers.

Possible Solutions

- Create a program for increasing users' information and sense of responsibility for protecting the school system's data.
- Acquire antivirus checking equipment, keep it reasonably current, and use it.
- Make certain all school personnel as well as students use it.
- Make sure that someone has the responsibility to keep up-to-date regarding the problem.

COMPUTER-ASSISTED CLASSROOM ADMINISTRATION

Electronic classroom management techniques go far beyond the gradebook concept. Although there are computer programs that test and enter the student's scores, there are better programs that permit teacher-created tests that have the advantage of being individualized for student use and also record their scores. There are also classroom management programs that support the portfolio approach to student achievement. These computer programs have the ability to preserve sound, pictures, video clips, and text, making possible a broader resume of student accomplishments and activities. The sound of the student reading a poem, a photograph of a sculpture the student created, a video of a dance performance, speech in foreign languages, or samples of written work, give a more complete picture of the student's growth. Student choices should be considered for inclusion in such a portfolio.

Identifying Positive Elements

- All teachers have their own computers on their desks.

- Training has been provided so that all teachers are comfortable and competent in electronic testing and portfolio preparation.
- Students are comfortable with these methods of assessing their work and appreciate the availability of documented progress.

Identifying Negative Elements

- Teacher insecurities were not addressed, which led to resistance.
- Response only to declared teacher interest has created a divisive atmosphere as well as inequities among the teachers and the students they serve.
- The electronic capabilities are available but are underutilized by including only gradebook type test scores or writing samples.

Identifying Missing Elements

- The concept of electronic portfolios has never been introduced.
- There is insufficient equipment to make the program viable.
- Peripherals such as scanners, digital cameras, video spigot needed to support the computer program capabilities are not available.

Possible Solutions

- Teacher training must be individualized to accommodate and match each teacher's own instructional style and needs.
- An employee or volunteer is available to transfer data into the electronic portfolios.

- Incorporate the use of portfolio documentation in parent conferences.

COMPUTER-ASSISTED LIBRARY
MEDIA CENTER ADMINISTRATION

Many clerical functions necessary for the smooth operation of the school library media center are performed more efficiently through the use of computers in the same manner that other building or systemwide operations are made more effective by their use. The use of the computer in school library media center management requires that personnel be trained in its use just as is the case in any office. When there is insufficient support staff, this can cause a problem. The school library media teacher will not have time during the school day to enter data. When there is insufficient staff on hand during the school day, it may be an option to pay someone to work after hours if the program is to function effectively.

Care must be taken to match the capabilities of a specific computer, the program selected, and the demands of the school library media program. Effective planning is required to make a smooth transition into computerized systems. It is important to realize that the transfer of records is accomplished only with the involvement of human beings. Equipment, people, time, and budget are all integral parts of the conversion program. All are essential to ultimate success.

School library media center functions that respond well to computerized methods include circulation of materials, listing overdues, creating on-line catalogs, placing orders, taking inventory, creating bibliographies, word processing, and creating signs and newsletters. These are all administrative functions and should not be confused with student use of the computer for educational purposes.

Recognizing Positive Elements

- Most school library media teachers have become comfortable with the use of computers and are eager to use them for administrative purposes.
- The materials and equipment collection inventories are entered onto computerized data files and backup copies are stored outside of the school building, safe from fire and other damage.
- Suitable utility discs have been purchased permitting the creation of data files, original catalog cards, and word processing which indicate that the personnel and program are ready to move forward to computerized circulation, on-line catalog, and reference networking.

Recognizing Negative Elements

- Requests have been made to include computers for use by the school library media teachers and staff, but they have been cut from the budget.
- The computers purchased are not properly maintained and so are unusable a good deal of the time.

Identifying Missing Elements

- The school library media teachers have shown no interest in the use of computers for any purpose at all.
- Inventorying of materials collection has not been done in too long a period because of the time required, and no one has realized how computerized circulation relates to computerized inventorying.
- The idea that a skilled student can create a suitable

computer program for the school library media center's need is proposed rather than budgeting for the purchase of a tested, commercially produced program.

Possible Solutions

- Recognize that computerized programs change rapidly, but that when the needs are completely and clearly identified, a suitable program can be purchased that will function successfully for some time. It is a mistake to wait for upgrading to halt before installing a computer program in the school library media center. Changes and improvements should be continuous.
- Visit other school library media centers where computerized functions are being used well and where the professionals are excited about the results, to learn how they work.
- If it proves impossible to acquire a school library media center computer through the budget process, initiate a fund-raising project specifically for the purpose.
- Begin by using one or two programs to build confidence in using computers for school library media center administrative functions, and develop from that point of introduction.
- Realize that "going online" will require entering complete cataloging information for every item in the collection into the computerized database. Frequently the school joins a network at the same time, which permits many improvements to be made during this conversion process. Investigate the conversion services that are available. Better results at

lower cost may be obtained by using these services than by using your own paid or volunteer help to do the conversion job.

- Remember that joining a network gives students access to significantly increased numbers of materials because of the pooling of resource listings in the database. It can also mean that interlibrary loan access is enlarged. For most schools, the process will raise the level of information available through the catalog. These are valuable improvements that become possible only because of computerized functions.

COPYING MACHINES

It is desirable to have a good quality copying machine located in the school library media center. Students rarely may use the office machine themselves, and easy copying of pages reduces dramatically the vandalism of tearing out pages and pictures. The machine should be capable of clearly reproducing pictures as well as print. Legitimate library media center copying includes duplicating short parts of reference materials in heavy demand, multiple entries found only in the same volume and needed by several students simultaneously, and illustrations and graphics.

On the other hand, copy centers in the school often have multiple and more sophisticated machines, as well as paid staff to do the copying. It is here that large runs are done. This system avoids misuse of the equipment and ensures less downtime and repair cost. Similarly, having a support staff person assigned to copy duty in the library media center will extend the service life of the equipment.

If the school system does not support free copying machine use, then a slightly-over-cost fee may be charged. In this way the cost of upkeep will be covered. In a busy school library media center enough money will be collected to pay for repairs and machine replacements as well. The machine can be self-supporting, but the fee per copy should be kept as low as possible to encourage student use. Arrangements for change-making and payments must be made. Sometimes coin operation devices are attached to the copying machine itself. Keeping a separate account for copying machine operations facilitates the assessment and evaluation of the copying machine service.

Recognizing Positive Elements

- There is a dependable copying machine in the school library media center that makes good copies of both print and pictorial material.
- Students as well as adults may use this machine, and do so frequently.
- If coin operated, the device is emptied daily, and monies are deposited in the office safe or with the finance officer.
- There is an IOU system established for students momentarily unprepared to pay the fee.
- There is a low level of vandalism evident in school library media center periodicals, newspapers, and books.
- Classroom teachers do not accept clipped pictures as illustrations for reports—only copies or drawings.

Recognizing Negative Elements

- Pages are often ripped from reference and popular books.
- Periodicals are constantly vandalized.

- The only copying machine is in the main office and it is unavailable to students, thereby causing teachers or other adults to spend time copying for student use.

Identifying Missing Elements

- No copying service is available to students within the school building.
- Teachers are not aware of how adversely their assignments affect the school library media center when members of several classes—or even all the members of just one class—are given assignments requiring the use of the same few reference tools and there are no copying facilities.

Possible Solutions

- A class gift, PTA, or other fund-raising event for the purpose of installing a copying machine in the school library media center is encouraged and supported.
- The budget includes money for lease or purchase of a copying machine to be placed in the school library media center.
- The budget provides a copy center that handles large runs.

DATABASE SEARCHING

Students who have access to the wide range of electronic learning tools will surely have access to databases among their choices. Their use is important when what they provide helps students learn better and teachers teach better.

However, the idea that the online database access will supplant much of what is already done by other means is not tenable. The significance of the database is its potential currency of information, as well as its varied range of types of information sources. Through the database there will be access to materials and current affairs services that the individual school library media center could never hope to subscribe to or own.

Electronic resources require careful evaluation just as non-electronic resources do. No single tool solves every information problem or best meets every information need. The database(s) chosen must mesh with the other resources available in the library media center, fill a gap, or create an extension of opportunity for the students. Having databases in the collection just to have them cannot be justified. Using them to provide access to a vastly expanded universe of information and opportunity to learn and practice lifelong problem-solving skills certainly can be. Regardless of technical changes in speed of response, breadth of information included, or other aspects of the equipment, the mental approaches used to deal with huge amounts of information are essential. They include cutting it into segments that are manageable and bear directly on the topic being studied without missing valuable material, and are the basis of a very important set of information literacy skills.

Identifying Positive Elements

- Students' work requires currency.
- Teachers use currency to enhance all aspects of their teaching.
- Database use is made selectively and interspersed with use of other information sources.
- Students apply Boolean logic, proximity searching, natural language processing, and relevance ranking

techniques to search multiple databases. They learn to add search terms or use truncation to enlarge searches and to select search terms judiciously to narrow their searches.

- A gradually increasing expectation of student use based on realistic goals is evident in the work being done by students.
- Students demonstrate application of serious evaluation when choosing among multiple electronic information tools.
- Students develop and apply strong, logical problem-solving skills.
- Database sources serve effectively in classes studying rapidly changing fields and for which there are no textbooks; e.g., advanced biology.
- Teachers have come to live with the unpredictability of what students will interject based on their electronic searching.
- Information tools serve as a link rather than a separation between the library media center and the classrooms.
- Classroom and library media teachers team to evaluate, teach, and use the most appropriate information sources available to solve student search problems.

Identifying Negative Elements

- Users believe that complete information on a topic is to be found in a database.

Identifying Missing Elements

- Students have established neither the keyboarding nor search planning skills needed to effectively use database information.

- Teachers have not had the opportunity to learn to use the tool in their teaching.

Possible Solutions

- Provide staff development instruction opportunities for teachers to learn best uses of database information.
- Initiate the search concept with the youngest students through use of CD-ROM sources.
- Incorporate learning keyboard skills in the lowest grades so that students may develop these skills as soon as they are suitably developed physically.
- Incorporate Boolean and evaluative search skills in introductory forms to youngest children and to others as needed.
- Plan to introduce database searching skills incrementally begining with students where they are. For example, high school freshmen may have come from literacy and learning-deficient backgrounds that mandate basic instruction.
- Establish a mentoring system among students to provide more assistance for students needing help in the lab.

DATABASES

Computer databases are compendia of information in picture, sound, or print format or any combination thereof. They may be purchased as a complete unit or as a continuing subscription with weekly, monthly, or annual updates. They may be programs to be installed in computers, on CD-ROM, or both. Databases may also be shared in a network. When considering the acquisition of access to a database, the size, power, and type of hardware requirements must be carefully examined. The frequency or amount of use a database will have should determine how many workstations will be set up to access it. In a school that makes many assignments requiring information from periodical or newspaper databases, for example, students may need access every hour of the day. Additional access workstations will need to be provided to meet increased demand.

When databases are provided as part of the library media center program, instruction in their use is required. Keyword searching is an indexing skill that needs to be in all areas of the curriculum and taught developmentally beginning in the primary grades. Instruction and practice are also necessary for effective searching of the library media center's electronic card catalog. Learning to be selective about requests from a database is extremely important. It has direct bearing on the cost of the search, whether it is online (and the school is paying for the time per request or at a set monthly rate) or leads to excessive use of computers, printers, and printouts. Business and industry recognize built-in costs but schools seldom do.

Recognizing Positive Elements

- The school has online, in-house and/or networked databases.
- Learning to make effective use of databases is evident in all areas of the curriculum at all grade levels.
- The databases are used with ease by students and staff because of ready access.
- There is ongoing observation and monitoring of database use to ensure equity and limit waste.
- Acquiring new and improved database access is an ongoing operation of the library media program.

Recognizing Negative Elements

- Workstations that provide database access are not added even when heavy demand indicates need.
- Only shared or networked databases are used. Those that require monetary commitments are not used.
- Neither students, faculty, administration, nor staff are given instruction in database searching.

Identifying Missing Elements

- There is no access to databases in-house, online, or networked.
- Neither the curricula nor assignments call for database searching.
- Although the faculty and administration recognize that some students have parents who provide them with database access, it is not seen as an equity issue by the school.

Possible Solutions

- A careful study should be made of what databases are available and at what cost (hardware, software, quantity needed, installation and upkeep), and budget accordingly.
- Plan for accompanying instruction in their use for students, faculty, administration, and staff.
- Assessment of the use made of databases should be done on a regular basis to determine needs, encourage proper use, and ensure equity.

DEMANDS OF TECHNOLOGY

Technology tools belong in the school library media center when they contribute to the overall library media program, to its administration through circulation and record keeping, and to students' learning opportunities. To be justified they must be used well; certainly not allowed to sit unutilized or be used simply for games and amusement, or for dull drill and practice. They offer many ways to develop higher-order thinking skills in the hands of skillful, energetic teachers.

Individual pieces of equipment should be identified for specific purposes and reserved for those uses just as some phone lines are given over to dedicated uses. Users need to be instructed in the use of both hardware and software. Attention should be given to how best to provide this instruction. Sometimes whole classes in the computer lab or hub is the answer. Sometimes small groups have a momentary need not shared by the entire class. Sometimes individuals need independent introduction to a specific function. It is certain that when group instruction is provided there will be need for individual follow-up and reinforcement.

The library media or classroom teacher may be available to provide the needed help to the student. There may be instructional guide posters in the lab or near the equipment in the library media center that will give cues. There may be individual learning packages prepared to provide step-by-step guidance in using the different types of equipment and materials so that students can have assistance any time they choose.

One of the pitfalls is the tendency to purchase software without a clear picture of how it will be used and what exactly it will contribute to students' learning. There is a huge difference between taking advantage of the computer's ability to branch and make nonlinear connections and programs that are just electronic versions of storybooks or workbooks. Everyone is faced with financial constraints that require thoughtful evaluation and selection of materials. When computer software is merely a replication of the book, at many times the cost, it is logical to use the printed text rather than the computer. Access to computers is limited and should emphasize use of programs that take full advantage of the capabilities of the computer. For example, the CD-ROM version of Macaulay's book *The Way Things Work* allows students to experience the added feature of motion when exploring how machines function. Connections can readily be made between the object and the scientific concepts involved along with the biographical information concerning the developer. This is in contrast to the Living Books or Discuss Books series which reproduce a story book. An audio tape listening station does nearly as much for a lot less cost. With limited funds the software purchased should emphasize open-ended utility programs that allow students to create graphs, spreadsheets, databases, and multimedia productions. Programs of this sort require students to think, organize information, and create a product rather than merely be entertained. This involves a higher level of teacher involvement in developing assignments. While there is a motivation factor to be gained through the use of computerized drill and practice programs, much of their educational value can be obtained through the use of less expensive formats.

Identifying Positive Elements

- Computers used for circulation and administrative functions are used for nothing else. Staff time is allowed before and after closing hours to set up or close down properly. Backup discs are routinely prepared.

- Some computers are assigned for word processing by either students or teachers.
- Sufficient computers are reserved for CD-ROM use. (See "CD-ROM" in this chapter.)
- Sufficient computers are reserved for indexing services.
- Software is selected for its excellence, not for merely having something in that format.
- Teachers make overall creative and demanding assignments for students fitted to individual needs. Electronic "workbooks" are avoided.

Identifying Negative Elements

- Insufficient computers are reserved for CD-ROM use so that there are long lines waiting for access.
- Discs are not properly cared for and there is no clear indication of who may change them or when they may be changed, if at all.
- Users change computer set-ups to accommodate their immediate needs and do not return to the original set-up upon leaving.
- Teachers prefer computer programs that fit in with the tradition of assigning students a given number of pages to work with; i.e., twenty minutes at the machine with an unclear educational purpose.

Identifying Missing Elements

- Staff development efforts have not stressed teaching with the kinds of software that call for creative teacher use.
- Little or no assessment or evaluation of teacher use of technology is made by the administration.

- Student computer output is not evaluated in terms of learning.
- Students receive little or no prompting or assistance in program use from staff, posted guides, or locally prepared independent learning packages.

Possible Solutions

- Make a thorough evaluation of the supply and use of technology in the school and especially in the library media center.
- Where improvement is needed, develop a materials selection program, a staff development program, and a plan for evaluating teacher and student outcomes.

ELECTRONIC MAIL

Use of electronic communication, or e-mail, has developed almost unaided. Internet has been discovered the world over as an easy introduction to telecommunications, one that is enjoyable and profitable in a learning sense. Because the mass of information distributed is not edited or controlled, users must quickly become aware that they are responsible for determining the accuracy, bias, or value of the ideas exchanged. Evaluation of sources is not a new concept regarding search techniques, just a frequently neglected one. However, learning/teaching opportunities abound.

E-mail has created an interactive global classroom for students and teachers. Connections are made with peers and with professional specialists. Simple research data can be compared and contrasted by classroom groups and expert advice can be obtained by advanced students regarding sophisticated inquiry. On a day-to-day basis helpful experiences are exchanged that make personal and educational problems shrink or disappear. Whether the e-mail correspondent is the recipient or the provider of the help, good feelings usually go along with the exchange.

Identifying Positive Elements

- Teachers use Internet to participate in educational exchanges with colleagues.
- Teachers use Internet to enhance classroom learning.
- Students are involved in e-mail exchanges with other students and helpful adults around the world.
- A systemwide approved network use policy is in effect.

Identifying Negative Elements

- A rigid schedule makes using e-mail difficult.
- Teachers and students are not sufficiently aware of the need to be evaluative concerning the content of e-mail messages.

Identifying Missing Elements

- E-mail plays no part in the school program.
- There is no board policy concerning student access to networked information resources, and no set of procedures, rules, or sanctions delineating student responsibilities.

Possible Solutions

- Institute flexible scheduling not only in the library media center but throughout the school day so that classes or parts of classes can have sufficient time to take advantage of e-mail exchanges.

- Encourage someone you know to send an e-mail message to a reluctant teacher or student through the library media center's e-mail address so that the hesitant ones will experience a personal encounter.
- Share some of the messages you read (printed out to begin with) with reluctant users, choosing ones that mesh with the classroom activity of the moment or as an extension of some element of the class curriculum.
- Demonstrate the potential for curriculum enhancement of such shared information as migratory trackings or keypal exchanges (like penpal exchanges) on an elusive or popular topic in order to help get teachers and students involved.

NETWORKS

Connecting the school to the world of information via computers is referred to as "networking." This is a modern term for the traditional concept of sharing. It means formalization of longtime informal practices. School library media teachers have always made independent and informal contacts with friends, colleagues, and other libraries to acquire the use of a specific title or item that was not available within their own collections. They continue to borrow privately for the benefit of their students, but they now have many formalized networking services to draw upon.

Membership in networks has budgetary implications because there are costs of copying pages and mailing them, sending entire books, or using computerized equipment and modem lines to transmit information. The idea that money is saved by belonging to a network because of the access afforded to materials in someone else's collection is incorrect. The network permits access to a wide range of materials, it is true, and therefore better service to users. Good planning may reduce redundancy in purchasing, and thereby recoup some dollars. However, materials do not "borrow" themselves and staff is needed to implement the borrowing and searching that users come to expect.

Schools may be members of local, state, regional, and national networks. Many have been participants in county systems for years. Some states are helping to fund the creation of a statewide network that includes every library in the state through the use of technology. Larger academic and municipal libraries can afford to purchase services such as OCLC, ERIC, or RLIN or even access to several databases offered by vendors, such as DIALOG and BRS. Networking can give schools these same advantages.

Because networking provides access to materials all across the United States (and beyond), and because some forms of networking are available to everyone, students must become knowledgeable about their use. It is not necessary to have access to databases in-house in order to provide useful preparatory instruction in their use. Prior to going online to conduct a search, much intelligent manual use of indexing, subject heading terminology, controlled vocabulary lists, and examining contents of databases must be done. These indexing skills should be a part of students' curriculum experiences, whether to be used with computerized databases or other resources of information such as books and periodicals.

The term *network*, whether used as a noun or as a verb, has many interpretations depending on the common understanding of speaker/listener or writer/reader. A network, in school library media center parlance, usually refers to some alliance of other libraries and the computerized listings of their collections. These cooperative libraries may be within the same school system, throughout the town, county, state, or region. The network enables their staffs and users to share services and information. Compatible hardware or interfaces are needed depending on the programming, number of participants, and distances involved. The Internet is an example of a network of networks made accessible in a number of ways. These are all networks linking the library media programs to others outside the school. A large amount of downtime on the network is probably a signal for needed upgrading.

Recognizing Positive Elements

- There is very little computer downtime.
- The library media center is networked with other libraries in the city, county, state, and beyond.
- Students and faculty regularly prepare and make searches using network access.
- Elementary students are introduced to basic indexing skills and Venn diagram concepts in the primary grades.

Recognizing Negative Elements

- Computers in the library media center are used only for circulation, cataloging, inventory, word processing, and/or CD-ROMs.
- Costs of database searching are too high because of insufficient instruction and practice in narrowing topics and using correct terminology.
- Membership in a network is underutilized because of lack of interest or information about services.
- There is insufficient feedback to the network re-

garding services that are needed or improving those that are being provided.

- Teachers who are computer users have been told to buy their own modems for home use in place of school access if they want to surf the net.

Identifying Missing Elements

- There is no staff technology teacher or technician.
- There is no overall technology plan involving the computers in the school at present or for the future.
- The school's wiring and the phone lines to classrooms are inadequate.
- There is no instruction given students that prepares them to use the expanded opportunities for locating materials through networks.
- There is no board policy in place concerning student use of networks.
- There is no opportunity within the school for students to make use of networking services.
- No consideration has been given to the educational values of networking by the school library media teachers or the administrators.

Possible Solutions

- Devise at once a technology plan, required by many states or individual school systems, involving the computer users of the school and with advice from state department of education experts, vendors, other school systems technology personnel, and business people.
- Wiring and phone lines necessary for networking should be installed with a view toward future growth and use, not just for immediate needs.

- Budget implications include replacement and up-grading costs, not just new purchases.
- Include in the curriculum K-12 opportunities to learn about the use of information networks.
- Work with the public or academic libraries in the area to develop a plan of access for students and faculty to networks and databases available through these agencies.
- Investigate network and database services that would be of benefit to the school and work toward budgeting for the acquisition of at least one basic service by the school library media center.

NETWORKS WITHIN THE SCHOOL

Within the school, all the computers in the building may be "networked" so that some or all software or programs are distributed over the network (for which an extra charge may be made by the manufacturer or publisher—referred to as "site license" or "network version") rather than on stand-alone computers. Through the setting of access privileges passwords can provide various levels of network security. Thus, access to some information such as student records or personnel files can be limited. Students, faculty, and staff may log-in from any terminal needing only their own data discs to which they may download information. Users may be given accounts on network file servers allowing for personal storage space on the network. They may also print on an attached printer or designated printer at specific locations. Information can be preset so that student users do not need passwords for ordinary use and their names will automatically bring up classroom or homeroom teacher, room number, graduating class, or whatever other information is considered useful in that school. Laptops and desktops located outside the school building may also access the network within the school and allow for faculty, administration, staff, students, parents, and community members to avail themselves of needed information via computers with modems.

Identifying Positive Elements

- All computers in the school are networked.
- The library media center collection on database is networked with the whole school.
- Students and faculty regularly use the network whenever they are in the school building or at home.

Identifying Negative Elements

- Computers in the school are mostly stand-alone stations; only the computer lab is networked.
- There are problems with limiting software use to specific individual classroom computers.
- Computers in the library media center are used only for the latter's management.
- Teachers who borrow school computers for home use cannot access the school's software unless they borrow that as well.

Identifying Missing Elements

- The wiring for in-school networking is inadequate.
- There are insufficient fileservers to network the school.

Possible Solutions

- Begin with a networked research learning hub within the library media center accessed by all students.
- Wire the entire building so that as computers are added they can be connected to the network.
- Make long-range plans for funding and/or search for grants and local partnerships to purchase equipment.

TELEVISION AND VIDEO

The impetuous young love affair with television in the 1960s has settled into a mature relationship in the 1990s. Where educators once saw television as the panacea for all educational ills, many are now enamored of personal computers, citing for the new technology the same expectations they had for its predecessor. While there is much less clamor for complete TV studios to be built in each school, there remain many good arguments for having one studio in the school system or in a region that serves all the member schools. Less expensive hand-held or mobile cameras can fulfill most instructional needs at the building level. Special programming can be provided through the systemwide or regional operations.

There are properties of television that are invaluable and unique. When teachers view tapes made of lessons they have given, they learn more about student reactions and weak points that need correction than a dozen checklists will tell them. Exciting events at the school, field trips taken, guest lecturers, poets or artists-in-residence can be recorded and enjoyed by those unable to attend the original activity, or enjoyed again by those who did. Edited versions of these recordings are cataloged and become part of the library media center collection.

When students learn the whys and hows of television through hands-on experience, they are less likely to be the uncritical audiences the TV programmers and advertisers have judged them to be. As students learn to recognize bias, innuendo, cliché, and opinion in books, magazines, and newspapers, they must also be able to identify these elements in the visual media. Videotapes of important historical events are among the primary resources vital to the school library media collection.

The videocassette player has had a tremendous impact on instructional processes because of the relative ease with which programs can be taped from commercial, educational, and cable offerings. This is an activity that must be monitored assiduously lest there be illegal use or copyright infringement.

Many school systems play an active role in local cable productions. Some use cable education channels to acquaint the communities served with what the schools are doing. But all educators need to keep up-to-date on what the national, state, and local regulations and developments are regardless of how active their schools are in local programming.

Identifying Positive Elements

- All TV equipment is the responsibility of the school library media center.
- The library media center keeps informed about upcoming commercial or cable programming and assists teachers and students with discussion, reading, and other means of reinforcing and extending the programs' learning potential.
- Records are kept of the amount of use made of all equipment.

- Provision is made for regular servicing and immediate repair.
- Visual literacy is a part of the approved curriculum.
- Copyright laws are adhered to.
- Videocassettes or videotapes that are retained in the collection are cataloged.

Identifying Negative Elements

- Television, like film, is not used for educational or instructional purposes relative to what is being studied.
- Students and teachers use television for its entertainment rather than educational or instructional features.
- Studios or TV production equipment remain largely unused.

Identifying Missing Elements

- There is little or no classroom preparation or follow-up on TV viewing.
- There has been little or no evaluation made of the cost effectiveness of TV use.
- Neither TV use nor visual literacy are incorporated in the general curriculum.
- No use is made of cable television opportunities.

Possible Solutions

- Evaluate the educational return being received from the school's investment in TV equipment.
- Make certain that all teachers know why, when, and how best to use television in their teaching.

- Investigate local cable television for offerings and opportunities that will benefit students.
- Make sure that adequate, competent personnel are responsible for integrating television into the curriculum, and provide staff development opportunities.

PART THREE
Appendixes

Appendix A
Sample Evaluation Forms:
Montgomery County Public Schools

COMPARISON OF EVALUATION CRITERIA
USED FOR LIBRARY MEDIA TEACHERS AND
CLASSROOM TEACHERS

The Department of Personnel Services of Montgomery County (Md.) Public Schools has developed different criteria for evaluating library media teachers and classroom teachers. The two forms used are identical except for the *criteria* used for evaluation of the two types of teachers and the *indicators of effective performance.*

A comparison of the lists of performance criteria follow: Numbers 1, 6, 7, 9, and 10 (as shown on the Media Specialist Services form) use the same wording. Numbers 2, 3, 4, 5, and 8, although similar, reflect differences. There is an added number 11 for the media specialist. The different wording used on the classroom teacher's form follows:

2. Establishes learning objectives consistent with appraisal of student needs, requirements of MCPS curriculum framework, and knowledge of human growth and development.
3. Plans and provides for involvement of students in the learning process.
4. Plans for and uses those instructional methods that

motivate and enable each student to achieve learning objectives.

5. Plans for and utilizes those resources that motivate and enable each student to achieve learning objectives.

8. Appraises his/her own effectiveness and demonstrates successful application of skills and information acquired to increase effectiveness.

Evaluation of Media Specialist Services
Department of Personnel Services
Montgomery County Public Schools
Rockville, Md.

Name, (Last, First) Date (-) First Year in County (-) Tenure (-) After Tenure (every 3rd year) (-) Tenure (if AP or SP Certificate)
Position Location (-) Other

Soc. Sec. No./Grade/Step/LonE/Cert.Type/Cert.Class/Date issued/Date expires

A. Objectives jointly developed by the Media Specialist and the Evaluator for the current year:

1. Objectives
2. Evidence of Attainment

B. Performance Criteria Evaluation

Performance Criteria Supporting Statement

Effective

Needs Improvement

Not Effective

1. Appraises student learning levels, interest, and needs (-) (-) (-).

2. Directs, organizes, and supervises the personnel and services essential to a unified media program (-) (-) (-).

3. Directs, organizes, and supervises resources and facilities essential to a unified media program (-) (-) (-).

4. Assumes responsibility for evaluating, selecting, and acquiring materials and equipment to support the instructional program and to meet the varied interests, abilities, and maturity levels of the students served (-) (-) (-).

5. Participates in the planning, development, and implementation of the school program of instruction (-) (-) (-).

6. Plans for and utilizes evaluation techniques that measure the effectiveness of the media program to determine which practices or objectives to maintain or modify (-) (-) (-).

7. Establishes and maintains a media center environment that motivates and enables students and teachers to use the facilities and resources to attain instructional

and personal objectives (-) (-) (-).

8. Appraises the effectiveness of his/her teaching practices, managerial practices, and instructional program not only in terms of achieving personal objectives but also in terms of the total school instructional program (-) (-) (-).

9. Participates in school management activities related to policies, regulations, and general school atmosphere (-) (-) (-).

10. Establishes relationships with colleagues, students, parents, and community that reflect recognition of and respect for every individual (-) (-) (-).

11. Identifies areas for growth necessary to maintain or improve effectiveness, acquires appropriate training or information, and demonstrates successful application (-) (-) (-).

C. Additional Information.
Name of second observer as required for probationary media specialist only:

D. Overall Evaluation (including suggestions for further training).

Dates of observations and Conferences: Observations Conferences

List dates of classroom observations of at least 20 minutes and/or conferences with the media specialist on which this evaluation is based and for which notes are filed in the school (and will be held for 6 months after this evaluation is received by Professional Personnel office).

E. Recommendation (Check one).

(-) Continued Employment

(-) Dismissal Date

(-) Non-Renewal of Contract

(-) Second Class Certificate

F. Signatures.

Evaluator(s) - Date -

*Person Evaluated - Date -

*By signing this evaluation,

G. Comments of person evaluated. The employee verifies the record of the observations and conferences but does not necessarily have to agree with the contents. If he or she wishes, comments may be added.

H. Date received in the Department of Personnel Services: MCPS Form 430–79, April 1975,

Information Found on Reverse Side of Evaluation of Media Specialist Services Form

Both pages of this form provide the framework for the evaluation of media specialist services. The form is completed according to the instructions below.

Instructions

A. Objectives jointly developed by the Media Specialist and the Evaluator for the current year.

    1. Objectives: Each year the media specialist and evaluator jointly develop one or more objectives. The objectives for the school year in which the media specialist's performance is to be evaluated are recorded on this form. These objectives are derived from an analysis of the media specialist's performance and should be relevant to at least one of the performance criteria. They should also contribute to achievement of school program improvement objectives.

    2. Evidence of Attainment: Enter a summary statement describing the meeting of the objectives set forth in Item A-1. above.

B. Performance criteria evaluation.
Media specialist performance is evaluated in relation to the eleven (11) criteria listed on the reverse side of page 2. Indicators for each performance criterion are provided as guides for data collection by observers and by the media specialist. Based upon the evidence collected, the evaluator indicates the media specialist's effectiveness in meeting each criterion as follows:

Effective. The criterion is attained and the quality is consistently acceptable, ranging from acceptable through exceptional. Note exceptional performance as such; give
specific facts that identify exceptional results achieved
with students or impact upon the school program.

Needs Improvement. The quality of the attainment of the
criterion is not consistently acceptable.

Not Effective. The criterion is not attained. #(-) # Must
be accompanied by a supporting statement identifying
recommended improvements.

(-) The criterion must become an objective of the media
specialist for the following year, with the completed work
sheet (MCPS Form 425–121) entered into the media
specialist's permanent personnel records.

C. Additional information.
   List media specialist's assignments for the period since
   the last evaluation and any other information that adds
   another dimension to the media specialist's performance.

D. Overall evaluation.
   After a careful analysis of the information reported in A,
   B, and C record a summary statement of the media
   specialist's performance, and as appropriate, suggestions
   for further training.

E. Recommendations.
   The evaluator determines the recommendations to be
   made, using the following standards:

   1. If a media specialist's performance is deemed effec-

tive or needing improvement on all but four (4) or fewer of the criteria, the recommendation must be Continued Employment.

2. For the media specialist whose performance is deemed not effective on five (5) or more of the criteria, the recommendation must be for Non-renewal of Contract (probationary media specialist only), Second Class Certificate, or Dismissal (tenured media specialist only) because the overall performance of the media specialist is deemed not satisfactory.

Performance Criteria and Indicators of Effective Performance: Media Specialist

1. Appraises student learning levels, interests, and needs indicators:

   a. Consults with teachers, counselors, or specialists.

   b. Maintains communication with media specialists who have worked, or will be working, with the same student(s) in MCPS.

   c. Observes students as a group and consults with them individually.

   d. Establishes and maintains procedures whereby students are able to communicate concerns and utilizes resultant data.

   e. Gathers information from student records, when necessary.

    f. Utilizes appropriate diagnostic tools to determine student media skill competencies.

    g. Analyzes circulation records and other pertinent data to determine needs and interests of the students and faculty.

2. Directs, organizes, and supervises the personnel and services essential to a unified media program.

Indicators:

    a. Provides leadership for the involvement of students and staff in the development of written guidelines and procedures for governing the services and uses of the media center and school media program.

    b. Provides in-service opportunities for students and staff.

    c. Defines, assigns, and supervises the duties of media center staff and volunteers.

    d. Assesses competencies of media center staff and provides opportunities for growth.

    e. Participates in the evaluation of instructional materials aides and equipment aides.

    f. Works with principal and staff to establish and administer local school procedures regarding acquisition, processing, distribution, circulation, and inventory of media materials and equipment.

g. Involves principal and staff in devising an effective loan system and implements MCPS circulation policies that provide maximum availability of all materials and equipment.

h. Communicates with students, teachers, and parents about the media program's guidelines and procedures, services, and new materials.

i. Consults with area and central office personnel on items such as policies and procedures, summer assignments, or renovations.

3. Directs, organizes, and supervises resources and facilities essential to a unified media program.

Indicators:

a. Plans a tentative media budget after consulting with the faculty, students, and administration about the instructional materials and equipment needs of the school.

b. Manages expenditures from the media center account and coordinates uses of this account with other accounts within the school (such as textbooks, instructional materials, equipment, reading, and special education) and follows the MCPS ordering cycles for materials and supplies.

c. Participates in the design, development, and writing of proposals for acquisition for local, state, or federal funds to support and extend the media program.

    d. Coordinates maintenance and repair of media materials and equipment to insure maximum utilization by and safety of students and staff.

    e. Takes initiative to see that educational media (materials and equipment) are inventoried, classified, or cataloged regardless of where they are housed or how acquired.

    f. Directs and is responsible for maintenance of media center records regarding inventory of holdings, budget, circulation, use of media center, and equipment repair.

    g. Coordinates the use of the media center facilities and provides accessibility to materials and equipment.

    h. Prepares and submits monthly activities reports and annual local, state, and federal reports as well as special reports when required.

4. Assumes responsibility for evaluating, selecting, and acquiring materials and equipment to support the instructional program and to meet the varied interests, abilities, and maturity levels of the students served.

Indicators:

    a. Follows MCPS policies and procedures (MCPS Regulation 365–3) for evaluating, selecting, and ordering materials and equipment and regularly communicates these policies and procedures to both students and staff, and to the community, as needed.

    b. Utilizes professional reviewing media and visits the Division of Evaluation and Selection (DEMAT) a minimum of one-half day monthly to examine new materials.

    c. Utilizes media selection tools, courses of study, curriculum guides, and subject bibliographies to select instructional materials.

    d. Develops cooperatively with students and staff procedures for the evaluation and selection of materials and equipment in the local school.

    e. Assesses the collection with the assistance of the students and the faculty to identify areas that need development and items that need to be replaced, duplicated, or withdrawn.

5. Participates in the planning, development, and implementation of the school program of instruction.

Indicators:

    a. Assists in identifying the interests and needs of both students and staff for the purpose of continuous program planning.

    b. Participates in planning for curriculum implementation and/or innovation.

    c. Coordinates the implementation of the MCPS media research and communications skills program in the school.

d. Consults with students and staff in the selection and utilization of materials and equipment.

e. Communicates to students and staff, through orientation and relevant instruction, information regarding materials, equipment, and services available in the media center.

f. Utilizes instructional methods designed to motivate and enable students to achieve learning objectives.

g. Cooperates in the implementation of learning activities within the media center designed to meet a variety of needs, interests, and abilities.

h. Provides instruction for students and staff in production techniques and operation of equipment.

I. Assists students and staff in designing and producing materials to achieve instructional objectives.

j. Provides access to MCPS materials housed outside the local school; i.e., film library, EML, area-based resources.

k. Directs students and staff to available community resources.

l. Notifies the public library staff of student information needs.

m. Notifies the students and staff of cultural, educational, and recreational opportunities.

6. Plans for and utilizes evaluation techniques that measure the effectiveness of the media program to determine which practices or objectives to maintain or modify.

Indicators:

   a. Plans and conducts periodic evaluation of specific aspects of the media program with the assistance of students, staff, and community.

   b. Evaluates new services to determine their effectiveness.

   c. Uses available evaluative criteria in assessing the program.

   d. Solicits cooperation of the faculty in evaluating programs of students in media skills development.

7. Establishes and maintains a media center environment that motivates and enables students and teachers to use the facilities and resources to attain instructional and personal objectives.

Indicators:

   a. Organizes media center facilities to provide appropriate work areas for a variety of activities.

   b. Organizes materials and equipment through a system of cataloging, classifying, and indexing that will facilitate accessibility for the user.

   c. Adjusts physical arrangements and/or modifies noise levels in order to provide for a variety of learning styles and activities.

   d. Follows and expects students to use democratic procedures that show consideration for the rights of others.

   e. Plans and provides for a pleasing, attractive environment.

   f. Deals promptly with behavior that may be detrimental to the health or physical safety of others.

8. Appraises the effectiveness of his/her teaching practices, managerial practices, and instructional program not only in terms of achieving personal objectives but also in terms of the total school instructional program.

   Indicators:

   a. Assesses each lesson and/or unit in terms of student response to the techniques, activities, and materials, and also in terms of student attainment of the objectives.

   b. Uses results of lesson and/or unit assessments to continue to modify his/her instructional program and to plan further teaching-learning activities.

   c. Evaluates short-range achievement of objectives and long-range progress toward goals of the instructional program.

   d. Works with colleagues and students to evaluate the total program's effectiveness.

9. Participates in school management activities related to policies, regulations, and general school atmosphere.

   Indicators:

   a. Participates in the development and review of school guidelines and regulations.

   b. Observes school system policies and legal regulations.

   c. Cooperates with colleagues and students to maintain good atmosphere.

   d. Shares ideas, materials, and methods with other teachers.

   e. Encourages special interest activities for students and staff.

   f. Cooperates in relating school activities to community needs.

   g. Shares responsibility for care of equipment and facilities.

10. Establishes relationships with colleagues, students, parents, and community that reflect recognition of and respect for every individual.

    Indicators:

    a. Utilizes such human relations techniques as acceptance, praise, and humor when appropriate.

b. Maintains objectivity in relations with others.

c. Maintains a positive attitude in working situations.

d. Fosters an open atmosphere in which others feel free to express themselves.

e. Listens and responds to the concerns of others.

f. Cooperates in making the community feel a part of the school.

g. Communicates effectively with the community about the school and the Montgomery County Public Schools.

11. Identifies areas for growth necessary to maintain or improve effectiveness, acquires appropriate training or information, and demonstrates successful application.

Indicators:

a. Applies knowledge and skills gained from coursework, conferences, workshops, in-service activities, travel, or other enrichment activities.

b. Reads professional and other published materials pertinent to the profession or specific subject areas to improve instruction.

c. Participates in organizations or conferences supportive of professional responsibilities.

d. Demonstrates awareness of current events and cultural trends.

e. Seeks MCPS or area services available to help increase personal effectiveness.

f. Appraises own professional growth using data related to professional coursework, in-service activities, and professional reading.

g. Takes advantage of opportunities to learn from colleagues, students, parents, and community.

Performance Criteria and Indicators of Effective
Performance: Classroom Teacher

1. Appraises student learning levels, interests, and needs.

Indicators:

a. Uses information in cumulative folders and in other school records.

b. Uses individual and group observations.

c. Consults with parents.

d. Selects and utilizes appropriate diagnostic instruments (MCPS standardized and teacher-made).

e. Surveys students as a group, and consults with them individually.

f. Consults with previous teachers, team teachers, and/or specialists.

g. Makes referral to EMT based on appropriate assessment of student needs.

2. Establishes learning objectives consistent with appraisal of student needs, requirements of MCPS curriculum framework, and knowledge of human growth and development.

    Indicators:

    a. Follows the Program of Studies in appropriate subject areas as it relates to units of instruction, objectives, time allocations, and skills.

    b. States instructional objectives in terms of student behaviors.

    c. Establishes performance objectives for class and homework assignments in each unit and instructional activity.

    d. Establishes performance objectives for affective, cognitive, and psychomotor outcomes.

    e. Develops different performance objectives for each group of students based on ability and achievement, experience, vocational goals, and cultural values.

    f. Incorporates in daily planning content and skills of previous levels for reinforcement and anticipates content and skills of future grade levels to insure continuity and sequence.

    g. Maintains balance among various subject areas and within the subject itself.

    h. Collaborates with other teachers in coordinating objectives for the student's total program.

3. Plans and provides for involvement of students in the learning process.

   Indicators:

   a. Helps students understand performance objectives, procedures, activities, and the evaluative process.

   b. Encourages students to suggest interest areas, plan classroom activities, and evaluate units of instruction and the course.

   c. Works with students to establish and carry out classroom rules and procedures.

   d. Expects and encourages students to use all class time on learning tasks.

   e. Assists students in organizing their work so that they learn how and when to work independently and how and when to seek help.

   f. Provides opportunities for students to demonstrate critical and reflective thinking, resourcefulness, responsibility, and creativity.

   g. Organizes the class to encourage student leadership and develop student skill in group decision-making.

   h. Solicits and accepts honest feedback from students including "The Mutual and Reciprocal Evaluation."

4. Plans for and uses those instructional methods that motivate and enable each student to achieve learning ob-

jectives and interest by varying the difficulty of experiences, by differentiating instruction and assignments, and by allowing students to pursue topics independently.

   b. Helps students develop efficient learning skills and work habits.

   c. Uses a variety of appropriate teaching techniques, avoiding excessive use of any one technique.

   d. Communicates clearly and correctly in speech and writing and encourages and expects students to do the same.

   e. Conveys sense of enthusiasm.

   f. Demonstrates flexibility by responding to immediate learning needs of students.

   g. Demonstrates knowledge of the subject matter and of human growth and development.

   h. Reexamines and adjusts teaching strategies when students are experiencing learning difficulties.

   i. Makes every effort to devote additional time necessary to meet student needs even though it may require more time than the normal work day.

5. Plans for and utilizes those resources that motivate and enable each student to achieve learning objectives.

   Indicators:

   a. Utilizes and encourages students to utilize a variety of reference and other printed materials.

b. Utilizes and encourages students to utilize nonprint and audiovisual materials.

c. Utilizes media center resources including securing instruction for students in media center skills.

d. Utilizes human and material resources in community and school.

e. Makes use of the physical school environment to support current learning activities.

f. Consults with area and central office personnel and arranges for their working with students.

6. Plans for and utilizes evaluation techniques that motivate and enable each student to achieve learning objectives.

Indicators:

a. Follows MCPS guidelines for evaluation of student work as outlined in policy on Grading Reporting.

b. Uses evaluation methods, materials, and standards for each unit consistent with performance objectives and instructional activities.

c. Uses prompt, frequent, and accurate feedback in class to make learning tasks meaningful.

d. Evaluates clearly and accurately all tests and assignments and returns them promptly.

e. Reviews with students each test and assignment before assessing the same objectives again.

    f. Shows students how and gives them opportunities to analyze, evaluate, and revise their own work.

    g. Allows students to demonstrate achievement of objectives in a variety of ways.

    h. Confers with students not making progress to bring about improvement and informs parents as appropriate.

    i. Collaborates with other professional staff members to develop common and fair standards for evaluating students' work.

7. Establishes and maintains the environment required to motivate and enable each student to achieve learning objectives.

Indicators:

    a. Follows and expects to use democratic procedures that show consideration for the rights of others.

    b. Utilizes appropriate behavior-management strategies.

    c. Follows school disciplinary procedures and works cooperatively with students, parents, and administrators to implement these procedures.

    d. Maintains a classroom atmosphere conducive to good health and safety.

e. Adjusts physical arrangements and modifies noise levels in order to provide for a variety of learning styles.

f. Selects activities appropriate to the physical attributes of the work area.

g. Follows MCPS policy on Students Rights and Responsibilities.

8. Appraises his/her own effectiveness and demonstrates successful application of skills and information acquired to increase effectiveness.

Indicators:

a. Assesses each lesson and unit in terms of student response to the techniques, activities, and materials in terms of student attainment of the objectives.

b. Uses results of lesson and unit assessments to continue or modify his/her instructional program and to plan further teaching-learning activities.

c. Evaluates both long-range progress toward goals and short-range achievement of objectives of classroom activities.

d. Works with colleagues, including administrators and supervisors, to evaluate the total program's effectiveness.

e. Uses MCPS resources available to improve instruction.

f. Participates in organizations and conferences supportive of instructional responsibilities.

g. Applies knowledge gained from travel, course work, reading, and other enrichment activities.

9. Participates in school management and shares responsibility for the total school program.

Indicators:

a. Participates in the development and review of school policies and regulations.

b. Observes school policies and legal regulations.

c. Encourages habits of good citizenship and good behavior and works with students to reduce vandalism.

d. Enforces Board policies relating to pupils and unauthorized visitors in the building and on school grounds.

e. Cooperates with colleagues and students to maintain good atmosphere.

f. Shares ideas, materials, and methods with other teachers.

g. Encourages special interest activities with community needs.

h. Shares responsibility for care of equipment and facilities.

10. Establishes relationships with colleagues, students, parents, and community that reflect recognition of and respect for every individual.

Indicators:

a. Demonstrates sensitivity to individuals who are of another race, culture, religion, sex, or are handicapped.

b. Utilizes such human relations techniques as acceptance, praise, and humor when warranted.

c. Puts problems in perspective.

d. Responds positively to challenges.

e. Fosters an open atmosphere in which others feel free to express themselves.

f. Listens and responds to the concerns of others.

g. Seeks to make the community feel a part of the school.

h. Communicates effectively with the community about the school and the Montgomery County Public Schools.

i. Uses MCPS [sources] available to address human relations issues.

[Note: Section 1, f; Section 3, f; Section 4, b; Section 5, a, b, c; Section 6, i; and Section 9, h of the classroom teacher's Indicators List involve utilization of the School Library Media Program and teacher.]

Appendix B
Sample Job Description and Job Function Documents

There is substantial difference in the content of job description and job function documents. Both are needed because they serve different purposes. The following sample job description and job function documents are included here to illustrate the difference in content and wording (see "Job Description Documents" in chapter 3). The first set is from a computerized secondary school. The second set is for an elementary school. The third set is for a media clerk or aide and includes a sample for a manual operation as well as a computerized one. Both sets are included because each illustrates the differences these documents may take on when written for different schools, and thereby emphasizes the need to tailor the documents to the library media center operation they are describing—an aim of this section.

PART I: SECONDARY SCHOOL

Library Media Specialist, Grades 7–12: Job Description

Major Responsibilities: Organization and Management

Demonstrated ability to:

- organize and maintain an orderly and efficient physical arrangement of library media furnishings, equipment, and collection holdings;
- develop and implement documentation that identifies library media program philosophy, goals, objectives, activities, operating policies, collection development procedures, and management procedures;
- supervise students in the library media center setting;
- develop and maintain a library media collection of print and nonprint resources correlated with the school's curricula and with students' identified information needs;
- develop and maintain daily operating procedures to provide for optimum student access to the library media center and for orderly use of its resources and facilities;
- maintain a card catalog providing access to all library media materials, according to professional standards;
- maintain an efficient and accurate circulation and inventory control system, and manage the clearance of student obligations for borrowed materials;
- direct the acquisition and optimum use of advanced instructional media and information technologies

consistent with the needs of post–high-school education and employment;

- develop and implement an annual budget, applying district-approved procedures for the acquisition of library media materials, equipment, and furnishings;
- conduct formal and informal evaluation of the library media program and use of resources, and implement revisions as necessary to redirect program offerings.

Major Responsibilities: Instructional Development and Teaching

Demonstrated ability to:

- consult with teachers and department heads, participating in curriculum development at the building-wide, department, and classroom levels;
- collaborate with teachers in the development and application of instructional projects and activities, integrating library media resources and information into course content;
- develop a comprehensive information curriculum providing instruction in the access, retrieval, evaluation, and application of information from multiple sources;
- instruct students—individually, in small groups, or as whole classes—in the access, selection, and effective use of library media materials, and in the development of assigned teachers' projects;
- instruct the use of instructional media technology for optimum information retrieval;
- develop and conduct a program to motivate a life-long interest in reading for pleasure and for seeking information for continuing self-education;

- work successfully with a schoolwide faculty and administration to meet the instructional goals and objectives of the school.

Library Media Specialist, Grades 7–12: Job Functions

The functions listed below are in alphabetical order; at any given time in the work day or work year, priorities can and do change for the provision of specific functions.

Budget Planning and Management

- Prepare priority lists of library media resources for potential purchase, linked to curricular needs;
- consult with department heads and staff members to determine or to verify curricular/instructional requirements for library media materials;
- determine proposed budget request levels and allocations, consistent with library media program needs and curricular implementation;
- develop budget request documentation as per the current district-wide budget planning process;
- determine purchase priorities with respect to the level of materials account budgeting approved by the Board of Education, upon receipt of B of E office documentation assigning budget amounts;
- prepare data for typing of requisitions for purchase of specific library media resources;
- maintain a file folder and a computer database managing the budget-accounting process—including copies of requisitions and corresponding purchase orders, receipt and verification of ordered materials, supplies and equipment, sign-off of Purchase Or-

ders, and cumulative encumbrances on account balances.

Cataloging and Media Organization

- Prepare original cataloging worksheets for all purchased and donated library media materials (descriptive cataloging, subject heading analysis, and Dewey Decimal Classification, prepared in MARC tagging format);
- correlate cataloging of newly accessioned materials with existing items within the library media materials collection;
- organize the shelving and display of all library media collection materials for efficient access by users;
- reorganize the shelving and display of collection materials as library media program priorities are modified;
- weed outdated or damaged materials on a periodic basis, as funding allows for the replacement of collection materials.

Computer Technology Management, Supervision, and Maintenance

- Develop long-range plans for the applications and acquisition of computer technology in the library media center, for information retrieval and organization and library media program and library media center management;
- organize procedures for the effective and efficient use of computer technology by students and staff, in retrieving and organizing information;
- evaluate, select, and acquire equipment according to professional models, to meet the needs of library

media programming, consistent with existing computer equipment;

- supervise the use of computer equipment to insure proper techniques of operation by all users;
- maintain the physical condition of library media center and computer laboratory computer equipment;
- maintain the physical security of library media center equipment against theft.

Instruction in Uses and Applications of Library Media Center Resources and Equipment

- Plan and provide "point-of-need" instruction for whole classes in the availability and uses of library media. Are sources relevant to ongoing subject-area assignments or projects?
- provide instruction in the use of the index to periodicals and its varied databases for whole classes and individual students;
- demonstrate the information sources provided via CD-ROM technology;
- assist students in the use of the microfilm reader.

Instructional Design and Curricular Integration of Library Media Resources

- Develop systematic instructional packages for curricular-linked information search, describing the rationales, objectives, procedures, criteria, and library media resources required for a given assignment, with or for subject-area teachers;
- develop instruction sheets or packages describing procedures for efficient and effective location, evaluation, and retrieval of information from diverse types of library media resources.

Library Media Center Facilities Organization and Management

- Evaluate periodically the physical layout and organization of the library media center, including shelving arrangement, furniture, and equipment, to provide for modifications in programming and facilities use;
- rearrange shelving, furniture, and equipment as needed to implement modifications in programming and services.

Library Media Center Supervision

- Develop policies to guide the behavior of students using library media center facilities, appropriate such as to promote the most effective use of facilities and the most conducive work environment for *all* students;
- monitor the daily use of the library media center to promote cooperataive, positive use of library media center facilities and resources;
- develop policies and procedures for access to the library media center and recordkeeping of daily attendance, period-by-period.

Library Media Clerk Supervision

- Develop specific descriptions of clerical job functions;
- prioritize job functions of the library media clerk, as needed—daily, weekly, monthly, or by marking period;
- retrain, as necessary, to improve the library media clerk's skills in specific job functions.

Library Media Program Management

- Develop policies and procedures to define the operations and services of the library media center;
- prepare, and revise as necessary, a library media program manual for inclusion in the schoolwide faculty handbook describing program and service offerings;
- prepare and revise as necessary, a "Library Media Center" section in the student handbook describing library media center services, policies, and procedures as they affect students.

Library Media Resource Evaluation, Selection, and Acquisition

- Maintain a "consideration file" to assist in planning for the purchase of library media resources;
- consult with department heads and staff members regarding curricular needs and related recommendations for the acquisition of library media resources;
- consult professional guides that evaluate library media resources, to provide data in selecting resources for purchase;
- meet with sales representatives and vendors to determine the availability and contents of print and nonprint information resources or the quality and functions of equipment;
- attend professional conferences viewing new materials and typing up notes on meetings and workshops to share with other library media teachers and/or staff;
- determine long-term (multiple year) and short-term (single year) priorities for the acquisition of library media resources;

- prepare data for typing requisitions for the purchase of library media resources.

Periodicals Ordering, Processing, and Maintenance

- Develop an annual list of periodicals for acquisition and display, linked to curricular usage, students' recreational reading, and professional usage;
- determine current costs for periodical titles from the current vendor;
- prepare data for typing a requisition for the purchase of an annual list of periodicals;
- manage a database to verify the receipt and expiration dates of new and renewal titles of periodicals; prepare data for communication to the current vendor regarding duplicate or missing issues of periodicals;
- prepare data for communication to the current vendor regarding duplicate or missing issues of periodicals;
- revise, as needed, a backfiling system for storage of, and access to, all periodicals.

Services to Nonteaching Staff

- Supervise and train library media clerks;
- recruit, train, and supervise volunteers.

Services to Students

- Assist or instruct students in using the computer to search for periodical articles on a given topic;
- assist students in locating and retrieving information from CD-ROM data discs;
- assist students in selecting and evaluating LMC resources for a class project or assignment;

- instruct students in the drafting of bibliographic entries to cite library media resources in class projects or assignments;
- assist students in the drafting of thesis statements as may be required for term papers or class projects;
- assist students in interpreting or analyzing the objectives of specific class projects or assignments;
- provide services for photocopy reproduction of all library media resources;
- provide services for reproduction of periodical articles.

Services to Teaching Staff

- Prepare selected bibliographies of resources available on a given topic;
- develop instruction packets for subject-area assignments, linking library media resources to assignment contents;
- develop group-teaching materials for library media information skills instruction;
- recommend library media resources for application to class assignments or projects;
- collaborate in planning subject-area lessons;
- provide for the acquisition of library media materials upon recommendation from a staff member or a department.

[NOTE: Used by permission. Dr. Michael D. Leahy, Eastern High School Library Media Center, Bristol, Conn.]

PART 2: ELEMENTARY SCHOOL

Library Media Specialist, Grades K-6: Job Description

Nature and scope of position: Develops and maintains the library media collections, equipment, and programs for the school.

Major Responsibilities: Organization and Management

Demonstrated ability to:

- involve administrators and teachers in developing flexible scheduling;
- develop physical facilities to accommodate library media center resources and instructional services;
- develop and implement documentation that identifies goals, objectives, activities, collection development procedures, and management procedures for the operation of the school library media program;
- develop and maintain library media collections of print and nonprint resources correlated with the school's curriculum and with students' identified information needs;
- develop and implement procedures for students' access to, and their supervision within, the library media center;
- develop and maintain indexing to provide access to all library media materials, according to professional standards;
- maintain an efficient and accurate circulation and inventory control system for the library media center, and manage the clearance of student obligations for borrowed materials;
- supervise the management of adult volunteer services in the library media center;

- develop and implement an annual budget for the library media center, applying district-approved procedures for the acquisition of library media materials, equipment, and furnishings;
- conduct formal and informal evaluation of the library media program and use of resources, and implement revisions as necessary to redirect program offerings.

Major Responsibilities: Instructional Development and Teaching

Demonstrated ability to:

- consult with teachers and elementary school administrators, participating in curriculum development at the buildingwide and classroom levels;
- collaborate with teachers in the development and application of instructional projects and activities integrating library media resources and information into classroom curricular content;
- develop a comprehensive information curriculum providing instruction in the access, retrieval, evaluation, and application of information from multiple sources;
- instruct students—individually, in small groups, or as whole classes—in the access, selection, and effective use of library media materials and in the development of assigned teachers' projects;
- develop and conduct a program to motivate a lifelong interest in reading for pleasure and for seeking information, with students of grades K through 6;
- work successfully with a schoolwide faculty and administration to meet the instructional goals and objectives of the school.

PART 3: LIBRARY MEDIA CLERK AND CIRCULATION DESK AIDE

Library Media Clerk: Job Functions

Computerized System

The functions listed below, under the given categories, are not listed by priority. At any given time in the work day or work year, priorities can and do change, for the provision of specific functions. It is expected that skills and technologies new to the library media clerk will be learned and mastered in a timely fashion.

Working Philosophy and Policy

- Know and support the implementation of library media center philosophy, policy, and operating procedures statements, as presented in the faculty handbook and the student handbook.

Computer and Equipment Operations

- Use, accurately and efficiently, computer programs and equipment required to meet the service and management functions of the library media program currently including:
- CD-ROM magazine index;
- the various word-processing and database modules;
- library automation software, including circulation, data entry, inventory, and report functions;
- bar code production software;
- operate computers to retrieve and print information from various selected CD-ROM data discs;

- load paper into printers connected to computers;
- operate microfiche reader/printer to reproduce periodical articles;
- add photocopy paper to microfiche reader/printer, as needed;
- replace microfiche reader/printer toner/drum cartridges as needed;
- notify library media teacher of operation malfunctions with microfiche reader/printer, as they occur;
- operate photocopier as appropriate to provide reduction of reproductions, for practical conservation of supplies;
- operate photocopier as required to provide enlargement of reproductions;
- add photocopy paper to photocopier, as needed;
- add toner to photocopier and discard toner containers, as needed;
- notify library media teacher of operation malfunctions with the photocopier, as they occur.

Student Support Services

- Provide photocopying for students and staff, promptly upon request, of any and all *library media center materials (only)*—including periodicals, newspapers, reference collection resources, and circulating collection resources;
- interpret contents of computer printout, to retrieve all available periodical articles requested, in either microfiche or hard copy format, as appropriate;
- provide assistance to students for the following requests: retrieval of backfiled periodicals and newspapers; location of shelved materials; dispensing of writing paper, selected titles of periodicals, cellophane tape, scissors, and stapler.

Routine Daily Tasks

Attendance Verification

- Verify "head count" of students against period attendance sheet;
- investigate/verify student sign-out from study hall, when a student is missing from the library media center.

Circulation of Library Media Materials

- Operate circulation system to charge out or clear the return of library media materials;
- process overdue book/fine notices, as necessary;
- distribute overdue book/fine notices to homeroom teachers, mailboxes, as necessary;
- collect overdue/lost materials fines, as necessary, and process them according to the current model of procedure.

Fax Machine Operation

- Operate the LMC-installed fax machine, sending facsimile messages as required to conduct LMC business.

Library Media Center Maintenance

- Maintain orderly arrangement of library media center tables and chairs at the end of each class period;
- maintain orderly arrangement of periodicals display racks;
- clean table surfaces, as necessary;
- maintain flush-frontfiling order of bookshelves.

Mail Pick-up and Sorting

- Pick up library media center mail from the main office, daily;
- sort out mail: periodicals; vendors' catalogs; first-class mail; information resources; and parcel post materials.

Materials Shelving and "Shelf-Reading"

- File newly processed or returned books according to Dewey Decimal Classification system numbering, and standard alphabetizing and shelf-filing rules;
- read shelves to organize and refile books, as necessary, according to Dewey Decimal Classification system numbering, and standard alphabetizing and shelf-filing rules.

Periodicals Display, Filing, Storage, and Retrieval

- File new periodicals on display racks, upon receipt, and backfile periodicals in short-term or long-term filing locations, as necessary, according to existing models and standards;
- file serial information resources (e.g., Facts on File; CQ Researcher) upon receipt;
- retrieve backfiled periodicals as necessary to fill requests of students and staff for use or reproduction of contents;
- reorganize backfile storage of periodicals, as necessary, to provide for ongoing long-term storage.

Supplies Inventory

- Maintain an inventory of library media center operating and processing supplies;

- compile semiannually a needs list of supplies and materials as required.

Telephone Protocols

- Answer the telephone according to existing model, and write messages as necessary;
- make telephone calls, as requested, to vendors and school department personnel.

Vendors' Catalog Filing

- File the daily receipt of commercial vendors' catalogs and product information mailings, according to existing model and procedures.

Requisition Preparation

- Type requisitions, as necessary, according to existing model and standards.

Online Electronic Catalog Maintenance

Materials Accession and Processing (tasks to be performed according to existing models and professional standards)

- Type entries into accession database, for each item to be cataloged and entered into the library media collection;
- stamp library media center identification and accession number for each accessioned item;
- operate circulation computer software to enter MARC data cataloging entry information into the electronic catalog database for each accessioned item;

- maintain a file of cataloging data sheets, annotated with date of computer processing and clerk's initials;
- operate barcode production software to create identifying title, call number, and barcode number labels for each accessioned item;
- affix computer-generated call number label to the book spine of each accessioned item;
- affix computer-generated barcode label to the pocket page of each accessioned item;
- affix plastic label protectors covering the spine label and barcode label of each accessioned item.

Inventory, End-of-year

- Operate portable inventory barcode reader to conduct an annual end-of-year inventory of the complete library media center collection.

Inventory Follow-up

- Prepare end-of-year inventory reports.

[Adapted and used by permission. Dr. Michael D. Leahy, Eastern High School Library Media Center, Bristol, Conn.]

Library Media Circulation Desk Aide: Job Functions (Beginning at 7:30 A.M.)—Manual System

1. Is responsible for daily total operation of circulation desk: checking out and checking in of materials, borrowers' card files, daily circulation and usage statistics, restrictions on delinquent borrowers, reserves, generating overdue lists.
2. Records daily data entries.

3. Answers phone calls and relays messages, provides change for the copier and office supplies for students.

4. Sorts books daily onto carts and shelves when requested.

5. Copes with high-volume periods of stress requiring technical skills, accuracy, speed, and tact.

6. Maintains a firm, consistent, but friendly and cooperative interpretation of the rules, primarily within viewing range of the circulation desk.

7. Has a broad knowledge of all library aspects and procedures but has the judgment to know when to tackle problems and when to refer them to the library teachers.

8. Supervises security system and copy equipment.

9. Provides instruction to students in use of copier and, when library teachers are occupied, in use of microfilm readers. Assists in the orientation of students in the use of library materials. Refers students with academic questions to the professional instructional staff.

10. Performs additional clerical duties as requested (typing, card filing, microform filing, bulletin board displays, vertical file folders) that can be carried out at circulation desk.

11. Assists with inventory as requested.

12. Carries out such other reasonable duties and responsibilities as the library teachers may assign.

*Library Media Circulation Desk Aide: Job Functions—
General Responsibilities*

Procedures for September Opening Jobs—Circulation
Desk

1. Read and become familiar with the student/faculty handbook.
2. Post new time schedules at several places throughout the library media center.
3. Post new intercom telephone list by telephones.
4. Have copies of school map at desk for use by new students. Note changes.
5. Clean and oil chargeout machines. Set dates and check tape roll. Decide on tape color sequence for the year.
6. Set time clock.
7. Prepare teachers' sign-up book with dates for the entire year based on school calendar.
8. Prepare statistics, notices, and other forms, and establish clipboard of school notices.
9. Check inventory of school supplies in desk—composition paper, small and large scrap paper, blue passes, discipline forms, pens, pencils, scissors, stapler, tape, ruler, protractor.
10. Have change for copy machine.
11. Verify the borrowers' cards. Erase old overdue marks and remove yellow tabs.
12. Punch new cards and interfile correctly. Remove Senior cards from previous year.
13. Verify alphabetic order and be alert to identical (or nearly so) student names. These will be trouble spots unless noted early.
14. Verify carryover obligations and place black tabs on

borrowers' cards. Be sure our records and office records agree.

15. Recall any unreturned summer borrowing materials.

Library Media Circulation Desk Aide: Job Functions—Daily Procedures

Before Students Are Admitted

1. Plug in copy machine and other electrical equipment.
2. Roll cart with Rolodex borrowers' cards to desk area.
3. Unlock desk and telephone.
4. Rearrange furniture if disarranged because of night meeting.
5. Check time clock for accuracy of setting.
6. Verify that security system is functioning.

Admit Students

1. Check in overnight books. Unclip overdue markers where appropriate (paper clips) from borrowers' cards.
2. Set overnight books aside to be sorted and shelved first. These are usually marked either "Ref." or "Reserve."
3. Check remaining (uncleared) overnight cards and clip borrowers' cards with a paper clip for *each* overdue overnight book. Write date in bottom left hand corner of borrower's card (in pencil). These dates, when accumulated to three, will call for affixing fluorescent red sticker to card to indicate no further use of overnight borrowing privileges.

4. Collect newly returned books from book drop and check them in. Remove appropriately colored clips from borrower's card corresponding to returned overdue books. This process should be accomplished at least twice a day.
5. Check out books to students wishing to borrow. (Procedure described elsewhere.)
6. Refile borrowers' cards as time permits. Place a penciled tick mark on the reverse side of card before refiling to indicate use record.
7. Arrange book cards from books borrowed according to Dewey order and file or interfile them as much as possible throughout the day.
8. Update notices on clipboard at desk. Remove those that are too old to be of value.

ACCURACY IS MORE IMPORTANT THAN SPEED!!!!

Library Circulation Desk Procedures

Daily Closing Procedures

1. Sort and arrange book cards according to Dewey order and interfile within the borrowing date. File in desk drawer for students and for faculty sections.
2. Sort and file overnight cards placing them in file on top of desk.
3. Sort and file borrowers' cards. Mark each with a pencil tick in lower left hand corner of back side before refiling.
4. Fill in statistical record with daily count of people (number on dial from security system counter) and books borrowed (number from both machines). Compute daily totals.

5. Turn page on class sign-up book to next day; note any special comments.
6. Change date on chargeout machines "s" levers to next date. On Friday *only*, change date on "7" levers to the next Wednesday due date (two weeks). Change tape color according to predetermined pattern.
7. Have excess money from copy machine processed.
8. Lock white phone.
9. Lock desk drawer.
10. Put Rolodex cart in inner office.
11. Deliver any discipline slips, memos, or letters to the main office on way out.
12. If the last staff person to leave, see that lights are out, all people are out, and that the doors are locked.

Weekly Procedures

1. Wednesday mornings, after usual morning routine is completed, start clipping borrowers' cards for books due that day. Books become overdue at 2:15 P.M. Be sure to remove overdue clips if a book is returned or renewed during the day.
2. Fridays, at the end of school, change date and tape on chargeout machines as needed.

Monthly Procedures

1. Change date on time clock. It is not automatic for 29-, 30-, and 31-day months. Month, day, and dates must be shifted manually.

2. Put out new log sheets for telephone use. Take old log to the principal's office.

Notice Clipboard

All notices of general interest circulated from the main office are kept on a clipboard at the circulation desk for all to see. These are retained beyond the use date for referral until the stack becomes unmanageable.

Teacher Sign-Up Book

This book is kept at the circulation desk, open to the current date so that it may be easily checked by any teacher or student. Teachers must sign up in advance to reserve space for their classes. Telephone requests and notes sent by runners are honored. If a class arrives with no reservation, the library teachers should be informed. Classes should sit in the area reserved for them. Other students occupying that space should be requested to relocate. The accompanying classroom teacher is responsible for the behavior of that class.

The first teachers signing for space should follow the plan that social studies will be in the northeast corner, science in the 500s alcove, and English along the wall by the 800s. The purpose is to place the group nearest the bulk of the materials they will be using. An art or music class should use the west wall if it is not already in use by an English class.

If a class is to use special material areas (microfilm, periodical room, etc.) in addition to or instead of the traditional areas, this should be noted in the sign-up book. Also, indicate number of students if the group is to be only a partial class. The desk clerk should indicate on the appropriate page special scheduled events such as class assemblies, Winter Carnival, or any other event that may affect teacher usage. Teacher or administrator conferences with the library teachers should be indicated on the appropriate page as should classroom appointments for the library teachers.

Book and Body Counts

In the back of the teacher sign-up book are forms to be filled out daily indicating the chargeout machine count and the turnstile count. The dates should be filled in from the bottom of the page upward to facilitate arithmetic computation. One page per month is used, and a summary is prepared at the end of the school year.

[NOTE: Designed and used by Dr. Hilda L. Jay]

Appendix C
Student Evaluation Questionnaires

STUDENT EVALUATION OF ELEMENTARY
SCHOOL LIBRARY MEDIA PROGRAM

Room _____ Date _____

Students should be instructed to circle Y for *yes*; N for *no*; and ? for *sometimes* or *don't know* answers.

Y   N   ?   1. The media teacher helps me when I need it.

Y   N   ?   2. The media teacher gives me ideas about ways to do assignments.

Y   N   ?   3. The media center has books I can use for assignments.

Y   N   ?   4. The media center has books I can read for fun.

Y   N   ?   5. The media center has fair rules.

Y   N   ?   6. The media center enforces the rules fairly.

Y   N   ?   7. I have been taught how to find things in the media center.

Y   N   ?   8. I have been taught how to use the media center computers.

Y   N   ?   9. The media teacher shows me how to use computer software.

Y   N   ?   10. I want to learn more about how to use the media center.

Y   N   ?   11. The media teacher does things to make me want to come to the media center.

Y   N   ?   12. I do the bulletin board learning centers.

Y   N   ?   13. I learn things by doing them.

Y   N   ?   14. They are too hard for me.

Students should be instructed to place a (1) before the choice they like best, a (2) before their next choice, and so on.

1, 2, 3, 4   15. When we come to the media center as a class group I like to:

_____ Listen to a story

_____ Use computers

_____ Search for information

_____ Learn how to use the media center

_____ Work in cooperataive groups

_____ Make multi-media productions

[NOTE: Designed and used with students by Dr. M. Ellen Jay.]

STUDENT EVALUATION OF SECONDARY SCHOOL LIBRARY MEDIA PROGRAM

Please circle your grade: 9   10   11   12

and track: Special   Standard   Honors

1.   How many study halls do you have each week? _____

term papers to write this year? _____

2.   Check the amount of use you make of the center for each of the following purposes:

Hardly ever go	Teacher takes or sends	Several times a week	Almost every day	Purpose
(__)	(__)	(__)	(__)	A. Find materials for assignments
(__)	(__)	(__)	(__)	B. Find materials for pleasure
(__)	(__)	(__)	(__)	C. Do textbook work for _____ (subject)
(__)	(__)	(__)	(__)	D. Meet friends
(__)	(__)	(__)	(__)	E. Socialize before school
(__)	(__)	(__)	(__)	F. Study before school
(__)	(__)	(__)	(__)	G. Wait for something after school
(__)	(__)	(__)	(__)	H. Study after school
(__)	(__)	(__)	(__)	I. Other: _____

3. Do you use other libraries than ours? (__) Once in a while; (__) often; (__) never.

4. If you do, which libraries do you use? (Omit interlibrary loan or personal services from our staff)

   (__)   Town public library
   (__)   Public library in (town) _____
   (__)   College library in (town) _____
   (__)   Have other people bring materials from _____
   (__)   Personal or home library

5. Why do you use these libraries? _____

6. Comment on the adequacy (or lack of it) of our center:
   A.   Space to work (tables, carrels, chairs) _____
   B.   Computers for online or CD-ROM information _____
   C.   Computers for word processing _____
   D.   Accessibility (getting in, hours) _____
   E.   Assistance provided to answer questions _____
   F.   Collection (books, films, tapes, periodicals, software, etc.) _____

7. Are there subjects for which your teachers require little or no use of the center? (List *subject name* only!) _____

8. How many books have your read so far this year for classwork other than textbooks? _____ For pleasure? _____

9. Do you find materials for assignments (___) almost always; (___) sometimes; (___) hardly ever; (___) don't try to get any.

10. Do you find materials for pleasure (___) almost always; (___) sometimes; (___) hardly ever; (___) don't try to get any.

11. If you have not found what you needed in our center, indicate what these shortages have been. (PLEASE BE SPECIFIC). It does not help us purchase if you say "Social Studies," but it does help if you indicate a specific area such as, "Hoover's presidency," "Cuban Missile Crisis," or "Desert Storm Operation." Give specific authors and titles of books, if you wish. _____

12. Make additional suggestions for improving the center on the back of this sheet. Thanks for your help.

[NOTE: Designed and used with students by Dr. Hilda L. Jay.]

Appendix D
Student Access to Networks

At the time of writing, there is much concern being expressed over student access to potentially undesirable materials available on uncontrolled networks. Regardless of what the federal or state governments might legislate, it is likely that schools will want to set their own network use policies and library media teachers will share responsibilities for implementing them. For that reason the work done by the Bellingham (Wash.) School District to create their Board Policy has been included (by permission) as a possible model document.

BELLINGHAM (WASH.) SCHOOL DISTRICT 501 BOARD POLICY 2313: STUDENT ACCESS TO NETWORKED INFORMATION RESOURCES

The Board recognizes that as telecommunications and other new technologies shift the ways that information may be accessed, communicated, and transferred by members of the society, those changes may also alter instruction and student learning. The Board generally supports access by students to rich information resources along with the development by staff of appropriate skills to analyze and evaluate such resources. In a free and democratic society, access to information is a fundamental right of citizenship.

Telecommunications, electronic information sources, and

networked services significantly alter the information landscape for schools by opening classrooms to a broader array of resources. In the past, instructional and library media materials could usually be screened—prior to use—by committees of educators and community members intent on subjecting all such materials to reasonable selection criteria. Board Policy 2311 requires that all such materials be consistent with district-adopted guides, supporting and enriching the curriculum while taking into account the varied instructional needs, learning styles, abilities, and developmental levels of the students. Telecommunications, because they may lead to any publicly available fileserver in the world, will open classrooms to electronic information resources that have not been screened by educators for use by students of various ages.

Electronic information research skills are now fundamental to preparation of citizens and future employees during an Age of Information. The Board expects that staff will blend thoughtful use of such information throughout the curriculum and that the staff will provide guidance and instruction to students in the appropriate use of such resources. Staff will consult the guidelines for instructional materials contained in Board Policy 2311 and will honor the goals for selection of instructional materials contained therein.

Students are responsible for good behavior on school computer networks just as they are in a classroom or a school hallway. Communications on the network are often public in nature. General school rules for behavior and communications apply (see Board Policy 3200). The network is provided for students to conduct research and communicate with others. Access to network services will be provided to students who agree to act in a considerate and responsible manner.

Independent student use of telecommunications and electronic information resources will be permitted upon submission of permission forms and agreement forms by parents of minor students (under 18 years of age) and by students themselves. Regional networks such as WEDNET require agreement by users to acceptable use policies outlining standards for behavior and communication.

Access to telecommunications will enable students to explore thousands of libraries, databases, and bulletin boards while exchanging messages with people throughout the world. The Board believes that the benefits to students from access in the form of information resources and opportunities for collaboration exceed the disadvantages. But ultimately, parents and guardians of minors are responsible for setting and conveying the standards that their children should follow when using media and information sources. To that end, the Bellingham Public Schools support and respect each family's right to decide whether or not to apply for independent access.

The Board authorizes the Superintendent to prepare appropriate procedures for implementing this policy and for reviewing and evaluating its effect on instruction and student achievement.

Adopted: April 27, 1995
Bellingham School District 501
2313P
Administrative Procedures

Procedures

Program Development

In order to match electronic resources as closely as possible to the approved district curriculum, district personnel will review and evaluate resources in order to offer home pages and menus of materials that comply with Board guidelines listed in Board Policy 2311 governing the selection of instructional materials. In this manner, staff will provide developmentally appropriate guidance to students as they make use of telecommunications and electronic information resources to conduct research and other studies related to the district curriculum. All students will be informed by staff of their rights and responsibilities as users of the district network prior to gaining access to that network, either as an individual user or as a member of a class or group.

As much as possible, access to district information resources will be designed in ways that point students to those that have been reviewed and evaluated prior to use. While students may be able to move beyond those resources to others that have not been evaluated by staff, they shall be provided with guidelines and lists of resources particularly suited to the learning objectives. Students may pursue electronic research independently of staff supervision only if they have been granted parental permission and have submitted all required forms. Permission is not transferable and may not be shared.

Internet Rules

Students are responsible for good behavior on school computer networks just as they are in a classroom or a school hallway. Communications on the network are often public in nature. General school rules for behavior and communications apply.

The network is provided for students to conduct research and communicate with others. Independent access to network services is provided to students who agree to act in a considerate and responsible manner. Parent permission is required for minors. Access is a privilege, not a right. Access entails responsibility.

Individual users of the district computer networks are responsible for their behavior and communications over those networks. It is presumed that users will comply with district standards and will honor the agreements they have signed.

Network storage areas may be treated like school lockers. Network administrators may review files and communications to maintain system integrity and insure that users are using the system responsibly. Users should not expect that files stored on district servers will always be private.

During school, teachers of younger students will guide them toward appropriate materials. Outside of school, families bear responsibility for such guidance as they must also exercise with information sources such as television, telephones, movies, radio and other potentially offensive media.

The following are not permitted:

1. Sending or displaying offensive messages or pictures.
2. Using obscene language.
3. Harassing, insulting, or attacking others.
4. Damaging computers, computer systems, or computer networks.
5. Violating copyright laws.
6. Using others' passwords.
7. Trespassing in others' folders, work, or files.
8. Intentionally wasting limited resources.
9. Employing the network for commercial purposes.

Sanctions

1. Violations may result in a loss of access.
2. Additional disciplinary action may be determined at the building level in line with existing practice regarding inappropriate language or behavior.
3. When applicable, law enforcement agencies may be involved.

Approved: April 27, 1995
Dale E. Kinsley, Superintendent of Schools
Contact can be made by using <jmckenzie@msmail. bham.wednet.edu> or http://www.bham.wednet.edu.

Appendix E
A Note Regarding Inclusion of American Library Association Documents

Principals have indicated that they have some difficulty finding supportive materials when they need them to deal with local situations. Although they may freely contact the American Library Association, 50 East Huron Street, Chicago, IL 60611, or use the (800) 545–2433 phone number, this information may not be widely enough known. For this reason examples of the ALA/AASL documents are printed here. Inasmuch as they are revised from time to time, it would be well to check with ALA to make certain the latest document is in hand. There may appear to be redundancy, but each document addresses a separate facet of concern although all are interrelated and based on the *Freedom to Read* statement and the *Library Bill of Rights* document. The position statements are documents published by the American Association of School Librarians [AASL] that pertain to staffing, scheduling, training, and the value and operation of the library media center program by the library media specialist, as well as to intellectual freedom.

THE FREEDOM TO READ

The freedom to read is essential to our democracy. It is continuously under attack. Private groups and public authorities in various parts of the country are working to remove books from sale, to censor textbooks, to label "controversial" books, to distribute lists of "objectionable" books or authors, and to purge libraries. These actions apparently rise from a view that our national tradition of free expression is no longer valid; that censorship and suppression are needed to avoid the subversion of politics and the corruption of morals. We, as citizens devoted to the use of books and as librarians and publishers responsible for disseminating them, wish to assert the public interest in the preservation of the freedom to read.

We are deeply concerned about these attempts at suppression. Most such attempts rest on a denial of the fundamental premise of democracy: that the ordinary citizen, by exercising critical judgment, will accept the good and reject the bad. The censors, public and private, assume that they should determine what is good and what is bad for their fellow-citizens.

We trust Americans to recognize propaganda and to reject it. We do not believe they need the help of censors to assist them in this task. We do not believe they are prepared to sacrifice their heritage of a free press in order to be "protected" against what others think may be bad for them. We believe they still favor free enterprise in ideas and expression.

We are aware, of course, that books are not alone in being subjected to efforts at suppression. We are aware that these efforts are related to a larger pattern of pressures being brought against education, the press, films, radio, and television. The problem is not only one of actual censorship. The shadow of fear cast by these pressures leads, we suspect, to an even larger voluntary curtailment of expression by those who seek to avoid controversy.

Such pressure toward conformity is perhaps natural to a time of uneasy change and pervading fear. Especially when so many of our apprehensions are directed against an ideology, the expression of a dissident idea becomes a thing feared in itself, and we tend to move against it as against a hostile deed, with suppression.

And yet suppression is never more dangerous than in such a time of social tension. Freedom has given the United States the elasticity to endure strain. Freedom keeps open the path of novel and creative solutions, and enables change to come by choice. Every silencing of a heresy, every enforcement of an orthodoxy, diminishes the toughness and resilience of our society and leaves it the less able to deal with stress.

Now as always in our history, books are among our greatest instruments of freedom. They are almost the only means for making generally available ideas or manners of expression that can initially command only a small audience. They are the natural medium for the new idea and the untried voice from which come the original contributions to social growth. They are essential to the extended discussion that serious thought requires and to the accumulation of knowledge and ideas into organized collections.

We believe that free communication is essential to the preservation of a free society and a creative culture. We believe that these pressures towards conformity present the danger of limiting the range and variety of enquiry and expression on which our democracy and our culture depend. We believe that every American community must jealously guard the freedom to publish and to circulate, in order to preserve its own freedom to read. We believe that publishers and librarians have a profound responsibility to give validity to that freedom to read by making it possible for the readers to choose freely from a variety of offerings.

The freedom to read is guaranteed by the Constitution. Those with faith in free people will stand firm on these constitutional guarantees of essential rights and will exercise the responsibilities that accompany these rights.

We therefore affirm these propositions:

1. It is in the public interest for publishers and librarians to make available the widest diversity of views and expressions, including those that are unorthodox or unpopular with the majority.

Creative thought is by definition new, and what is new is different. The bearer of every new thought is a rebel until that idea is refined and tested. Totalitarian systems attempt to maintain themselves in power by the ruthless suppression of any concept that challenges the established orthodoxy. The power of a democratic system to adapt to change is vastly strengthened by the freedom of its citizens to choose widely from among conflicting opinions offered freely to them. To stifle every nonconformist idea at birth would mark the end of the democratic process. Furthermore, only through the constant activity of weighing and selecting can the democratic mind attain the strength demanded by times like these. We need to know not only what we believe but why we believe it.

2. Publishers, librarians, and booksellers do not need to endorse every idea or presentation contained in the books they make available. It would conflict with the public interest for them to establish their own political, moral, or aesthetic views as a standard for determining what books should be published or circulated.

Publishers and librarians serve the educational process by helping to make available knowledge and ideas required for the growth of the mind and the increase of learning. They do not foster education by imposing as mentors the patterns of their own thought. The people should have the freedom to read and consider a broader range of ideas than those that may be held by any single librarian or publisher or government or church. It is wrong that what one can read should be confined to what another thinks proper.

3. It is contrary to the public interest for publishers or librarians to determine the acceptability of a book on the basis of the personal history or political affiliations of the author.

A book should be judged as a book. No art or literature can flourish if it is to be measured by the political views or private lives of its creators. No society of free people can flourish that draws up lists of writers to whom it will not listen, whatever they may have to say.

4. There is no place in our society for efforts to coerce the taste of others, to confine adults to the reading matter deemed suitable for adolescents, or to inhibit the efforts of writers to achieve artistic expression.

To some, much of modern literature is shocking. But is not much of life itself shocking? We cut off literature at the source if we prevent writers from dealing with the stuff of life. Parents and teachers have a responsibility to prepare the young to meet the diversity of experiences in life to which they will be exposed, as they have a responsibility to help them learn to think critically for themselves. These are affirmative responsibilities, not to be discharged simply by preventing them from reading works for which they are not yet prepared. In these matters taste differs, and taste cannot be legislated; nor can machinery be devised that will suit the demands of one group without limiting the freedom of others.

5. It is not in the public interest to force a reader to accept with any book the prejudgment of a label characterizing the book or author as subversive or dangerous.

The ideal of labeling presupposes the existence of individuals or groups with wisdom to determine by authority what is good or bad for the citizen. It presupposes that individuals must be directed in making up their minds about the ideas they examine. But Americans do not need others to do their thinking for them.

6. It is the responsibility of publishers and librarians, as guardians of the people's freedom to read, to contest encroachments upon that freedom by individuals or groups seeking to impose their own standards or tastes upon the community at large.

It is inevitable in the give and take of the democratic process that the political, the moral, or the aesthetic concepts of an individual or group will occasionally collide with those of another individual or group. In a free society individuals are free to determine for themselves what they wish to read, and each group is free to determine what it will recommend to its freely associated members. But no group has the right to take the law into its own hands and to impose its own concept of politics or morality upon other members of a democratic society. Freedom is no freedom if it is accorded only to the accepted and the inoffensive.

7. It is the responsibility of publishers and librarians to give full meaning to the freedom to read by providing books that enrich the quality and diversity of thought and expression. By the exercise of this affirmative responsibility, they can demonstrate that the answer to a bad book is a good one, the answer to a bad idea is a good one.

The freedom to read is of little consequence when expended on the trivial; it is frustrated when the reader cannot obtain matter fit for that reader's purpose. What is needed is not only the absence of restraint, but the positive provision of opportunity for the people to read the best that has been thought and said. Books are the major channel by which the intellectual inheritance is handed down, and the principal means of its testing and growth. The defense of their freedom and integrity, and the enlargement of their service to society, requires of all publishers and librarians the utmost of their faculties, and deserves of all citizens the fullest of their support.

We state these propositions neither lightly nor as easy generalizations. We here stake out a lofty claim for the value of books. We do so because we believe that they are good, possessed of enormous variety and usefulness, worthy of cherishing and keeping free. We realize that the application of these propositions may mean the dissemination of ideas and manners of expression that are repugnant to many persons. We do not state these propositions in the comfortable belief that what people read is unimportant. We believe rather that what people read is deeply important; that ideas can be dangerous; but that the suppression of ideas is fatal to a democratic society. Freedom itself is a dangerous way of life, but it is ours.

This statement was originally issued in May of 1953 by the Westchester Conference of the American Library Association and the American Book Publishers Council, which in 1970 consolidated with the American Educational Publishers Institute to become the Association of American Publishers.

Adopted June 25, 1953; revised January 28, 1972, and January 16, 1991, by the ALA Council and the AAP Freedom to Read Committee.

A Joint Statement by: American Library Association & Association of American Publishers subsequently endorsed by:

American Booksellers Association
American Booksellers Foundation for Free Expression

American Federation of Teachers AFL-CIO
Anti-Defamation League of B'nai B'rith
Association of American University Presses
Children's Book Council
Freedom to Read Foundation
International Reading Association
National Association of College Stores
National Council of Teachers of English
PEN—American Center
People for the American Way
Periodical and Book Association of America
Sex Information and Education Council of the U.S.
Society of Professional Journalists
Thomas Jefferson Center for the Protection of Free Expression
Women's National Book Association
YWCA of the U.S.A.

"LIBRARY BILL OF RIGHTS"

The American Library Association affirms that all libraries are forums for information and ideas, and that the following basic policies should guide their services.

1. Books and other library resources should be provided for the interest, information, and enlightenment of all people of the community the library serves. Materials should not be excluded because of the origin, background, or views of those contributing to their creation.

2. Libraries should provide materials and information presenting all points of view on current and historical issues. Materials should not be proscribed or removed because of partisan or doctrinal disapproval.

3. Libraries should challenge censorship in the fulfillment of their responsibility to provide information and enlightenment.
4. Libraries should cooperate with all persons and groups concerned with resisting abridgment of free expression and free access to ideas.
5. A person's right to use a library should not be denied or abridged because of origin, age, background, or views.
6. Libraries which make exhibit spaces and meeting rooms available to the public they serve should make such facilities available on an equitable basis, regardless of the beliefs or affiliations of individuals or groups requesting their use.

Adopted June 18, 1948; amended February 2, 1981; June 27, 1967; and January 23, 1980 by the ALA Council.

AN INTERPRETATION OF THE "LIBRARY BILL OF RIGHTS": ACCESS TO RESOURCES AND SERVICES IN THE SCHOOL LIBRARY MEDIA PROGRAM

The school library media program plays a unique role in promoting intellectual freedom. It serves as a point of voluntary access to information and ideas and as a learning laboratory for students as they acquire critical thinking and problem-solving skills needed in a pluralistic society. Although the educational level and program of the school necessarily shape the resources and services of a school library media program, the principles of the "Library Bill of Rights" apply equally to all libraries, including school library media programs.

School library media professionals assume a leadership role in promoting the principles of intellectual freedom within the school by providing resources and services that create and sustain an atmosphere of free inquiry. School library media professionals work closely with teachers to integrate instructional activities in classroom units designed to equip students to locate, evaluate, and use a broad range of ideas effectively. Through resources, programming, and educational processes, students and teachers experience the free and robust debate characteristic of a democratic society.

School library media professionals cooperate with other individuals in building collections of resources appropriate to the developmental and maturity levels of students. These collections provide resources that support the curriculum and are consistent with the philosophy, goals, and objectives of the school district. Resources in school library media collections represent diverse points of view and current as well as historic issues.

While English is by history and tradition the customary language of the United States, the languages in use in any given community may vary. Schools serving communities in which other languages are used make efforts to accommodate the needs of students for whom English is a second language. To support these efforts, and to ensure equal access to resources and services, the school library media program provides resources that reflect the linguistic pluralism of the community.

Members of the school community involved in the collection development process employ educational criteria to select resources unfettered by their personal, political, social, or religious views.

Students and educators served by the school library media program have access to resources and services free of constraints resulting from personal, partisan, or doctrinal disapproval. School library media professionals resist efforts by individuals to define what is appropriate for all students or teachers to read, view, or hear.

Major barriers between students and resources include: imposing age or grade level restrictions on the use of resources; limiting the use of interlibrary loan and access to electronic information; charging fees for information in specific formats; requiring permissions from parents or teachers; establishing restricted shelves or closed collections; and labeling. Policies, procedures, and rules related to the use of resources and services support free and open access to information.

The school board adopts policies that guarantee access to a broad range of ideas. These include policies on collection development and procedures for the review of resources about which concerns have been raised. Such policies, developed by persons in the school community, provide for a timely and fair hearing and assure that procedures are applied equitably to all expressions of concern. School library media professionals implement district policies and procedures in the school.

Adopted July 1986; amended January 1990 by the ALA Council.

THE UNIVERSAL RIGHT TO FREE EXPRESSION: AN INTERPRETATION OF THE "LIBRARY BILL OF RIGHTS"

Freedom of expression is an inalienable human right and the foundation for self-government. Freedom of expression encompasses the freedoms of speech, press, religion, assembly, and association, and the corollary right to receive information.

The American Library Association endorses this principle, which is also set forth in the "Universal Declaration of Human Rights," adopted by the United Nations General Assembly. The Preamble of this document states that " . . . recognition of the inherent dignity and the equal and inalienable rights of all members of the human family is the foundation of freedom, justice, and peace in the world . . . " and " . . . the advent of a world in which human beings shall enjoy freedom of speech and belief and freedom from fear and want has been proclaimed as the highest aspiration of the common people. . . . "

Article 18 of this document states:

> Everyone has the right to freedom of thought, conscience, and religion; this right includes freedom to change his religion or belief, and freedom, either alone or in community with others and in public or private, to manifest his religion or belief in teaching, practice, worship, and observance.

Article 19 states:

> Everyone has the right to freedom of opinion and expression; this right includes freedom to hold opinions without interference and to seek, receive, and impart information and ideas through any media regardless of frontiers.

Article 20 states:

> 1. Everyone has the right to freedom of peaceful assembly and association.
> 2. No one may be compelled to belong to an association.

We affirm our belief that these are inalienable rights of every person, regardless of origin, age, background, or views. We embody our professional commitment to these principles in the "Library Bill of Rights" and "Code of Professional Ethics," as adopted by the American Library Association.

We maintain that these are universal principles and should be applied by libraries and librarians throughout the world. The American Library Association's policy on International Relations reflects these objectives: " . . . to encourage the exchange, dissemination, and access to information and the unrestricted flow of library materials in all formats throughout the world."

We know that censorship, ignorance, and limitations on the free flow of information are the tools of tyranny and oppression. We believe that ideas and information topple the walls of hate and fear and build bridges of cooperation and understanding far more effectively than weapons and armies.

The American Library Association is unswerving in its commitment to human rights and intellectual freedom; the two are inseparably linked and inextricably entwined. Freedom of opinion and expression is not derived from or dependent on any form of government or political power. This right is inherent in every individual. It cannot be surrendered, nor can it be denied. True justice comes from the exercise of this right.

We recognize the power of information and ideas to inspire justice, to restore freedom and dignity to the oppressed, and to change the hearts and minds of the oppressors.

Courageous men and women, in difficult and dangerous circumstances throughout human history, have demonstrated that freedom lives in the human heart and cries out for justice even in the face of threats, enslavement, imprisonment, torture, exile, and death. We draw inspiration from their example. They challenge us to remain steadfast in our most basic professional responsibility to promote and defend the right of free expression.

There is no good censorship. Any effort to restrict free expression and the free flow of information aids the oppressor. Fighting oppression with censorship is self-defeating.

Threats to the freedom of expression of any person anywhere are threats to the freedom of all people everywhere. Violations of human rights and the right of free expression have been recorded in virtually every country and society across the globe.

In response to these violations, we affirm these principles:

- The American Library Association opposes any use of governmental prerogative that leads to the intimidation of individuals which prevents them from exercising their rights to hold opinions without interference, and to seek, receive, and impart information and ideas. We urge libraries and librarians everywhere to resist such abuse of governmental power and to support those against whom such governmental power has been employed.
- The American Library Association condemns any governmental effort to involve libraries and librarians in restrictions on the right of any individual to hold opinions without interference, and to seek, receive, and impart information and ideas. Such restrictions pervert the function of the library and violate the professional responsibilities of librarians.
- The American Library Association rejects censorship in any form. Any action which denies the inalienable human rights of individuals only damages the will to resist oppression, strengthens the hand of the oppressor, and undermines the cause of justice.
- The American Library Association will not abrogate these principles. We believe that censorship corrupts the cause of justice and contributes to the demise of freedom.

Adopted by the ALA Council, January 16, 1991.

STATEMENT ON LABELING:
AN INTERPRETATION OF THE
"LIBRARY BILL OF RIGHTS"

Labeling is the practice of describing or designating materials by affixing a prejudicial label and/or segregating them by a prejudicial system. The American Library Association opposes these means of predisposing people's attitudes toward library materials for the following reasons:

1. Labeling is an attempt to prejudice attitudes and as such, it is a censor's tool.
2. Some find it easy and even proper, according to their ethics, to establish criteria for judging publications as objectionable. However, injustice and ignorance rather than justice and enlightenment result from such practices, and the American Library Association opposes the establishment of such criteria.
3. Libraries do not advocate the ideas found in their collections. The presence of books and other resources in a library does not indicate endorsement of their contents by the library.

A variety of private organizations promulgate rating systems and/or review materials as a means of advising either their members or the general public concerning their opinions of the contents and suitability or appropriate age for use of certain books, films, recordings, or other materials. For the library to adopt or enforce any of these private systems, to attach such ratings to library materials, to include them in bibliographic records, library catalogs, or other finding aids, or otherwise to endorse them would violate the "Library Bill of Rights."

While some attempts have been made to adopt these systems into law, the constitutionality of such measures is extremely questionable. If such legislation is passed which applies within a library's jurisdiction, the library should seek competent legal advice concerning its applicability to library operations.

Publishers, industry groups, and distributors sometimes add ratings to material or include them as part of their packaging. Librarians should not endorse such practices. However, removing or obliterating such ratings—if placed there by or with permission of the copyright holder—could constitute expurgation, which is also unacceptable.

The American Library Association opposes efforts that aim at closing any path to knowledge. This statement, however, does not exclude the adoption of organizational schemes designed as directional aids or to facilitate access to materials.

Adopted July 13, 1951; amended June 25, 1971; July 1, 1981; June 26, 1990, by the ALA Council. [ISBN 8389–5226–7]

LIST OF ADDITIONAL ALA/AASL DOCUMENTS RE-LATED TO THE "LIBRARY BILL OF RIGHTS"

"Access for Children and Young People to Videotapes and Other Nonprint Formats: An Interpretation of the Library Bill of Rights." Adopted June 28, 1989, by the ALA Council; the quotation from "Free Access to Libraries for Minors" was changed after Council adopted the July 3, 1991, revision of that interpretation. [ISBN 8389–7351–5]

"Access to Library Resources and Services Regardless of Gender or Sexual Orientation: An Interpretation of the 'Library Bill of Rights.'" Adopted by the ALA Council, June 30, 1993. [ISBN 8389–7701–4]

"Access to Resources and Services in the School Library Media Program: An Interpretation of the Library Bill of Rights." Adopted July 2, 1986; amended January 10, 1990, by the ALA Council. [ISBN 8389–7053–2]

"Challenged Materials: An Interpretation of the Library Bill of Rights." Adopted June 25, 1971; amended July 1, 1981; January 10, 1990, by the ALA Council. [ISBN 8399–6083–9]

"Diversity in Collection Development: An Interpretation of the Library Bill of Rights." Adopted July 14, 1982; amended January 10, 1990, by the ALA Council [ISBN 8389–6552–0]

"Economic Barriers to Information Access: An Interpretation of the Library Bill of Rights." Adopted by the ALA Council, June 30, 1993. [ISBN 8389–7702–2]

"Evaluating Library Collections: An Interpretation of the Library Bill of Rights." Adopted February 2, 1973; amended July 1, 1981, by the ALA Council. [ISBN 8389–5406–5]

"Exhibit Spaces and Bulletin Boards: An Interpretation of the Library Bill of Rights." Adopted July 2, 1991, by the ALA Council. [ISBN 8389–7551–8]

"Expurgation of Library Materials: An Interpretation of the Library Bill of Rights." Adopted February 2, 1973; amended July 1, 1981; January 10, 1990, by the ALA Council. [ISBN 8389–5419–7]

"Free Access to Libraries for Minors: An Interpretation of the Library Bill of Rights." Adopted June 30, 1972; amended July 1, 1981; July 3, 1991, by the ALA Council. [ISBN 8389–7549–6]

"Library-Initiated Programs as a Resource: An Interpretation of the Library Bill of Rights." Adopted January 27, 1982; amended June 26, 1990, by the ALA Council. [ISBN 8389–6528]

"Meeting Rooms: An Interpretation of the Library Bill of Rights." Adopted July 2, 1991, by the ALA Council. [ISBN 8389–7550–X]

"Restricted Access to Library Materials: An Interpretation of the Library Bill of Rights." Adopted February 2, 1973; amended July 1, 1981; July 3, 1991, by the ALA Council. [ISBN 8389–7552–6]

Appendix F
American Association of School Librarians (AASL)
Position Papers

AASL, a Division of ALA, has prepared a number of position papers based on the "Library Bill of Rights" and addressing concerns of those involved in providing school library media programs. Like the position papers adopted by ALA, those of AASL are written emphasizing a particular point that has strong support in the basic documents quoted at the beginning of this section. One position statement, that on flexible scheduling, is given as an example.

AASL POSITION STATEMENT ON
FLEXIBLE SCHEDULING

Schools must adopt the educational philosophy that the library media program is fully integrated into the educational program. This integration strengthens the teaching/learning process so that students can develop the vital skills necessary to locate, analyze, evaluate, interpret, and communicate information and ideas. When the library media program is fully integrated into the instructional program of the school, students, teachers, and library media specialists become partners in learning. The library program is an extension of the classroom. Information skills are taught and learned within the context of the classroom curriculum. The wide range of resources, technologies, and services needed to meet students' learning and information needs are readily available in cost-effective manner.

The integrated library media program philosophy requires that an open schedule must be maintained. Classes cannot be scheduled in the library media center to provide teacher release or preparation time. Students and teachers must be able to come to the center throughout the day to use information sources, to read for pleasure, and to meet and work with other students and teachers.

Planning between the library media specialist and the classroom teacher, which encourages both scheduled and informal visits, is the catalyst that makes this integrated library program work. The teacher brings to the planning process a knowledge of subject content and student needs. The library media specialist contributes a broad knowledge of resources and technology, an understanding of teaching methods, and a wide range of strategies that may be employed to help students learn information skills.

Cooperative planning by the teacher and library media specialist integrates information skills and materials into the classroom curriculum and results in the development of assignments that encourage open inquiry.

The responsibility for flexibly scheduled library media programs must be shared by the entire school community. The Board of Education endorses the philosophy that the library program is an integral part of the district's educational program and ensures that flexible scheduling for library media centers is maintained in all buildings and at all levels.

The District Administration supports this philosophy and monitors staff assignments to ensure appropriate staffing levels so that all teachers, including the library media specialists, can fulfill their professional responsibilities.

The Principal creates the appropriate climate within the school by advocating the benefits of flexible scheduling to the faculty, by monitoring scheduling, by ensuring appropriate staffing levels, and by providing joint planning time for classroom teachers and library media specialists.

The Teacher uses resource-based instruction and views the library media program as an integral part of that instruction.

The Library Media Specialist is knowledgeable about curriculum and classroom activities, and works cooperatively with the classroom teacher to integrate information skills into the curriculum.

Adopted June 1991.

LIST OF ADDITIONAL AASL POSITION PAPERS

"Appropriate Staffing for School Library Media Centers." Adopted April 1991.

"Confidentiality of Library Records." ALA Policy 52.4, 54.16.

"Information Literacy: A Position Paper on Information Problem Solving." Based on a 1993 document of the Wisconsin Educational Media Association. Adopted by AASL in 1994, and by the National Forum for Information Literacy, an umbrella group of over 60 organizations.

"Preparation of School Library Media Specialists." Adopted 1994.

"Resource-Based Instruction: Role of the School Library Media Specialist in the Whole Language Approach." Adopted June 1993.

"Role of the School Library Media Program." Adopted October 1990.

"Role of the School Library Media Specialist in Outcomes-Based Education." Adopted February 1994.

"Role of the School Library Media Specialist in Site-Based Management." Adopted 1993.

"Value of Independent Reading in the School Library Media Program." Adopted June 1994.

"Value of Library Media Programs in Education." Adopted 1994.

SUGGESTED READINGS

American Association of School Librarians and Association for Educational Communications and Technology, *Information Power: Building Partnerships for Learning* (Chicago: ALA, 1998).

American Library Association Presidential Committee on Information Literacy: Final Report (Chicago: ALA, 1989).

Lance, Keith Curry, et al. *The Impact of School Library Media Centers on Academic Achievement* (Castle Rock, Colo: Hi Willow Research & Publishing, 1993).

Michigan State Board of Education, "Position Paper on Information Processing Skills" (Lansing, Mich.: Michigan State Board of Education, 1992).

"Restructuring and School Libraries," (Special Section) *NASSP Bulletin* 75 (May 1991): 1–58.

(A Special Section on the School Library for the Nineties). *Phi Delta Kappan* 73 (March 1992): 521–537.

U.S. Department of Labor, The Secretary's Commission on Achieving Necessary Skills, *Learning a Living: A Blueprint for High Performance* (Washington, D.C.: U.S. Government Printing Office, 1992).

Notes

INTRODUCTION

1. Samuel B. Bacharach and Sharon C. Conley, "Education Reform: A Managerial Agenda," *Phi Delta Kappan* (May 1986): 644.
2. Ibid.
3. E. D. Hirsch, Jr., "The Core Knowledge Curriculum: What's Behind Its Success," *Educational Leadership* (May 1992): 29.
4. Ibid.: 30.

CHAPTER 1

5. James R. Marks, Emery Stoops, and Joyce King-Stoops, *Handbook of Educational Supervision: A Guide for the Practitioner* (Boston: Allyn and Bacon, 1971).

CHAPTER 2

6. Clifford Stoll, "The Internet? Bah!," *Newsweek* (February 25, 1995): 41.
7. "The Haves and Have-Nots," *Newsweek* (February 25, 1995): 52.
8. Ibid.
9. Richard A. Durost, "Integrating Computer Technology: Planning, Training, and Support," *NASSP* (September 1994): 49.

10. Stephen K. Stoan, "Research and Library Skills: An Analysis and Interpretation," *College and Research Libraries* (March 1984): 99–107.
11. Vicki Hancock, as quoted by Philip Cohen, "Putting Resource-Based Learning to Work," *ASCD Education Update* (March 1995): 6.
12. Barbara Campbell, as quoted by Philip Cohen, Ibid.
13. Margaret Jorgensen, "Assessing Habits of the Mind," *Eric Document ED 372951*: 12.

CHAPTER 3

14. Ibid: 15–16.

CHAPTER 5

15. Benjamin S. Bloom, *Taxonomy of Educational Objectives. Handbook I: Cognitive Domain* (New York: David McKay, 1956).
16. Robert Marzano et al., *Dimensions of Thinking* (Alexandria, Va.: Association for Supervision and Curriculum Development, 1986).
17. Leslie Hart, *Human Brain and Human Learning* (New York: Longman, 1983).
18. Christina S. Doyle, "Eric Digest," *Emergency Librarian* (March–April 1995): 32.
19. Jo Ann Kerr, "Collaborative Assessment," *Eric Document ED 376961*: 8.
20. Ibid.
21. Christina S. Doyle, "Eric Digest," *Emergency Librarian* (March–April 1995): 32.
22. Grant Wiggins, "Creating Tests Worth Taking," *Educational Leadership* (May 1992): 27.

Glossary

Terms that have special meanings or interpretations in school library media programs have been chosen for this list. To amplify these, annotations—rather than definitions—have been used.

AACR2 *Anglo-American Cataloguing Rules*, second edition, revised, and *Amendments*, second edition, revised (1993), are basic rules used to catalog library materials. They were designed to increase international uniformity among libraries of all types and sizes, essential in networking.

ACCESS In a catalog or index the name, term, or code that is being looked up provides an access point to a reference on the topic. Access to materials means the rights of students to use all of the materials in the collection. It relates not only to intellectual freedom but also to the absence of physical and psychological barriers and to the presence of appropriate opportunities. ACCESS TO INFORMATION means that students will be able to gain information regardless of where it may be located through networking, interlibrary loans, databases, or other collections. Access to the school library media center should not be curtailed by arbitrary rules, contractual commitments, or insufficient equipment, personnel, or space.

ACCESSION FILE A computerized record of acquisition and disposal of each item that has ever been in the collection. This is a complete record of orders, gifts, and withdrawals.

ACCESSION NUMBERS Unique identification of materials in the order in which they were added to a collection, often in numerical form with the first two digits indicating the year, as in "96–114, 96–115," and so forth. This information is retained in the shelflist and/or accession file. (cf. bar codes).

ADDED ENTRIES Access to an item in a catalog through joint author, translator, illustrator, editor, compiler, collaborator, or series. These are in addition to main author, title, and subject entries in catalogs.

AFTER-HOURS MEETINGS Unless clear-cut policies are made and enforced, after-hours meetings can be the source of many misunderstandings and problems.

AIR CONDITIONING Not a luxury and not just for people comfort. When microforms and electronics are included in the collection, their preservation is affected by heat and moisture which air conditioning can help control.

ALPHABETIZING The alphabet is applied in two ways, known as word-by-word and letter-by-letter systems. Another explanation is to say we alphabetize using 27- or 26-character strings. In the 27-character system, a space is considered a character that precedes any letter. Dictionaries tend to use the letter-by-letter system. The older card catalogs were usually arranged word-by-word. Various reference books used whichever system the editor preferred. Computer programs usually alphabetize using the word-by-word system. Students need to be fluent in both.

AMERICAN LIBRARY ASSOCIATION The principal national professional association for librarians. A division known as American Association of School Librarians (AASL) is especially concerned with the operation of school library media center programs. School library media teachers benefit from membership. The address is: 50 East Huron Street, Chicago,

Illinois, 60611. Some white papers and policy statements and others listed by topic appear in Appendix E.

ANALYTIC Another form of added entry in the catalog that permits locating a play, poem, or story that is in a collection, or locating a lone chapter on a topic in a book that might otherwise be missed. Often used for locating obscure but frequently needed information.

ANNOTATION The note on a catalog entry or a bibliography that indicates the contents of the cataloged item.

ANNUAL A publication that comes out once a year such as an almanac or a yearbook. It can be desirable to have these purchased on a standing order plan to have them as soon as they are published.

ARCHIVES A type of reference library collection made up of public papers, documents, records, and other primary sources.

ATMOSPHERE In a school library media center the term applies to the inviting feeling users do or do not experience. It reflects the school library media teachers' personalities and is enhanced by easy chairs, color, plants, decorations such as good pictures and posters, carpeting, good maintenance.

AUDIOVISUAL MATERIALS The nonprint materials that teach through sound and sight. They should be stored with consideration given to the availability of equipment needed for listening and viewing, and they should be cataloged with access records filed in the main library media center catalog.

AUTHORITY FILES The records of the correct forms of names or terms used in the catalog. Their purpose is to maintain uniformity of entries.

BACKUP FILES These are master copies of computer software, audio tapes, guidebooks, or any other items likely to be lost. Only copies of the masters are circulated. When creating files by use of a computer program, it is customary to make a second disc that contains a copy of the materials created in case the original is damaged or lost.

BAR CODES The device made up of varying width lines (bars) that represent numbers used to code materials in a collection. Activated by a light wand, their use in materials circulation and inventory replaces accession numbers.

BASIC COLLECTION The minimum collection that should be ready for use opening day. There are bibliographies published that are helpful in establishing the initial collection, but they need to be adapted to suit local and individual school needs.

BAUD RATE Rate at which characters are transmitted by telephone lines.

BIBLIOGRAPHIC RECORD A catalog entry in any format—card, microform, online, machine-readable printout—that gives full cataloging information for the item.

BIBLIOTHERAPY The use of books and stories to help troubled readers deal with personal problems through information gathered or identification with characters.

BIDDING The business practice of seeking the lowest possible price for an item prior to purchase. In the book trade, firms cannot give across-the-board discounts because of the many variables of publishing, e.g., bindings. Not all business managers seem to be aware of the problems created through demanding bids on books. Many book jobbers are not interested in accepting accounts that require bidding.

BILL OF RIGHTS The American Library Association and its divisions have prepared documents that express support for the citizens' right to read. They have also prepared statements concerning ethics in serving library media center users. Media professionals support the principles stated in these documents. Titles of a number of interpretative documents based on the "Library Bill of Rights" appear in Appendix E.

BINDINGS One of the reasons for varying discounts on books is the binding in which the item appears. Paper, trade, text, and library-reinforced bindings have different wearing qualities and, therefore, manufacturing costs.

BIT Smallest unit of data used in computerized storage.

BOOK FAIRS Book sales sponsored by the PTA, class groups, or the school library media center itself, which encourage interest in book ownership and reading and often prove to be money-raising events. They can also be integrated into the curriculum and developed as excellent curricular and learning catalysts.

BOOK JOBBER The jobber can supply materials from many publishers or producers thereby reducing the number of purchase orders to be handled in the school library media center and by the business department. It is sometimes possible to visit the jobber's warehouse and make selections directly from the shelves. This allows first-hand inspection of the materials before purchase. Close to the end of a budget year, this system ensures full use of monies available as none are left unspent because of unfilled orders. When using this system, take along a letterhead statement of credit and a purchase order number.

BOOK REBINDING A portion of the school library media center budget should be reserved for rebinding. Expensive reference books and other heavy books tend to show wear and come apart with use. When these are useful items that should be retained, and when the text is current enough and the page paper is in good enough condition, it may be worthwhile to have the item rebound.

BOOK REINFORCEMENT Paperbound books wear longer when covered with clear plastic reinforcement sheeting or kits especially made for the purpose. Text and library bindings are strengthened with the insertion of fabric or plastic strips and stronger sewing of signatures so that they wear longer. These preventive measures add to the cost of the book. Pamphlets may be reinforced through hand stitching so that middle pages are not lost.

BOOK REPAIR Someone on the staff should be trained to make simple repairs on print and nonprint holdings when they become damaged. Students should be discouraged from trying to mend torn pages and loose bindings themselves because they do not have the proper materials. Special glues and techniques are needed to mend rather than further ruin a damaged book. Freezing is employed when there has been flood damage, and it also helps with removal of chewing gum.

BOOK REVIEWS *See* REVIEWS

BOOKSTORE The school bookstore may be operated as a part of the Distributive Education classwork at the high school level. Middle and elementary schools sometimes combine bookstore operation with the school library media program to encourage book ownership among students. Whereas book fairs are annual events, the bookstore program is ongoing.

BOOKTRUCK Often there are not enough booktrucks in the school library media center to permit filling several simultaneous requests for classroom reserve collections. Using booktrucks for these collections permits rolling them into classrooms for the periods needed and returning them to the center for everyone's use the rest of the time. When there are insufficient numbers of booktrucks available, those normally needed for center housekeeping have to be taken over for reserves, interfering with routine. A similar situation arises with equipment carts unless a cart is purchased routinely when an additional piece of machinery is acquired. Standards, which usually address the functional needs of the center rather than the program needs, rarely call for a sufficient number of booktrucks.

BORROWERS' CARDS When circulation is managed using charge-out machines or computerized methods, each student and teacher must be issued a borrower's card to activate the equipment. Some schools keep these cards on file at the circulation desk to avoid loss or use by someone else. These cards should include photo identification made current annually to ensure accuracy of use. When computerized systems are used, they also carry a bar code to identify the borrower.

BYTE Eight bits constitute a byte, the unit of data needed to represent one character such as a letter, a number, or a punctuation symbol. KILOBYTE equals 1,024 bytes of data; MEGABYTE equals 1 million bytes of data.

CALL NUMBERS These numbers, coded to the content, are affixed to the spines of books and to each nonprint item as an indicator of storage location. They are used for reshelving as well as for locating after a reference to them has been found in the catalog. They should be clearly legible, machine-lettered, use the author's complete last name (as opposed to one to three letters only), and should be placed on materials in a consistent location so that they are easily found and have a uniform appearance.

CARPETING The use of carpeting in school library media centers has become customary. Its acoustical qualities are noteworthy, and it contributes to the atmosphere through color, texture, and design. When carpeting is being chosen it should be of the best commercial quality to withstand wear. There can be a problem with carpeting if insufficient custodial staff or unsuitable cleaning equipment are assigned to the school library media center. Spills need to be attended to immediately. One major annual cleaning is insufficient.

CARREL A private study desk usually equipped with sides and a book shelf. It may be electrified to permit plugging in of equipment for listening, viewing, or computing.

CATALOG The traditional catalog entries have been prepared on 3 x 5 cards and filed in drawers with retaining rods. Catalogs have also been prepared in computer printout book format or read from microform. Current catalogs are accessed online through computer terminals. Regardless of format used, decisions must be made regarding arrangement, filing orders, and subject heading terminology to be used. Local cataloging preferences are not always compatible with network catalogs.

CATALOGING The process of preparing entries for a catalog; that is, indexing the collection.

CD-ROM (compact disc—read only memory) A form of data storage using laser optics rather than magnetic means for reading the data. Holds very large quantity of information including sound and motion picture or video clips as well as print and pictures.

CENSORSHIP The term used to indicate attempts from outside the school to control what information students may be able to access. The process of selection should never deteriorate into a form of censorship, and is unlikely to when the library media teachers and subject teachers feel secure in their support by the board of education and administration and in the presence of a written policy and procedure for handling censorship attempts.

CENTRALIZED PROCESSING Any cooperative plan that allows for one agency to provide a combination of ordering, cataloging, and technical functions for a group of libraries such as those of a school system or a combination of school, public, and special libraries.

CIP Cataloging-in-Publication, a program begun in 1971 by the Library of Congress and cooperating publishers in which a partial bibliographic description is provided on the verso (reverse side) of the title page of a book.

CIRCULATION The activities involved in lending materials and equipment to departments, classroom teachers, or individual students for varying periods of time, keeping records of these transactions, and retrieving and reentering these items into the collection.

CLASSIFICATION SYSTEMS Any of several schemes used for the arrangement of instructional materials according to subject or form. These include the Dewey Decimal System, which is the chief system used by schools and small libraries, and the Library of Congress System, which is used by universities and large municipal public libraries.

CLASSROOM COLLECTIONS Small groups of materials loaned by the school library media center for a limited time, changed frequently to match classroom activities, and subject to recall for broader use in the center or to meet an individual's need. They should not be referred to as "libraries."

CODE BOOK A manual or handbook in which all statements of philosophy, goals, policies, procedures, job descriptions, job functions, and forms used in the operation of the school library media center are written out to ensure consistency and continuity. New staff members use it to find out what has gone on before. Pages can be duplicated for instruction of volunteers and substitutes.

COLOR CODING A system in which color signifies location or format. Once used in card catalogs to indicate nonprint materials by adding a colored strip or plastic cover to a catalog card.

COMMUNICATION Technological advances permit instant communication by means of voice, e-mail, facsimile transmission, pagers, carphones, television, and more. Faster may not be better if attention ceases to be given to creating messages that have courtesy, clarity, completeness, or show emphasis, concern, or emotion regarding the information being transmitted.

COMMUNITY RESOURCES A broad term encompassing educational facilities within the community that are not part of the school. Also applied to skilled people willing to share their expertise with students or classroom groups. Reference is made in the catalog to the Community Resources File.

COMPUTER LAB The room or area in which computers are collected and their use by students supervised. Classroom groups or individual students and teachers may make use of the lab.

COMPUTER USE MANAGEMENT The computers in the school may be located in a number of places and used in a variety of ways. Those for student use may be concentrated in a lab, assigned to classrooms, assigned to the school library media center, or housed in the center and sent out to classrooms as requested. Often administrators and teachers are provided and use a different set of computers, programs, and networks. Training for and the educational use made of computers, along with the care of the software, is often the responsibility of school library media teachers even when supplementary computer staff is provided.

COMPUTER-ASSISTED INSTRUCTION Individualized, interactive drill and practice, tutorial, simulation, and problem-solving instructional formats. Students move through checkpoints in the educational programs at different rates of speed and approaches.

COMPUTERIZED LIBRARY ADMINISTRATION Many functions such as circulation, overdue notices, ordering, cataloging, inventory, and the creation of bibliographies can be done better through the use of a computer. To institute and continue with a computerized administrative program in the school library media center calls for the dedicated use of one or more computers. The computer does not operate itself, so there are personnel and budgetary considerations involved.

COMPUTER-MANAGED INSTRUCTION Method of managing information about students' performance based on administration of diagnostic tests. Scores tests, enters grades, and prescribes next steps. Gradebook programs calculate marks based on directions encoded to assign weight, drop, double, or average individually entered scores.

CONFERENCE ROOMS Small enclosed areas where individuals or groups of students may work together. These are necessary for recording practice speeches or for small-group discussions, neither of which work well in the main school library media center.

CONNECTIVITY When referring to SOFTWARE, means software packages with built-in conversion capability; i.e., these files can be used with different operating systems and still produce the original text-formatting features leaving such features as boldface, underscore, or italic intact. When referring to WIRELESS, means combining laptop or handheld computers with cellular fax modems, making it possible to have school information available at any place or time.

CONTESTS So long as the competition level does not become excessive and self-defeating, schoolwide contests that are curriculum-oriented and emanate from the school library media center can lead to improved and pleasurable learning.

CONTINUATION ORDERS Instead of cutting off an order that cannot be filled within a specified time, which requires reordering the same materials, this procedure permits the materials to be back-ordered. The benefit to the school library media program outweighs the inconvenience to the business office.

COPYING MACHINES Students need access to first-rate copying machines. Their use reduces vandalism and increases the amount of background reading students tend to do for assignments. When copying machines are installed in the school library media center, the students can operate them. When staff have to go to the school office to make copies for students, it is a poor use of professional time.

COPYRIGHT Respect for copyright privilege is a legal matter. The rules are clear-cut for print and continue to be clarified for nonprint materials. School library media teachers are expected to follow these laws themselves and to enforce them when doing work for other teachers or students. Probably the most difficult areas relate to the pirating of computer software and the increasing use of computer networks to share information. The school library media teacher benefits from definitive Board of Education policies and firm support from the administration.

COSTS It is useful to know the current average cost of books when one is establishing an annual budget request. These figures are available in the latest *Bowker Annual* (New York: Bowker).

CROSS-REFERENCES Known as "see" or "see also" references, students need to learn to differentiate between the two and to use them effectively. "See" is used to refer searcher to a different heading for any information on the subject; "see also" refers to other headings for additional information.

CYBERSPACE A science fiction term introduced in the novel *Neuromancer* (1984) by William Gibson describing the mix of the human mind and electronic capabilities in experiencing virtual reality.

DAMAGE Classroom teacher cooperation is essential to its prevention. When a cavalier attitude is exhibited regarding materials and equipment and their use, inconvenience is the least of the problems. Much money is lost when replacement is due to carelessness. The bigger problem is that replacement is often not possible, especially with the current status of tax laws which cause publishers and producers to issue fewer copies of an item making it go out of print faster. Classroom teachers who set a good example and who keep after their students make a significant contribution to the school library media center program.

DATABASES Computerized online bibliographies or subject-oriented content files that are used by researchers, usually for a fee. Depending on the information needed, they can save search time and they may be more current than printed indexes or bibliographies. However, they are no more inclusive of information than the cataloger or indexer's skills permit and should be used judiciously.

DESIDERATA *See* WISH FILE

DICTIONARY CATALOG The term applied to catalogs that interfile author, title, and subject entries in a single A to Z section.

DISC, FLOPPY Form of computer data storage, now 5 1/4 or 3 1/2 inch size. DENSITY of disc is determined by the spacing (number) of concentric rings called "tracks." The closer they are, the higher the density of the disc. HARD DRIVE is another form of computer data storage, normally an internal rigid disc in a sealed case. Not removable in the manner of floppy discs; it holds large quantities of data.

DISC DRIVE A peripheral computer device necessary to read and store material in floppy discs. May be built-in or external.

DISCIPLINE The school library media center should never be used as a means of punishment.

DISTANCE EDUCATION A means of bringing instruction into areas that cannot support the same instruction locally either because there are too few students or instructors are scarce, making the cost unjustifiable. Students in far-off locations who have access to cable or satellite receivers, phone lines, and video cameras can have access to teachers and subject content. Like any classroom experience, learning depends upon the skill of the instructor and the interest of the students. These classes employ one- or two-way audio and one- or two-way video. An extension of correspondence study, it provides equitable access to quality education through use of technology.

DIVIDED CATALOGS Term applied to catalogs that are in sections. Entries for authors and titles appear A to Z in one section, while entries for subjects appear A to Z in another.

EATING Food and school library media centers do not mix well. Libraries that permit eating or drinking within their facilities often provide snacking areas. Liquids spilled on pages, pictures, copying machines, and computer terminal keyboards leave expensive results. Food stashed behind rows of books in the stacks make a mess. Chewing gum stuck between pages and mashed into carpeting is most difficult to clean. A carrel in an out-of-the-way corner is a magnet to brown baggers who often do not bother to clean up. There is no easy solution to hungry students' wanting to use lunch hour to do some library-oriented work. (*See also* FOOD.)

EQUIPMENT Also referred to as "hardware," the machinery necessary for listening, viewing, copying, and computing operations. Each piece should be etched with its identifying number and owner. The electric stylus used for this marking may be borrowed from police departments, which encourage its use.

EQUITY The school library media program is a primary equalizer of educational opportunity. All students are persons with individual needs that must be met if we are to have true equality in education.

ERIC (Educational Research Information Centers) The school library media program should provide all teachers with the opportunity to obtain and view ERIC materials. Centralized professional collections may include access to ERIC indexing, microfiche, and CD-ROM items.

EVALUATION All school and library media center operations should be evaluated regularly by administrators, faculty teams, school library media personnel, students, and accrediting agencies. When questionnaires are used, a follow-up document should report answers to questions and explanations regarding what changes are being made, or cannot be made and why, as a result of the questionnaire.

EXTENDED HOURS When students have too few study hall or unassigned periods to enable them to use the school library media center adequately during the school day, the hours of the school library media program must be extended to address their needs. Professional staffing is as important as access to the center. Extended hours may require late bus runs.

FIELD TRIPS Information for making contacts and the evaluations and tips from field trip leaders are kept in the school library media center for use by other classroom teachers. Maintain a separate card file or place entries in catalogs, listing, under appropriate subject headings, information about places of interest for field trips. Classroom teachers new to the community or teaching courses new to them will benefit. So will students who want to make trips independently or with their parents.

FILING RULES Computerized databases have caused a reconsideration of filing. Outdated ALA filing rules contained a number of "as if" situations that were workable in a manual filing system. ALA rules have been revised to permit machine alphabetizing. The common rule now is to file "as is." Abbreviations are no longer uniformly filed "as if" they were spelled out. This causes the user to look in two places to make sure nothing has been missed—at the abbreviated spelling and at the full spelling. Compound words and names are entered as spelled and spaced. Students need to be taught to use catalogs and indexes that are in the old style arrangement as well as those that have been revised, as long as they are likely to use facilities that continue to use unchanged card catalog systems or reference books.

FINES Imposing a payment for each day a piece of borrowed material is overdue is designed to hasten the return of overdue materials or to encourage the on-time return of materials but often does neither. Students may believe that paying the fine legitimatizes keeping a book out, or they may decide to wait for an "amnesty day" to return it. Use of a fine system establishes a double standard that often appears to penalize honesty (especially when a maximum fine policy is established). Fines have no place as a budgetary supplement.

FIXED SCHEDULE Classes are scheduled for a specific day and time regardless of need. As a result, "library skills" become a separate subject taught in isolation. Student access to the library media center is limited to those specified times regardless of educational needs or personal interests. Classroom teachers tend to drop their classes off and not collaborate in the students' experiences in the center.

FLEXIBLE SCHEDULE Classes, small groups, and individual students are free to mix uses whenever need and interest arise. Library media and classroom teachers plan together regarding information needs arising from ongoing classroom instruction, and time spent in the center is reserved as needed. Teachers plan instruction collaboratively, skills instruction is integrated into the ongoing curriculum, and students use and check out materials as needed throughout the entire day every day. Classroom teachers remain with their whole classes and engage in the learning activities. However, on occasion classes may be split with part remaining in the classroom and part coming to the library media center.

FLOOR WORK A term used to describe the school library media teachers' being visible out "on the floor" and working with students as opposed to being seated behind a desk or in the workroom.

FOOD Eating is usually prohibited in the school library media center. Nevertheless, a coffee pot, a tea bag, and a slice of cake in the workroom do tend to bring in both administrators and classroom teachers. The serving of refreshments is an amenity that captures and holds a clientele for a few minutes. (*See also* EATING.)

FORMS The unique preprinted slips used to facilitate various school library media center functions. Examples include passes, evaluation forms for teachers to use when previewing or examining materials, or student requests for reserves or purchases.

FREE AND INEXPENSIVE MATERIALS These have their cost factor, if not in purchase price then in ordering, housing (vertical file maintenance), and use. Extra care needs to be taken with evaluation of their educational worth and the advertising bias that may be present.

FUNDS The support of the school library media program is provided by a tax-based budget. When a School Library Media Fund is established, individuals and organizations have a means to contribute without fear that the funds may be channeled elsewhere. PTA and other parent and friends groups often raise funds and manage grocery receipt drives and other community-based enterprises.

GAMES In addition to commercially prepared educational games, those which are teacher- or student-designed may be useful. Valuable ones should, therefore, be cataloged as a part of the library media center collection.

GOVERNMENT DOCUMENTS A valuable source of educational materials that is often underutilized by schools. Local, state, and federal sources are available.

GRANTS The titles of grants may not indicate that their monies may be used for libraries. Careful interpretation of their purposes and criteria may suggest applicability. For example, grants for humanities and selected disciplines could be sources of funds for collection development.

GRAPHS Students become familiar with graph making progressively, usually starting with pie or bar types. Graph construction programs are available for computer use and in addition to pie and bar types also include those known as stacked bar, line, x/y graph, scatter, boxplot, stem and leaf, best fit, and normal curve. Students benefit from recognizing and using the full range of graph construction.

GROUPWARE Programs that allow users of a computer network to jointly author, share, and disseminate electronic documents. One user starts a file and subsequent users read the work, react, and add comments and suggestions, including graphic images, sound, and video clips. The initial author then incorporates as much of the added material as desired. Another type of program allows network users to work together to brainstorm, question, analyze, rank items, and set priorities in order to make decisions.

GUIDE CARDS When the catalog is in card format, liberal use of guide cards facilitates filing and finding cards. A rule of thumb is to place guide cards approximately every inch, or wherever four or more access points are identical. The print on guide cards follows the standard formula of all capital letters for subject headings and upper and lower case for authors (inverted order).

HANG-UPS The trade name for plastic bags of varying sizes fitted with hooked closure handles that permit the hanging of nonprint materials or small pieces of equipment. Obtainable from Monaco Hangups, Bethel, CT 06801.

INDEPENDENT STUDY When there are formal programs of independent study, honors, gifted, or other educational programs that go beyond the standard classroom levels, they impact on the school library media collection, use of interlibrary loan, and the specialized network and off-site services of the school library media teachers. The planning for effective independent study programs must involve school library media teachers and be reflected in the budget.

INDIRECT SERVICES The selection of materials for purchase, processing, choice of subject heading terminologies for cataloging, and the determination to purchase database services are examples of indirect services school library media teachers provide for center users. Personnel should be evaluated on performance of these factors just as they should be on direct teaching and floor work services. The observable direct services are dependent upon successful indirect services.

INDIVIDUALIZED WORKSHEETS The use of identical questions or activities for student assignments in the school library media center is not effective. When each student has a unique assignment, series of questions, or suggested activity, little trading or sharing of answers can occur. Work is done by the student alone and the expected effort is produced. An entire class working on identical assignments creates a chaotic demand on the same materials and often leads to a dishonest approach to the assignment, thereby diminishing learning.

INFORMATION LITERACY The ability to find, interpret, evaluate, use, and communicate information gathered from a variety of sources.

INTERACTIVE MULTIMEDIA A computer technology that brings together information from a variety of sources, usually text, line drawings, maps and graphs, animated graphics, voice narration, music, and color video clips.

INTERCOM AS INSTRUCTIONAL TOOL Schoolwide contests, games, and attention-getting devices emanating from the school library media center as part of total school announcements can serve as effective educational experiences.

INTERLIBRARY LOAN The system of one library borrowing from another to fill a user's need. Standardized procedures and forms are used, and with the advent of networking, materials are located through the computerized databases. Frequently the needed materials can be received via fax processes.

ISBN International Standard Book Number, a distinctive number agreed upon internationally to identify a book. ISSN is used similarly with serials. These numbers are assigned by ISDS, International Serials Data System, a network of national and international centers sponsored by UNESCO. The book numbers consist of ten digits that indicate the language used, the publisher, and the publisher's in-house coding.

JOB DESCRIPTIONS A document listing the attributes and competencies and responsibilities required of the person who holds the job. It protects both the employer and the employee. It is used as a basis for evaluation of performance as well as of hiring job applicants. Every paid professional and nonprofessional staff position should have a job description. Additionally, job function documents need to be utilized.

JOB FUNCTIONS A companion document for use with job descriptions that describes in minute detail every step in a procedure or process. It is used by new employees, temporary substitutes, and to document changes in work load for salary evaluations.

LABELING Not only should individual items be clearly machine-labeled, but also the shelves, drawers, cabinets, or other areas of housing. This facilitates locating and refiling materials. Labeling, as in the practice of describing or designating materials by affixing a prejudicial label to predispose people's attitudes toward library materials, is a form of censorship.

LASER VIDEODISCS Laser videodiscs permit the user to interact with still or moving images in addition to print. A computer is not required. The disc player is operated by means of remote controls and bar code readers that locate and incorporate into multimedia presentations the desired images and information contained on the videodisc.

LEARNING PACKAGES A collection of materials pertaining to a unit or subject area meant to be used independently by the student. It may be a formal lesson with an expected outcome, or it may be an enrichment experience. Those made in-house that match curriculum areas and student capabilities are made from materials found in the school library media center collection. Commercially prepared packages usually do not serve specific needs as well because they must serve a general audience. Often they are based on only the most basic of references, and the lively school program will allow a student to progress much farther.

LEARNING PROMPTERS Students do not always learn the first time an explanation is given. Some are hesitant to ask when they believe they should know the answers to their questions. The use of learning prompters, that is, posted informational and directive signs where they are needed, provides for informal learning. For example, students from film study class who need to locate information about film directors benefit from signs listing the appropriate subject heading terminology used in various indexes. These should be posted where the film books or the indexes are located.

LIBRARY OF CONGRESS NUMBER Usually given on the verso (reverse side) of the title page of a book, this number begins with two digits (the year) followed by a hyphen and the rest of the number (e.g., 95–15695). This number is used as a unique identifier when using online databases. A similar number is assigned to nonprint materials. The Library of Congress number is not the same thing as the Library of Congress classification number that is used to place material on library shelves according to content.

LIGHT WAND The scanner used in some computerized circulation systems to read bar code labels.

LIMITED CIRCULATION When there are periods of high demand for a limited number of materials, a restructured circulation plan is called for. Reserve classification creates temporary reference status for these materials which are returned to their normal status as soon as the use crush is over.

LITERATURE SEARCH A systematic perusal in published sources for a piece or area of information. The school library media collection is the initial source of information, followed by search in local libraries, interlibrary loan services, and finally in databases. Students should be taught the techniques of fruitful search procedures, including use of Boolean terminology, standard indexing, and thesauri, before initiating database searches,

LM_NET A discussion and help exchange group on Internet for school library media professionals developed largely by Mike Eisenberg and Peter Milbury. Open to all school library media teachers and others involved in the school library media field worldwide since 1992.

MAIN ENTRY The complete record, that is, catalog entry, of an item in the form that uniquely identifies the item and usually includes the tracing that identifies all other catalog access points.

MARC Machine-Readable Cataloging, a program developed by the Library of Congress in which cataloging records are prepared in a format that enables the computer to recognize the elements and manipulate them for various purposes.

MEDIA In school library media centers, a medium is any means, agency, or instrumentality of communication regardless of format (print or nonprint).

MODEM Peripheral computer device that allows computers to communicate with each other via telephone lines. Modems operate at a wide range of speed.

MONITOR Peripheral computer device that is used to display information.

MULTIPLE COPIES Classroom size numbers of multiple copies are considered textbooks by definition of use rather than of format. When there are more than five copies of a title, these should be stored in the textbook stacks.

NETWORKING Networks of libraries are groups put together to share information, materials, and services. They can consist of just the schools within the district or region, a mix of public, academic, and special libraries, or can be computerized nationwide or link international information pools. Students and classroom groups make use of exchanges with other students and classes, as do teachers, to enlarge learning interests and information. There are networks that address any interest imaginable that permit popular individual exchanges. Many school library media teachers make extensive use of LM_NET, a part of Internet.

NONPRINT Carriers of information in other than print format. Pictures and sound are nonprint. Microforms, film, or computer discs may be classified as nonprint even though they feature print on surfaces other than paper and require hardware to be read.

OCLC Online Computer Library Center, a continuation of the Ohio College Library Center, is a bibliographic service center network with members throughout the United States and beyond. It is a source of cataloging information increasingly used by schools.

PAPERBACKS All materials in the school library media center collection should be listed in the catalog. When paperback racks are used for storage in a "go-fish" order, the system contradicts the philosophy of organization. A goodly number of nonfiction paperbacks are original works, not reproductions, and are worthy of intershelving.

PRECIS Preserved Context Indexing System, a British approach to subject retrieval in which an open-ended vocabulary can be organized according to a scheme of role-indicating operators for either manual or computer manipulation.

PRIORITY PURCHASE FILE A term meaning the same thing as "wish file" or "desiderata," but better understood by business managers.

PRODUCTION The actual physical production of all types of media, including audio, video, photographic, computer programs, or a combination of any of these. When a production program is encouraged there must be sufficient budget to support the needed materials, equipment, and staff time.

PROFESSIONAL COLLECTION A collection of books, journals, and other materials used mainly by teachers and administrators enrolled in coursework or for professional enhancement and advancement. The collection also is useful to students working on assignment topics involving education in the United States and abroad.

PROPERTY IDENTIFICATION The stamping of the school library media center's name and brief address on materials in the collection. Stamps should be applied in such a manner that the item, regardless of the position in which it is put down, exhibits a clearly readable property identification. On a book the stamp may be applied seven times, on endpapers, inside back and front covers, and on the three exposed edges.

REALIA Collections of real specimens and artifacts that are cataloged and used as learning devices. Rocks and minerals, bird nests, antique glass bottles, coins, whatever is useful to relate classroom teaching to real life, especially of people being studied—these are realia. Replicas are not realia. Both realia and replicas are considered objects by catalogers.

REFERENCE COLLECTION A group of sources within the collection containing authoritative information that is restricted to in-house or overnight use. The purpose is to assure school library media center users that materials needed to do assignments will be in school when needed. The problem of late returns is minimized when punishment for lateness is that the borrower may no longer take reference materials for overnight use.

REPLACEMENTS When materials have been lost or damaged, fees are collected equaling the replacement value. The problem here is that these fees often do not accrue to the school library media center funds but go directly into the general fund. This costs the library media center budget twice. It is a workable plan to require the errant borrower to personally purchase a replacement item. Accepting as clearance prepaid, noncancellable orders placed with a bookstore directed to deliver the material directly to the school library media center is another workable method. Some schools charge a replacement fee to cover the cost of processing. Others charge the current list price without an added fee.

REPORTS The school library media teacher files regular reports—weekly, monthly, and annually—in accordance with the school practice. Administrators can, with skillful reading, be alerted to potential problem areas, can make good use of the information for public awareness, and have documentation for planning.

RESERVE COLLECTION A temporary reference collection used to ensure availability to all during periods of high use as for a specific assignment given several classrooms at the same time. These may be retained on booktrucks and taken to classrooms or used in the school library media center. Like reference, tends to have overnight borrowing privilege accepted.

RETRIEVAL SUPPORT A responsibility of the administration to aid in securing the return, from students and teachers alike, of overdue materials, especially at term or year end and when families are moving out of town or teachers are changing schools.

RETROSPECTIVE CONVERSION The process of changing a card catalog to an online catalog. Combined in the process is weeding the collection, so that time and money are not spent on useless materials, and the update and improvement of cataloging when online MARC records are supplied for the collection. A time-consuming process sometimes undertaken by volunteers, paid converters, or more likely through a purchased service. Some equipment suppliers include retrospective conversion services as a sales incentive.

REVIEWS Sources of thorough reviews are important to proper materials selection, and these publications should be purchased as part of the school library media teachers' professional tools. School library media teachers need time to read reviews as a part of the selection process.

RUBRICS Criteria established by the teacher describing what a student must include in a finished product to achieve a given grade. E.g., "The butterfly mobile will be constructed following all ten of the construction directions provided. There will be a title and eight facts about butterflies included. Work will be done in an extremely neat and careful way. Due March 6." Lower-mark standards might use only eight or four construction directions, six or four facts, and accept less careful work. For additional points the student might also present an original poem about butterflies. Differentiation is addressed through the design of the range of rubrics presented.

SATELLITE Spacecraft used to send signals to Earth stations by means of microwave, telephone lines, or cable. Picked up by a DISH receiver.

SCHOOL LIBRARY MEDIA TEACHER When there are two or more professionals assigned to the same library media center, one is designated as department head or chairperson.

SEARCH SKILLS There is a distinct difference between search and research. Search is what most K-12 and undergraduate students do—seek out information and restructure it for a specific purpose. Research demands original thought and interpretation regarding some segment of a discipline. We teach search skills that can contribute to research when the scholar is ready to perform it.

SELECTION TOOLS The use of reviews appearing in respected journals, or of recognized basic bibliographies, is a standard selection practice among school library media teachers. A portion of the professional budget should be assigned to the purchase of such tools. However, complete dependence upon reviews and bibliographies is inappropriate. School policies and student needs are primary criteria. Whenever possible, actual examination of items should be encouraged.

SERVICE CONTRACTS Business managers have differing opinions regarding the use of service contracts for maintenance of machinery. School library media teachers always welcome the immediacy of response resulting from a service contract call for help. Downtime for a security system, for instance, can be costly, and for the circulation desk computer or the copying machine to be out-of-order contributes to frustration and poor public relations.

SHELFLIST The record of the instructional materials owned by the school library media center (regardless of where they are stored) and arranged in the order in which they are placed on the shelves. It is also the list that serves as an accurate base for inventory information.

SHELF READING Term applied to making certain each item is in its correct shelf order location. Students often place materials on shelves without regard to their proper location. These items remain "lost" until discovered by the shelf reader. Volunteers often help with this housekeeping task. It should be done weekly and throughout the entire collection.

SIMULATION Learning gained through simplification or abstraction of real-life processes or situations. Uses role playing and interactions to accomplish goals.

SPECIFICATIONS There is an art to writing specifications. Careful construction of requirements can manipulate the bidding system for desired results. When well written, specifications ensure that only the exact item wanted is purchased.

STACKS Stacks are bookshelves, and may be open or closed to student use. When closed, additional staff is needed to obtain materials for students and teachers. Closed stacks contribute to security but prohibit the advantages of browsing.

STANDARDS These may be set and mandated at state or national levels. Their impact will depend upon the degree to which they are enforced, funding or accreditation being withheld. National guidelines (not really standards because they carry no legal enforcement element) for school library media centers promoted by the professional associations were published in 1960, 1969, 1975, and 1987 and in 1998 as *Information Power: Building Partnerships for Learning*. (*See* AMERICAN LIBRARY ASSOCIATION.)

STANDING ORDER A system by which serial materials will be sent to a school library media center automatically immediately upon publication. Billing follows. The point is that the material would be purchased anyway, and this ensures not missing a publication and having it for use at the earliest possible moment. Reasonably accurate estimates can be used to encumber enough funds internally to cover the receipt of these needed materials. For example, next year's almanacs, yearbooks, or anticipated volumes of a title like *Contemporary Authors* are suitable for this type of ordering.

STORY HOURS To encourage children to enjoy literature is a universal goal, and story hours play an important part. Stories to be read should be selected with definite learning purposes in mind. Thinking skills can be practiced depending upon the way discussion is led or questions posed. These include having fun.

STORY TELLING An art form practiced by school library media teachers to share literature, make a point, or preserve a cultural heritage. Students may learn the art as a part of communications and language arts and can share their stories with younger students or peers.

SUBJECT HEADING A word or group of words indicating subject content of a cataloged item. Standardized lists are used to establish uniformity, but the lists differ. The Library of Congress Subject Heading List is used increasingly by networks and databases. While schools train students to use other libraries and purchase commercially processed materials that have MARC-generated indexing, all use LC headings, so that the LC terminology should not be changed. It is here to stay; it is the standardized terminology used when a system goes online. Time spent by school library media teachers in altering headings might better be spent in instruction. Special disciplines maintain their own lists such as the one found in the ERIC *Thesaurus*.

SUPPLIES While some items specifically designed for library use (such as flexible glues) can be purchased only from library supply houses, other standard items (such as tapes and computer paper) may be purchased at a lesser cost from other suppliers. It is more important to choose good quality supplies than less expensive but poorer quality substitutes.

TELECOMMUNICATIONS Telecommunications services permit establishing connections using a computer with modem and telephone line access to multichannel satellite and fiber-optic access. The value is in the up-to-dateness of information acquired through networks. Students may access publications, collect data through exchanges with specialists or peers, engage in e-mail communication, and participate in bulletin board and chat center conferencing. Contacts may be so local as to be within the school building or may be worldwide.

TELECONFERENCING Bringing meetings to people via technology. Saves travel time and expense and gets people together who might otherwise not attend. Exchanges are immediate and interactive.

TELEPHONE A telephone is an absolute necessity for the school library media center if the school library media teacher is to be able to efficiently provide full service. Immediate contact with other libraries and agencies extends the access to information. Having to leave the center to get to a phone or having to make all informational calls before and after school hours is wasteful and restricts the service. Controls on usage by unauthorized personnel are established through the switchboard or locking devices. Moreover, services dependent upon fax transmissions and computer modem connections require additional dedicated phone lines.

TIME CLOCK USE When passes are used to provide access to the school library media center, and classroom or study hall teachers need arrival or departure time verifications, signing and noting times for students is a poor use of time for the school library media personnel. More effective is the installation of a time clock in the center that students may use themselves upon entering and leaving.

TRACING The list of subject headings and added entries under which a cataloged item will appear in the catalog. It becomes essential when removing a record from the catalog to make sure all these references to the item are taken out.

TRADEBOOKS Refers to books published and sold for public consumption. The binding is often not reinforced for school or library usage. Some tradebooks will require almost immediate mending or rebinding. Most books in the library are tradebooks.

TYPES OF BOOKS Books are identified by their design of purpose. Government documents, atlases, gazetteers, almanacs, yearbooks, directories, pictorial histories, handbooks, encyclopedias, dictionaries, indexes, and bibliographies are examples. These types appear in most disciplines and therefore provide a suitable base for search instruction.

UNION CATALOG A catalog which includes the physical location of materials in a number of libraries such as an entire school system, the branches of a city library, or a regional network. By the use of the union catalog, one has used the combined catalogs of all the libraries in the system or network.

UNION SERIALS LIST A union catalog for periodicals.

VERTICAL FILE File cabinets in which folders full of clippings, pictures, and pamphlets are stored alphabetically by subject. These subject headings are the same as those used in the catalog. References to the contents of the vertical files are made in the catalog along with all other materials. Simple subject heading entries indicating the existence of a vertical file folder for the topic are sufficient.

VIRTUAL REALITY Employs three-dimensional environment obtained by use of special eyepieces to give a visual and kinesthetic sense of real life. The value is to move learning from a passive state to one in which students feel they have an active part. Term coined by Jaron Lamier.

VISUAL LITERACY For designers of visuals it pertains to imagery and imagery theory, visual symbols, visual verbal relationships, visual learning, cultural and technological coding of mass media images. For the library media and classroom teachers it means helping students recognize bias, persuasion, propaganda, and other symbolic or "hidden" visual messages just as is done with print messages.

VOICEMAIL A common touchtone telephone answering service available in many homes, businesses, and schools to take messages after hours or when personnel are not free to answer directly. Suitable for educational use to make contacts among teachers, students, and parents regarding homework comments and assignments, meetings, and conferences. By using personal information numbers privacy of information can be maintained.

WEEDING The process of systematically removing from the collection materials that have outlived their usefulness by becoming out-of-date, overly worn, no longer serving a curricular need, or are superfluous multiple copies taking up needed shelf space. In order not to be misled about use of materials that may be used frequently on reserve carts sent out as classroom collections, but show no circulation date as a result, it may be a good idea to date them in some way. LM_NET idea from Betty Dawn Hamilton is to use a rubber stamp saying "research" that also has the last two year digits, and stamp all books every time they go out on a cart. This could change the usage picture considerably.

WISH FILE The common term for desiderata, a file of items to be purchased when funds become available. Complete information needed for ordering (author, title, copyright date, publisher, ISBN number, list price, and edition) is entered initially, thus eliminating searching for this information later. The term used in this text is "priority purchase file."

WITHDRAWALS When materials have been removed from the collection through the weeding process, loss, or when they have become damaged beyond repair, all notations about them are withdrawn from the records. A policy should be in effect detailing the withdrawal process and the ultimate disposal process.

WORD PROCESSING Much has been learned about the use of word processing to improve the students' writing skills by increasing willingness to edit and revise. Currently use is being made of classroom sets of small portable word processors that can be stored and recharged on a rolling cart that provides security and flexibility. In some instances students may take these word processors home with them checking them out as they would any other piece of equipment or library book.

WORD-PROCESSING AREA A computer lab located in or near the school library media center, and separate from the business department classes, used to provide word-processing access to students working on assignments during unassigned time.

WORKSTUDY PROGRAMS Sometimes a satisfactory, mutually helpful arrangement can be developed in which workstudy students learn trade skills in the school library media center. This works well only when there is sufficient center personnel to permit assigning sufficient time to the students to ensure the intent of the workstudy program, and when the center program is sufficiently sophisticated to permit genuine real-world experience.

Index

About the Authors

Bernice L. Yesner is the Library Media Director of Beecher Road School in Woodbridge, Connecticut. Beecher Road School is a Pre-Kindergarten through 6th grade school serving 953 students. Mrs. Yesner has been an active member in regional, state, and national school library media associations for more than 40 years. Her previous writings include *Developing Literature-Based Reading Programs: A How-To-Do-It Manual for Librarians*, which Ms. Yesner co-authored with M. Mary Murray, and Neal-Schuman published in 1993.

Hilda L. Jay has experience in both school and public libraries, including 28 years in the library media program at Ridgefield (Connecticut) High School. She holds a doctorate in Education from New York University and has served as an adjunct faculty member at the University of Rhode Island, the University of Connecticut, and Southern Connecticut University. Dr. Jay has served on many committees in the American Association of School Librarians. She is a prolific author. Her many books include *The Library/Computer/Classroom Connection: Linking Content, Thinking, and Writing*, coauthored with one of her daughters, M. Ellen Jay, and published by Neal-Schuman in 1994.